AF504908

Nobody's Property

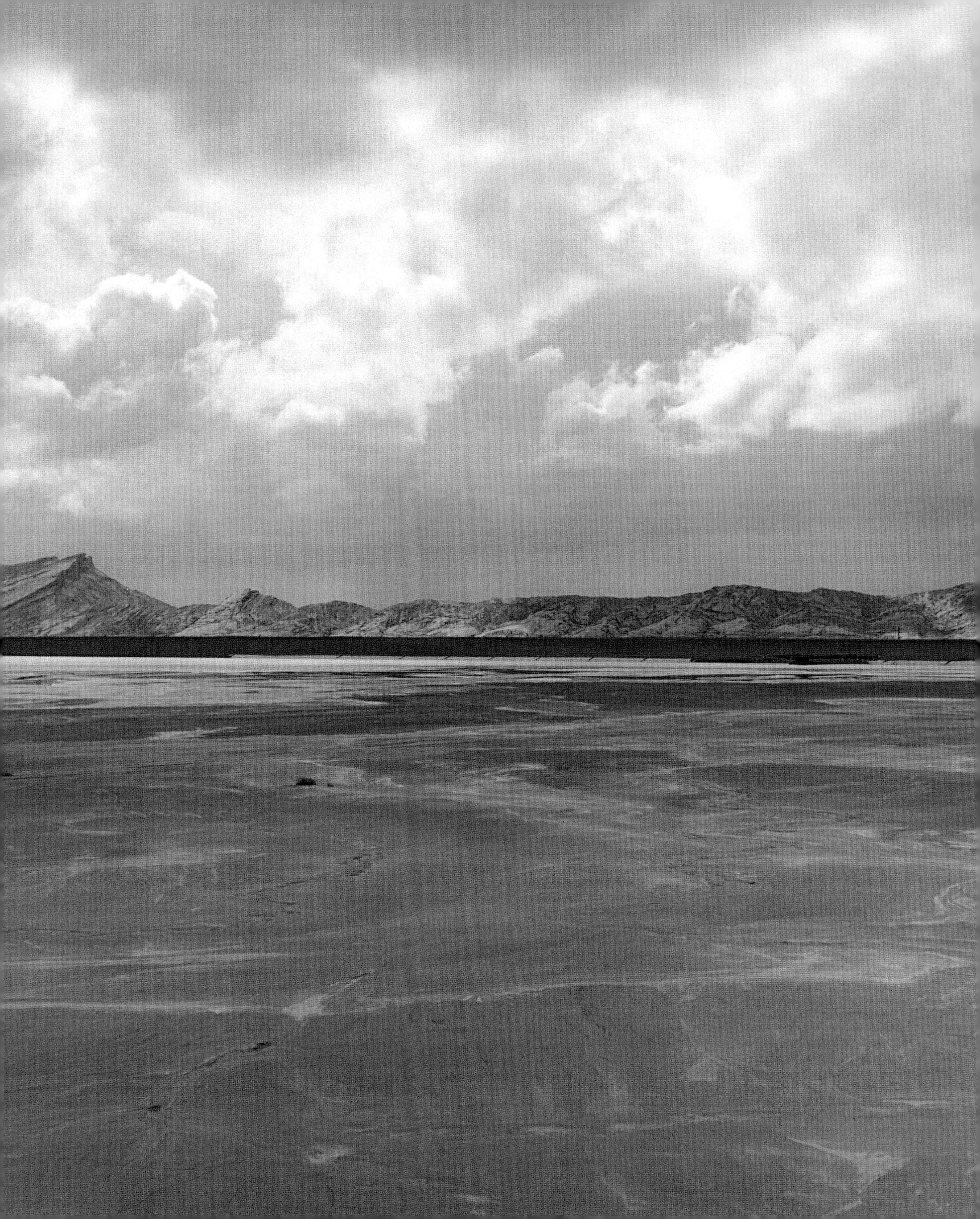

# Nobody's Property
## Art, Land, Space, 2000–2010

Kelly Baum


With contributions by
Yates McKee
Alex Bacon
Margo Handwerker
Michelle Lim
Kurt Mueller
Chris Reitz
Uriel Abulof
Rachael Z. DeLue
Jonathan Levy



Princeton University Art Museum
Distributed by Yale University Press, New Haven and London

Catalogue

# Foreword

Contemporary art often reflects incisively on the present day, and the works in *Nobody's Property: Art, Land, Space, 2000–2010* are no exception. In the videos, digital slide shows, photographs, performances, and assemblages featured, viewers will glimpse the physical and geopolitical landscape of the twentieth and twenty-first centuries, but not always in familiar or comforting form. Land and space have been irrevocably altered by conflict, urbanization, industrialization, and globalization. It is these very pressures that have driven artists to adopt "the environment" as a subject deserving of both aesthetic and critical investigation, leading us to see these artists as being engaged in some of the world's most complex issues as never before.

*Nobody's Property* signals the Princeton University Art Museum's commitment to an active and engaged program of contemporary art, one that serves members of the University community as well as the broader public, including the many thousands who visit the Princeton University campus and this Museum each year. The spirit of the exhibition and the works of art at its center are interdisciplinary in outlook, addressing issues that concern all of as human beings — globalization, war and conflict, industrial production, and environmental change, to name only a few. A glimpse at the day's news brings all this vividly home: the oil spill in the Gulf of Mexico remains uncapped as I write, with a continuing lack of consensus about how to treat the decades-long legacy of this spill; the war in Afghanistan is now the nation's longest. Land in its broadest sense is both central and contested the world over.

Tackling such extraordinary concerns through compelling works of art is a major topic, and one that is ambitious, timely, and exceptionally germane to the Museum's first permanently appointed curator of modern and contemporary art, Kelly Baum. Kelly has wisely, and effectively, sought to explore such concerns in ways that exemplify the collaborative spirit that exists between the Museum and the University as a whole. Extending well beyond our most closely related partners in the Department of Art and Archaeology to encompass faculty in the Department of History and the Liechtenstein Institute on Self-Determination in the Woodrow Wilson School, as well as graduate students in both Art and Archaeology and the School of Architecture, the project crosses boundaries and embodies our commitment to placing the Museum metaphorically at the heart of the University enterprise.

That this is possible is particularly a reflection of the fact that the focus of *Nobody's Property* aligns synergistically with a number of key initiatives at Princeton, most notably the initiative on globalism, announced as "Princeton in the World" by President Shirley Tilghman in 2007, in which she challenged

the Princeton University community to address events with
global ramifications, noting that "Students will have to be
knowledgeable about, and comfortable interacting with, cultures
different from their own. Researchers will have to become
more attentive to international issues and more sensitive to
the international dimensions of domestic problems." Similarly,
the project's concerns for the environment and global sustainability link clearly with the work of the Andlinger Center on
Energy and the Environment, itself a vital part of this renewed
emphasis on a world that is more intensely and self-consciously
international than ever before. With artists hailing from the
Americas, the Middle East, and Europe, *Nobody's Property*
crosses international boundaries with ease not only intellectu-
ally but also literally.

As a complex international exhibition, *Nobody's Property*
will be the focus of sustained investigation in the fall of 2010,
during the months it is on view in our galleries. It will leave a
more durable impact as well, not only through this scholarly
catalogue, featuring the work of nine authors of widely varying
intellectual specializations and points of view, but also because
works by two of the included artists or artist teams — Jennifer
Allora and Guillermo Calzadilla's *Land Mark (Foot Prints)*
(2000–2001) and sections from Andrea Geyer's *Spiral Lands/
Chapter 1* (2007) — were acquired by the Art Museum in 2009,

while a third — a strikingly powerful assemblage by Matthew Day
Jackson — was commissioned specifically for *Nobody's Property,*
and was purchased for the Museum's collection in 2010.

*Nobody's Property* could not have come from concept to
reality without the practical support and engagement of many,
including the Elizabeth Firestone Graham Foundation for a grant
in support of the exhibition catalogue; Gene and Sueyun Locks
for providing essential support for a multi-year commitment
to staffing in contemporary art; and the artists and catalogue
contributors, many of whom are Princeton University students
and faculty. I most especially, however, wish to recognize Kelly
Baum, who has served as a member of the Museum's staff
since December 2007 and was named the first Haskell Curator
of Modern and Contemporary Art in June 2010. This project is
the result of Kelly's vision, tenacity, and passion.

James Christen Steward
Director

# Acknowledgments

I am indebted to many individuals for helping make this exhibition and its accompanying catalogue possible. Special thanks go to director James Steward for his unflagging support of this project as well as my curatorship at Princeton. I am also grateful to Associate Director Rebecca Sender for helping guide *Nobody's Property* from its inception to its realization. Managing Editor Jill Guthrie and Assistant Editor Sophie Williams provided invaluable assistance on the catalogue and exhibition labels; Jennifer Alexander-Hill, Nancy Stout, and Eloise Tomei were particularly helpful with fundraising efforts. From our IT Department, Janet Strohl-Morgan, Cathryn Goodwin, and Daniel Brennan offered advice and support. Jeff Evans and Karen Richter oversaw matters related to photography. Photographer Bruce White contributed many arresting images to this publication. Caroline Harris, Johanna Seasonwein, and Elizabeth Lemoine in the Museum's education department helped conceptualize and organize a range of public programs. Registrars Francesca Williams and Alexia Hughes deftly managed loans and shipping. Chief Preparator Mike Jacobs and his dedicated team oversaw the installation of the exhibition, while Aaron Isler and Matt Suib of Greenhouse Media shared their expertise on all things digital, electronic, and technological. Jill Dawsey served as the catalogue's outside reader; Jane Boyd was its copy editor: for their incisive comments and assiduous attention to detail, I am very appreciative. The catalogue and exhibition design are by Joseph Cho and Stefanie Lew of Binocular. Joseph and Stefanie worked tirelessly on this project for nearly two years — their exquisite design sensibility as well as their commitment and patience are to be commended.

Warm thanks go to the donors and institutions who underwrote this exhibition and its related programs: the National Endowment for the Arts; the Virginia and Bagley Wright, Class of 1946, Program Fund for Modern and Contemporary Art; the Frances E. and Elias Wolf, Class of 1920, Fund; the Sarah Lee Elson, Class of 1984, Fund for the International Artist-in-Residence Program; and an anonymous foundation. Support for the catalogue has been provided by the Andrew W. Mellon Foundation Fund for Publications and the Elizabeth Firestone Graham Foundation. Additional support has been made possible by the Partners and Friends of the Princeton University Art Museum.

I would also like to thank the many galleries and gallery representatives for their assistance with both loans and catalogue illustrations: Carla Chammas and Elizabeth Deasey at CRG Gallery, New York; Donna Chu, Stephanie Daniel, Bellatrix Hubert, Carolyn Ramo, Chris Rawson, Cristina Revert, and Stephanie Stockbridge at David Zwirner Gallery, New York; Lara Blanchy at Galerie Chantal Crousel, Paris; Natalie Gaida at Galerie Thomas Zander, Cologne; Juliette Rizzi, Heidi Grivas, and Elena Crippa at Lisson Gallery, London; Simone Subal and David Blum at Peter Blum Gallery, New York; Sylvia Kouvali and Lara Fresko at Rodeo Gallery, Istanbul;

Ronili Lustig and Sivan Raveh at Sommer Contemporary Art, Tel Aviv. Many thanks to Karim Tabet, Mazen Makarem, and Dana Farouki for lending works by Joana Hadjithomas and Khalil Joreige to the exhibition and to Ilona Katzew, curator of Latin American Art at the Los Angeles County Museum of Art for approving a modified exhibition copy of Francis Alÿs's *The Green Line* for inclusion in *Nobody's Property*. For providing the contextual photographs that appear in this catalogue and for granting me permission to reproduce them, I am grateful to Greg Skinner; Lindsay Macdonald Danckwerth and Hannah Adkins at Galerie Lelong, New York; Allie Hughes at the Modern Art Museum of Fort Worth; Jeanne Dreskin at the Dia Art Foundation, New York; Elyse Goldberg of the Smithson Estate and James Cohan Gallery, New York; Christopher Rawson at James Cohan Gallery; and Ben Tufnell at Haunch of Venison, London.

Many friends and colleagues provided both intellectual and emotional support throughout this project. For their encouragement, I would like to thank Aron Johnston, Regine Basha, Jane Boyd, Amanda Bock, Charlotte Cousins, Rachael DeLue, Jeff Dolven, Laura Giles, Jessica Halonen, Chuck Isaacs, Mike Jacobs, Louise Kiefer, Karl Kusserow, Tom Levin, Carol Nigro, Gabriel Pérez-Barreiro, Joe Rucker, Rebecca Sender, Joel Smith, and Nancy Stout as well as my magnificent 2009 Venice and Istanbul traveling companions, Dan Bullock, Annette Carlozzi, Mike Chesser, Laurence Miller, Cynthia Toles, and Judy Willcott. Juliana Ochs led me to some important sources of information on the West Bank Barrier. I am very grateful to Paul Chan and Joe Scanlan as well as to Hal Foster and the students in our fall 2009 contemporary art seminar — especially Tessa Paneth-Pollak, Chris Reitz, and Laura Robertson — for providing excellent feedback on an early draft of my introductory essay. Special thanks go to Hal for being such a generous colleague, interlocutor, and mentor. Finally, I owe a special debt to Gene and Sueyun Locks for supporting my former position at Princeton — the Locks Curatorial Fellow for Contemporary Art — and to Preston H. Haskell for endowing my current position. Their generosity makes many things possible.

Heartfelt thanks go to the scholars who contributed their writing, thoughts, and considerable energies to this catalogue — Yates McKee, Alex Bacon, Margo Handwerker, Michelle Lim, Kurt Mueller, Chris Reitz, Uriel Abulof, Rachael DeLue, and Jonathan Levy — and to the artists whose insightful, poignant, and provocative works of art inspired me to pursue this exhibition in the first place: Jennifer Allora and Guillermo Calzadilla, Francis Alÿs, Yael Bartana, Andrea Geyer, Joana Hadjithomas and Khalil Joreige, Emre Hüner, Matthew Day Jackson, Lucy Raven, and Santiago Sierra. It was a privilege to work with and learn from all of them.

Kelly Baum
Haskell Curator of Modern and Contemporary Art

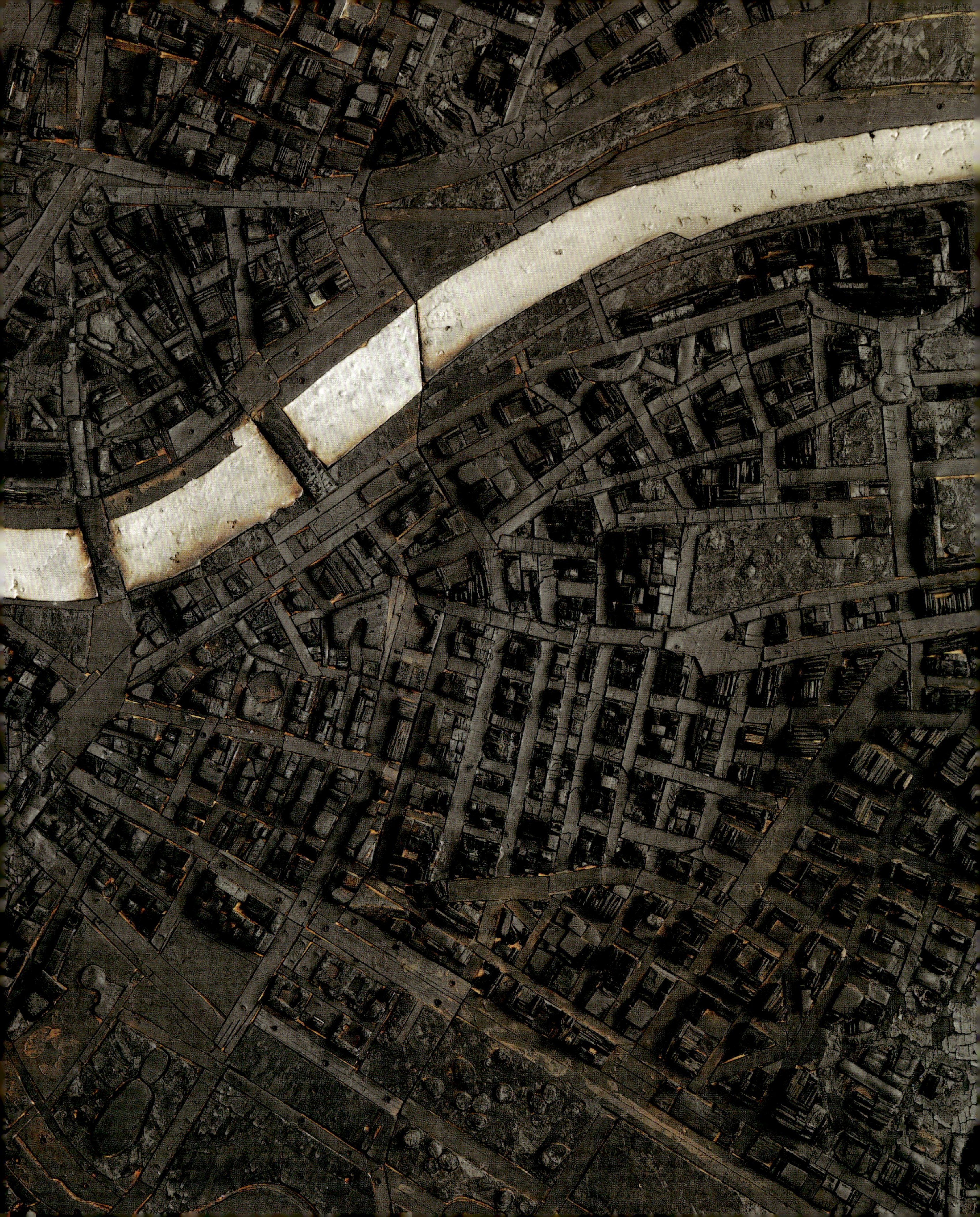

# Nobody's Property
Kelly Baum

*I am my relation to you.* Thus writes Judith Butler in her 2005 book *Giving an Account of Oneself*.[1] It is a sentence whose economy belies its profound implications, a sentence both descriptive and aspirational. We are constituted, Butler wants to say, of and by our relations with other human beings, and insofar as these relations both protect and expose us, they form the basis of our ethical responsibility to one another. To betray this responsibility, therefore, is to betray the very thing that introduces us into subjectivity and community alike.

If I begin my essay with these six words, it is because they signal so effectively and so gracefully this exhibition's meta-subject: the commons. Indeed, along with land, space, and territory, the commons forms my project's fourth compass point, the pivot around which so many of the works featured here revolve. To invoke the commons (as myriad authors do today) is to immediately raise the issue of human relations and their attendant social, political, economic, and spatial peculiarities. Generally speaking, *the commons* refers to places that prioritize accessibility and intersubjective exchange, as well as materials that belong to everyone and thus to no one in particular. Whether site (neighborhood park, community garden) or material (air, water, knowledge, DNA), the commons models a specific type of human relation, a relation based on sociability, commonality, and democracy.

As the artists in *Nobody's Property* are all too aware, however, ours is by no means a healthy, vigorous commons. Indeed, the rosy picture painted above is more wish than fact. With the advance of capitalism and the proliferation of war, the commons has declined considerably. Much that we share as human beings — natural resources and public spaces[2] as well as information and genetic codes[3] — has succumbed to privatization. Bit by bit, sale by sale, collectivity withers. Every time an army builds a wall, digs a tunnel, levels a village, or turns a mountaintop into a weapon, democracy likewise deteriorates. In each case, principles of exclusion and asymmetry supplant those of inclusion and equality. I introduce war and capitalism to make a larger point, the same one the artists in this exhibition are at pains to demonstrate: Any change to our physical environment, whether large or small, has a collateral impact on the social body.[4] The reverse is true as well: Space responds to every disruption, evolution, and recalibration of society.

*Nobody's Property* features the work of seven artists and two artist teams, all based in Europe, the Middle East, or the Americas: Jennifer Allora and Guillermo Calzadilla (Puerto Rico), Francis Alÿs (Mexico), Yael Bartana (Israel and the Netherlands), Andrea Geyer (Germany and the United States), Joana Hadjithomas and Khalil Joreige (Lebanon and France), Emre Hüner (Turkey and the Netherlands), Matthew Day Jackson

(United States), Lucy Raven (United States), and Santiago Sierra (Mexico). The subjects these artists address — land and space — are so omnipresent in contemporary art that the exhibition could have featured many more besides them (and it would have, if the museum's galleries had been larger). Despite its modest size, though, and despite the limits of its geographical range, *Nobody's Property* strives to represent, through the assiduous selection of projects, the aesthetic and methodological breadth of this most recent spatial turn in art.

The physical environment is many things to the artists in *Nobody's Property*. It is their subject, means, and stage. It is the stuff they study and depict, but it is also the material they alter, the backdrop against which they perform, and the arena in which they intervene, whether physically, symbolically, or politically. Using a wide variety of media, from assemblage and photography to video and performance, Alÿs, Raven, and the others subject land and space to a rigorous calculus. The majority address particular sites and the particular debates, struggles, and conditions in which they are enmeshed. Dispossession is a recurring theme, as are civil rights, national sovereignty, environmental welfare, and globalization. Other artists chose to survey that vast, seemingly boundless entity called space, but what their projects lack in territorial

specificity, they make up for in historical and ideological specificity. Two traditions of site-specificity are at play in *Nobody's Property*, therefore: an early version in which *site* signaled a discrete location in space, and a more recent iteration (astutely identified by Miwon Kwon), in which it corresponds to a "discursive vector," a category that might comprise a field of knowledge, a social issue, or a political debate.[5] Neither tradition preempts the other. Even the most obdurate of sites, the artists featured here insist, express discursive formations and relations of power that are no less particular, and demand no less thorough an examination, than the geographic coordinates to which they apply.

Deciphering space through strategic acts of intervention and representation, however, is not the only goal of the artists in *Nobody's Property*. Just as important are their efforts to make space signify against the grain, to make it speak otherwise, to make it *act* otherwise. Precedent aside, the ability of space to realize the social order as fact need not serve only the interests of power.[6] Space is not destined to reproduce the status quo, in other words. Thanks to writers such as Henri Lefebvre, we no longer mistake space for nature, nor do we exempt it from the historical forces that shape societies, human beings, and modes of production. Space is a cultural artifact, and an unfinished one at that. This has important

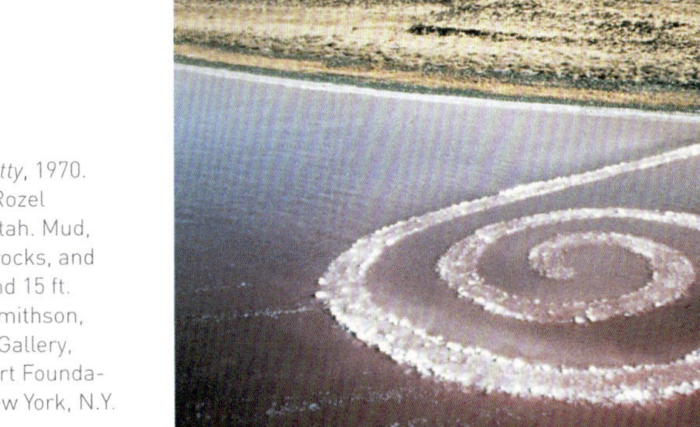

Robert Smithson. *Spiral Jetty*, 1970. Long-term installation in Rozel Point, Box Elder County, Utah. Mud, precipitated salt crystals, rocks, and water; coil: 1500 ft. long and 15 ft. wide. © Estate of Robert Smithson, Courtesy of James Cohan Gallery, New York. Collection Dia Art Foundation. Licensed by VAGA, New York, N.Y. Photo credit: Nancy Holt.

consequences for artists and activists alike: Since space is made, not given, it can be unmade, and since it can be unmade, it can also be repurposed. In the case of this exhibition, therefore, we might think of space as a medium that responds to artistic and political pressure alike.

The last ten years have seen a resurgence of interest in land and space among contemporary artists in general. This is by no means surprising. War, capitalism, globalization, and urbanization have all triggered dramatic changes to the planet, changes that artists are addressing alongside philosophers, social scientists, geographers, and nongovernmental activists.[7] Today we are also witnessing the *spatialization* of art — that is, the extension of art in and through space, its engagement with space as both form and material. This spatial turn is not limited to art, nor does it signal a historical rupture or dramatic paradigm shift. Indeed, the spatialization of art has been accompanied by the spatialization of the economy, on the one hand, and the spatialization of conflict and protest, on the other. Together these developments represent the culmination of a phenomenon that dates back to at least the 1960s and 1970s.[8]

To the extent that land (as distinct from space) is one of their principal points of reference, Bartana, Sierra, and the others constitute a new generation of Earth artists.[9] Teasing out the relationship between this generation of Land artists and those from the late 1960s and early 1970s is no easy task.[10] Everything depends on precisely which artist we consider paradigmatic of the conflicted, heterogeneous field that was historical Earth Art. Whereas contemporary Land artists have little in common with someone like Michael Heizer, for whom land constituted raw matter and remote retreat,[11] they demonstrate a profound affinity for Robert Smithson, who roundly rejected a romantic, mythopoetic view of nature. Nature, according to Smithson, was less the city's opposite — static, transparent, unadulterated — than its dialectical complement, and the same set of abstract, immaterial relations that underwrote cities also underwrote nature.[12]

Like many of the lessons handed down from the 1960s and 1970s, however, this one survives into the present only to be elaborated, inflected, and radicalized by contemporary artists. Indeed, what remains implicit or marginal in historical Earth Art — performance and interdiscursivity, along with the mutual imbrication of land, power, media, and technology — assumes a far more central role today.[13] Much has changed on the methodological level as well. As did their predecessors, contemporary Land artists tend to work with actors from many different fields (far more fields, in fact), but they do so in different ways and for different reasons. For the most part, their collaborations support larger political objectives and operate according to an ethic of reciprocity and exchange.[14] Much like Heizer and Smithson, moreover, Land artists still displace and manipulate raw matter, but their interventions are more akin to inscriptions, resulting in signs, not sculptures (as in the "earthwords" created by Sierra and Allora and Calzadilla).[15] No matter what form their work takes, though, artists today acknowledge their subject's always already textual nature. For them, land is as much stuff as it is effect: an effect of law, treaties, contracts, discourses, and systems of representation.[16] Finally, contemporary Land artists have embraced a range of new approaches, greatly expanding the menu endorsed by the previous generation. Exercises in fiction and narrative have become commonplace, while films, prints, and maps join digital slide shows, photographs, performances, assemblages, websites, pedagogical installations, platforms for exchange, and fabricated archives.[17] Documentation remains a prominent feature of much contemporary Land Art, but beyond preserving otherwise ephemeral activities or giving form to research-based projects, it also pressures the category of documentation itself. Insofar as their strategies are novel and their working definition of land highly nuanced, contemporary Land artists both revise and enrich traditional Earth Art, squaring *Earth* and *art* in ways appropriate to the twenty-first century.

TERMINOLOGY

*Nobody's Property* is organized around four compass points: land, space, territory, and the commons. Together they delimit this exhibition's field of inquiry, establish its conceptual parameters, and acknowledge its intellectual debts. I have already discussed the commons in some depth, but the other three terms remain to be unpacked.

Land: *Land* refers to the stuff of the earth, to dirt, and its presence in the title of this exhibition insists on the material reality and physical properties of the sites under discussion. As we already know, though, land is never just raw matter, nor is it immune to culture, history, or discourse.

Space: If *land* is mass, then *space* is void. Or is it? *Void* suggests a passive receptacle, an empty container waiting to be filled, but space is neither of these things — at least according to French sociologist Henri Lefebvre, whose 1974 book, *The Production of Space*, makes a strong, compelling case for the symbiotic relationship between space and power.

The now thriving field of Marxist geography owes an important debt to Lefebvre, who was one of the first to bring Marxism to bear on a subject long neglected by Marxists: space. Lefebvre also diagnosed a new stage in the history of space, one characterized by the interdependence of money, labor, commodities, and the physical environment. According to Lefebvre, every society possesses a specific mode of production, while every mode of production has specific spatial "peculiarities."[18] More than just these spatial peculiarities distinguish capitalism from earlier modes of production, however. Unlike its predecessors, capitalism aggressively exploits the strategic value of space, dedicating as many of its resources to producing the built world as it does the things we consume. "Today," Lefebvre confidently asserted in 1979, "we have passed from the production of things in space to the production of space itself."[19]

The space that capitalism creates is its ally in every way,[20] facilitating the flow of goods and bodies from market to market and reproducing the social relations on which capitalism depends. None of these developments would be possible without assistance from the state, which paves roads, subsidizes railroads, and develops land in keeping with the twin imperatives of efficiency and profitability.[21] The state also does its part to fortify capitalist society through the strategic organization of space: Neighborhoods are stratified, communities are ghettoized, and classes are relocated in a manner that best suits the economy.[22]

Four crucial points thus follow. First, space is always already social space.[23] Second, space is coextensive with the subjects and objects that comprise it. In other words, space does not exist prior to its occupation by subjects and objects, just as no subject or object exists independently of the space around it. Third, space is both prohibitive and prescriptive, forbidding certain behaviors and encouraging others.[24] Fourth, space is produced, but so too is it productive — that is, instrumental and operational.[25] Whether or not they have read Lefebvre and regardless of whether or not capitalism is their primary concern, all of the artists in this exhibition understand space in largely these terms.

Territory: The geopolitical categories of *territory*, *people*, and *state* comprise what Hannah Arendt once called the "national trinity."[26] According to conventional wisdom, territory is coterminous with the nation-state: the borders that delimit the nation also restrict the reach of the state. This is not always the case, however. Today, nation-states regularly exercise extraterritorial power — witness the American detention centers at Guantánamo Bay in Cuba, at Bagram Airfield in Afghanistan, and on the island of Diego Garcia in the Indian Ocean.[27] Long before the United States opened its extraterritorial prisons, however, the bond between nation, state, and territory was already under stress, due largely to overseas expansion and the epidemic of statelessness following World Wars I and II.[28]

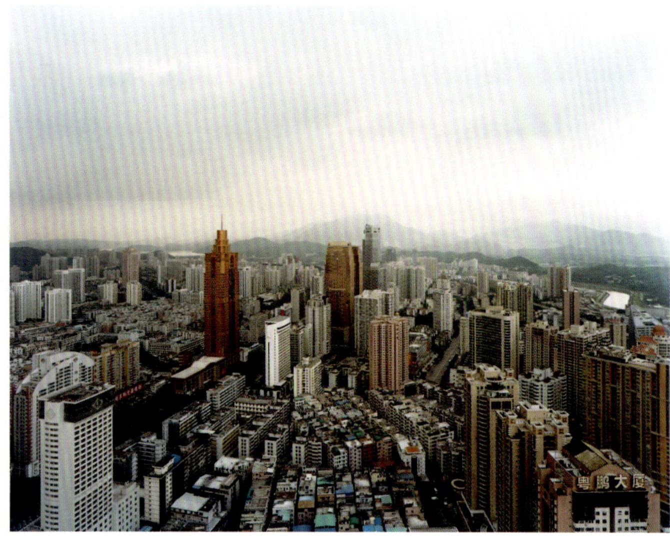

Sze Tsung Leong. *Luohu District, Shenzhen*, from the *Cities* series, 2008. Chromogenic photograph. Courtesy of the artist and Yossi Milo Gallery, New York. © Sze Tsung Leong.

Many argue that ours is an age defined by deterritorialization.[29] Globalization, mass migration, and the doctrine of free trade, along with the rise of transnational and nongovernmental organizations, have all but rendered the category of territory superfluous.[30] So, too, have changes to the nature of warfare. Instead of two or more nation-states with patent territorial ambitions and clearly articulated political goals battling for a limited period of time on a circumscribed area of land, we are just as likely to see drawn-out, delocalized conflicts between nation-states and non-state actors.[31] The extra-territorial conditions in which so many people, countries, and institutions now operate are by no means universal, however. Struggles for self-determination continue into the twenty-first century, and many, including those featured in the projects in this exhibition, make bold claims to territorial sovereignty.[32] When I use the word *territory*, therefore, I do so with awareness of the cloud of uncertainty that hangs over it.

## HISTORICAL BACKGROUND

Land, space, and territory have undergone dramatic transformations over the last century — that much is clear. Drilling, mining, farming, damming, industrialization, deforestation, and weapons testing have not only distressed vast portions of the planet, they have rendered it unfamiliar as well.[33] A mere 2 percent of Iowa, for instance, appears now as it did in the nineteenth century. The tall prairie grasses that used to cover the state have been replaced with fields of corn and soybeans that rival the density of Manhattan.[34] On the other side of the globe, construction of the Three Gorges Dam has displaced more than a million Chinese and inundated dozens of towns, farms, and archaeological sites.[35]

So great are the geopolitical changes that have occurred over the course of the twentieth and twenty-first centuries, a person living in 1900 would be hard pressed to recognize a world map from 2009.[36] The fall of the Ottoman Empire after World War I, for instance, triggered the wholesale reorganization of the Middle East. With approval from the League of Nations, Palestine and Transjordan were established as British mandates, and Syria and Lebanon as French mandates, in 1922 and 1923 respectively.[37] The Republic of Turkey came into being shortly thereafter, in 1923. In the mid 1940s, at the close of World War II, the Middle East underwent another series of seismic shifts. Syria and Lebanon gained their independence from the French in 1943, with the last troops departing in 1946, while the British released Transjordan that same year. Around the same time, in 1947, the United Nations moved to create a Jewish state in parts of Palestine, and in 1948, the British terminated its mandate in the area. Israel responded by declaring its

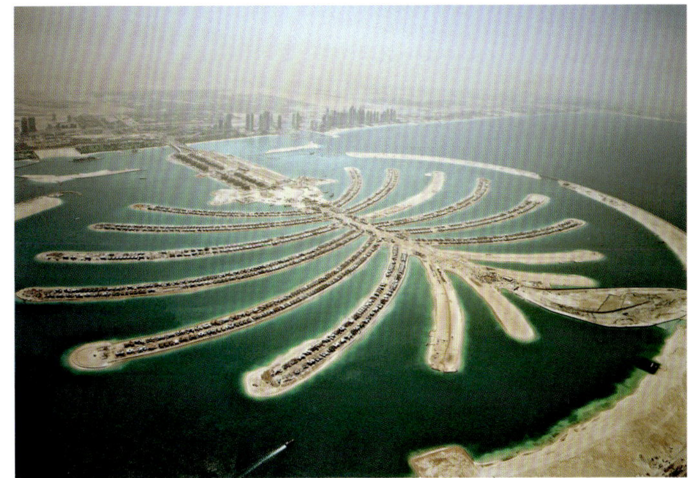

Robert Polidori. *Dubai (Palm Jumeirah)*, 2005. Chromogenic photograph. Courtesy of the artist.

independence. The United Arab Emirates emerged in 1971, after the British, who had maintained a presence in the Persian Gulf since the nineteenth century, departed. Asia and Europe have experienced similarly momentous realignments over the course of the twentieth century. Pakistan was carved out of India in 1947, while Yugoslavia underwent several iterations between 1918 and 2003, when it collapsed after nearly a century of political turmoil. Out of its dissolution emerged three new states: Montenegro, Serbia, and Kosovo (the latter still contested).

On the local and regional level, change has been equally drastic thanks to the dizzying pace of urbanization. We now find megalopolises like Shenzhen, Shanghai, and Abu Dhabi in places that were home as little as twenty years ago to farms, fishing villages, and, in some case, no land at all.[38] By 2010, urbanization will have swallowed up Kampong Buangkok, Singapore's last rural village.[39] Dubai, as large a construction site as Singapore, if not larger, is also being ecologically and architecturally reengineered. Hotels air-condition the outdoors; architects design indoor ski slopes; and developers dump soil on top of sand, all in effort to satisfy the desires of a wealthy transnational elite. Much like Singapore, moreover, Dubai has increased its overall area, especially its beachfront property, using dredged sand.[40] These efforts have resulted in a cluster of artificial archipelagoes, each with its own distinctive shape. The Palm Jumeirah resembles its namesake, while the Palm Jebel Ali spells out a poem written by Dubai's ruler, Sheikh Mohammed bin Rashid Al Maktoum. If configured as planned, another archipelago will simulate a world map.[41]

Urbanization is neither even nor steady, however. Nor is it immune to the vagaries of the market, as the events of the past three years have demonstrated. With the recession in full swing, a new global landscape is emerging — witness the skeletal, unfinished skyscrapers proliferating in cities around the world, the developments lying empty in American suburbs, and the tent cities springing up in Sacramento, Nashville, and St. Petersburg.[42] If the paradigmatic subject of five years ago was the globetrotting Iranian with apartments in Tehran, Dubai, and Paris, the paradigmatic subject of this new landscape is the former homeowner from Fresno, one of thousands to lose her house to foreclosure. We tend to think of poverty and deprivation as being invisible, as being written out of space, but that is less and less the case today, when capitalism's "other" seems more legible than ever. Never before have relations of power and property been inscribed so baldly in space.

Beyond the changes it has undergone and the crises it has suffered, land today is fraught with contradiction. Neither the way we apportion land nor the way we address others on

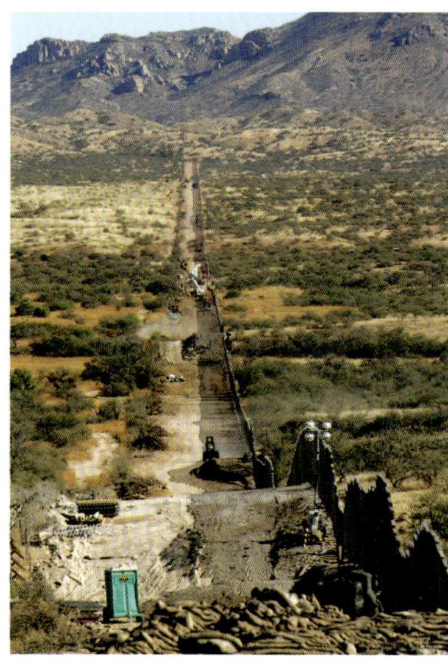

Dean Knuth. *Untitled (Border Fence between Mexico and the United States, Sasabe, Ariz.)*, November 2007. Chromogenic photograph. Courtesy of the artist and the *Arizona Daily Star*.

land displays a consistent logic; both seem to pitch in many different directions at once. Even though markets are integrating, nongovernmental organizations are multiplying, and populations are mixing, nativist, nationalist, and ethnophobic rhetoric is escalating. The "trinity of state-people-territory"[43] is slackening, but in many countries, *border patrol* and *homeland security* are championed with almost fanatical devotion.[44] The local is rapidly being subsumed into the global and integrated into vast networks of exchange, only to be resurrected as spectacle.[45] The horizontal exchange of goods, culture, and information is accelerating; still, the vertical transfer of ideas and values from west to east and north to south continues, stifling heterogeneity. As it turns out, these contradictions have a common source in capitalism and globalization.[46]

Over the last several decades, capitalism and globalization have worked in tandem to reorganize space. The fevered extension of capitalism beyond national boundaries, its restless search for new markets, resources, labor, and profits, has led to the globalization—or integration—of the world's economies, peoples, and cultures.[47] The movement characteristic of capitalism is deterritorialization. Capitalism is compelled to expand, and it can only expand if it destroys every barrier (legal, regulatory, and geopolitical) to that expansion.[48] The result is a deterritorialized field—a global spread—characterized by mobile populations, porous borders, and fluid relations of exchange.

Deterritorialization describes only some aspects of present-day space and spatial relations, however. What of the border fences and nationalist rhetoric? What of the sporadic efforts to restrict free trade and protect domestic producers? These express a counter-logic best called *reterritorialization*.[49] Against expansion, integration, and volatility, reterritorialization promotes contraction, differentiation, and stabilization. Insofar as it arrests the flow typical of globalization, reterritorialization is a fundamentally conservative, even defensive phenomenon. As such, it tends to emerge on the national and individual level as a reaction to precisely the sorts of changes triggered by deterritorialization. Yet reterritorialization is by no means foreign to capitalism, despite the latter's natural proclivity to deterritorialize. Especially in times of overproduction, capitalism works to capture the identity of particular demographics, establishing a "natural" affinity between groups and goods for which they have no preexisting desire.[50] The result is the consolidation of subject positions, a process whose spatial corollaries include the policing of borders, the imposition of tariffs, the hoarding of resources, and the targeting of local markets for overseas investment. It is the aim of many of the projects in *Nobody's Property* to sound out these contradictions, rendering them legible through strategic acts of investigation, representation, and intervention.

Along with capitalism and globalization, war has also has effected great changes to space, laying waste to the environment, flattening cities, dispersing communities, and expanding some borders while contracting others. We might expect war's collateral impact on space to constitute this exhibition's third discursive vector, but the artists in *Nobody's Property* are more interested in the *weaponization* of space. The dispossession of people in and by space is nothing new, of course. As Karl Marx, David Harvey, and the collective Retort have all asserted, primitive accumulation — the privatization of soil, forests, and natural resources — has long been used to enrich the few and disenfranchise the many.[51] Beyond these class-based struggles, though, land has proven to be an equally effective tool in geopolitical conflict.

We need not look very hard (or far) for a case study: the protracted war between Native Americans and the United States presents itself as a possibility, likewise the legal battle playing out over the island of Diego Garcia. Here, however, I have chosen to focus on the Israeli-Palestinian conflict. The latter not only plays a central role in two of this exhibition's projects (by Alÿs and Bartana); it is also the subject of a meticulous and illuminating study by Eyal Weizman: *Hollow*

*Land: Israel's Architecture of Occupation*, published in 2007.[52] A veritable treatise on the weaponization of space, *Hollow Land* inventories the constraints to which Palestinians have been subjected since Israel occupied Gaza and the West Bank in 1967.[53] These include the construction of fences and walls; the proliferation of checkpoints and settlements;[54] the ghettoization of neighborhoods; the destruction of orchards, camps, towns, and utilities;[55] the reduction of water quotas; the withholding of construction permits; the designation of strategic sites within Palestinian territory as historical or religious landmarks; and the rezoning of arable or inhabitable terrain as public space.[56] From the point of view of the Israeli government, these are defensive measures intended to protect Israeli citizens and preserve Jewish heritage, but their larger purpose, stated or not, includes the annexation of territory and the systematic isolation and pacification of the Palestinian population.[57]

Even though they lack the financial and technological resources of the Israeli military, Palestinians are by no means unschooled in the instrumentalization of land. Refugee camps provide shelter for families, but they also offer camouflage for both rockets and insurgents, and their dense network of alleyways do more than facilitate movement: they supply defense against surveillance, tanks, and soldiers as well. The tunnels carved out of the desert in Rafah, a town on the Egyptian border,

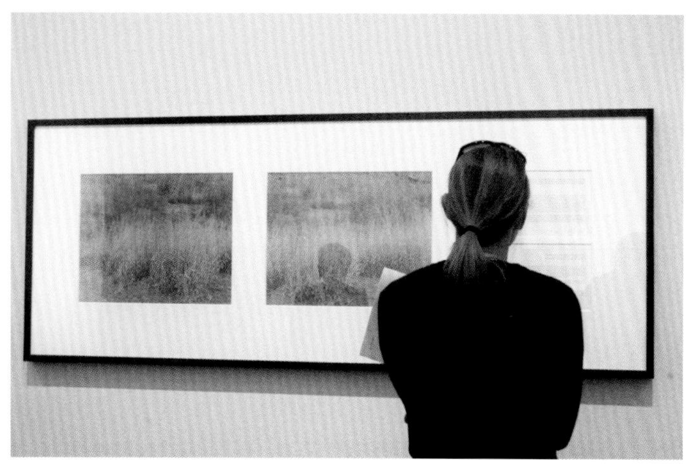



have been similarly repurposed. They not only support what is left of Gaza's economy, an economy crippled by the Israeli blockade; they also facilitate the import of weapons from Egypt and the export of Hamas militants into Israel.[58]

Weizman draws two important conclusions from the Israeli-Palestinian conflict in general and the Israeli strategy in particular. First, war and politics are increasingly "exercised in space making."[59] Second, power recruits space, while space disciplines on power's behalf.[60] If we speak of space as a "subject," Weizman's interlocutor Lefebvre once wrote, with "such and such an aim and with such and such means of action, this is because there really is a subject here, a political subject — power as such, and the state as such."[61]

## TYPOLOGIES

The nexus of capital, power, and space described above constitutes the historical backdrop against which the artists in *Nobody's Property* operate. It is their horizon of possibility, the field of social, economic, and political relations they aspire to represent. The key word here is *relation*. For Geyer, Raven, and the others, land emblematizes human relations. Land might be dirt, place, and effect as well, but first and foremost, it is a human relation made concrete.[62] What of these artists' methods, though? How does land appear in their work? Contemporary

Earth Art assumes a wide variety of forms — a far greater variety than historical Earth Art, certainly — but it is by no means diverse to the point of incoherence. A common organizing principle is at play, likewise a distinct typology of techniques: the investigatory, the parafictional, the interrogative, and the interruptive.[63] Individually, these terms will be familiar to curators, critics, and historians in the field, applying as they do to a wide range of artistic practices from the last two decades. *Nobody's Property* is the first time they have been formalized as a typology, however. It is also the first time such a typology has been developed for, and with the guidance of, contemporary Environmental Art.

**The Investigatory:** The *investigatory* is characterized by a unique sensibility as well as a specific set of working methods. The artists who operate in this mode have an affinity for research, and while planning a project, they often avail themselves of archives as well as meetings, negotiations, and interviews. These are not just fact-based pursuits, however, and the artists' goal is not simply the acquisition of knowledge. Indeed, as much as they manifest a palpable curiosity about the world, so too do they demonstrate a stubborn commitment to disclosing that which is overlooked, whether deliberately or accidentally.[64]

Among the works in this exhibition, Andrea Geyer's *Spiral Lands/Chapter 1* (2007), Lucy Raven's *China Town* (2009), and Yael

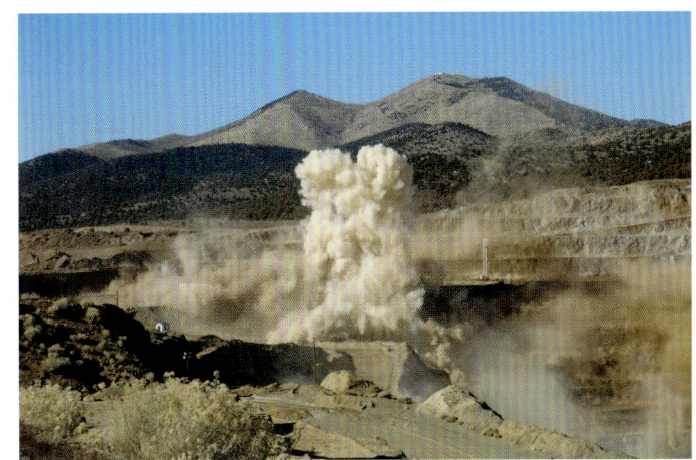

Lucy Raven. *China Town*, still, 2009. Photographic animation, color with sound, 51:30 minutes. Courtesy of the artist.

Bartana's *Kings of the Hill* (2003) best represent the investigatory ethos. Begun in 2003, *Spiral Lands/Chapter 1* is the first in a series of three projects concerning the long-standing conflict between the United States government and Native Americans. The lands that Geyer examines are embroiled in competing claims of sovereignty. To own them is a right, but this right is the basis on which other entitlements, such as the entitlement to self-determination, are alternately exercised or repealed. In *Spiral Lands/Chapter 1*, this tumultuous history takes the form of nineteen panels, each comprised of printed texts and two to three black-and-white photographs. The photographs depict landscapes both sublime and banal. All are associated with the indigenous peoples of Arizona and Nevada, and all are imbued with cultural, spiritual, and political significance. The printed texts include interviews with Native Americans, many of them Navajo; excerpts from the diary of an imaginary traveler whose voice mirrors, albeit imperfectly, the artist's own; and passages from a wide variety of archival and contemporary sources, such as colonial mandates, treaties, legal briefs, and manifestos from the American Indian Movement. Geyer counts herself an activist as well as an artist, and she considers *Spiral Lands/ Chapter 1* nothing less than a project for social justice. In this respect, her aim is far greater than that of merely excavating a repressed past and its consequences for the present. Insofar

as they appear at all, the past and the present are marshaled here in the service of a more equitable future. Geyer's work is investigatory, therefore, but it is also critical, ameliorative, and aspirational.

*China Town* (2009), a photographic animation by Lucy Raven, operates in the investigatory mode as well. Comprised of thousands of still photographs, *China Town* follows a few tons of copper ore as they are excavated from a mine in Ruth, Nevada, placed on a train bound for the port of Vancouver in Washington State, loaded onto a barge headed for Nanjing, China, transported up the Yangtze River, and, after various stops at factories in Shenzhen, Tongling, and elsewhere, transformed into spools of copper wire.[65] What emerges is a process few of us have ever seen, a process whose scale, elegance, efficiency, and destructive force approach the sublime. Raven's animation is no polemic on environmental welfare, and we should resist the temptation to infer a specific political agenda from it. Nonetheless, *environmental* accurately describes its overall point of view. Instead of exploring one aspect of copper production in isolation, Raven reconstructs the entire web of translocal and transnational exchange that makes possible this immense industrial ecosystem.

If I describe the work of Geyer and Raven as investigatory, and not documentary, I do so for good reason. Neither artist

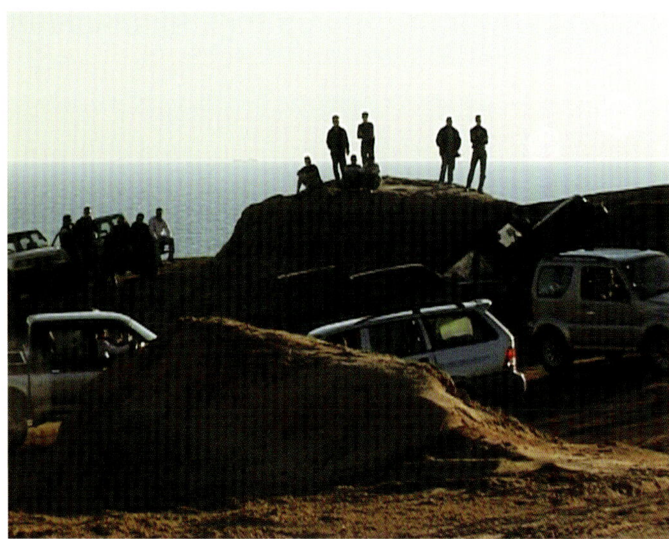

Yael Bartana, *Kings of the Hill*, still, 2003. Video, color with sound, 7:30 minutes. Courtesy of the artist, Annet Gelink Gallery, Amsterdam, and Sommer Contemporary Art, Tel Aviv.

claims to speak with complete neutrality or objectivity. Nor do they profess to render fully transparent the subjects they represent. Indeed, in many ways, some visual and others structural, both Geyer and Raven problematize the documentary aesthetic. Geyer does so by shooting the same landscape from slightly different points of view and then juxtaposing the images with a cacophony of disparate, often competing voices. In the process, two bedrocks of the documentary tradition are sacrificed: first, the notion of an absolute, inviolable truth, and second, the myth of a single, stable, authoritative subject.

Raven achieves much the same effect through different means. For example, the frame rate in *China Town* is inconsistent. It changes from slow to fast at irregular intervals, only occasionally synchronizing with the speed of the activity on the screen (and even then only imperfectly). Even when the photographs appear in rapid succession, moreover, the viewer is acutely aware that some crucial piece of information has been lost, whether it is the arc of an arm or the rotation of a tire. This is the nature of animation, and Raven exploits it to the extreme, forgoing any effort to create a seamless montage from the thousands of photographs she shot. She generates another kind of dissonance when she disarticulates sound from image. In the case of *China Town*, what we hear might be appropriate to what we see, but the mind has to work to reconcile these two

sets of sensory data. The result of Raven's interventions in the editing room is an animation that wears process on its sleeve. There is no escaping the fact that *China Town* is constructed, *made*. This, above all, is what distinguishes it from an ordinary document, which, while no less artificial, hides behind a spurious reality effect and obscures the conditions of its own production.

Israeli artist Yael Bartana works in the much the same tradition as Raven and Geyer, although she prefers the term "amateur anthropologist."[66] *Anthropological* is certainly one way to describe Bartana's videos, which inventory the rituals of everyday life in Israel, rituals that consolidate national identity around the twin imperatives of race and territory. We must understand *anthropological* the way Bartana does, though, as a highly nuanced point of view born of her conflicted position towards Israel. A member of the Israeli diaspora who maintains close ties to her family in Tel Aviv, and an opponent of the Israeli occupation who was raised in the Zionist tradition, Bartana is part insider, part detached observer, and part vocal critic. This has important consequences for her videos, including *Kings of the Hill* (2003). Shot in the upscale coastal resort of Herzliya Pituach, where a group of Israeli men assemble every Friday afternoon to ride the steep, pockmarked sand dunes in their SUVs, *Kings of the Hill* adopts a shifting mode of

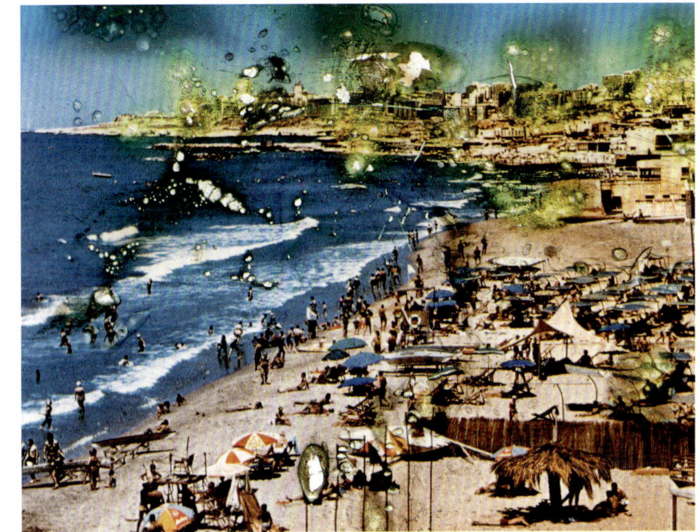

Joana Hadjithomas and Khalil Joreige. *Wonder Beirut #21 (Beaches in Beirut)*, from *History of a Pyromaniac Photographer)*, detail, 1998–2006. Lambda print mounted on aluminum, 70.5 × 105 cm (27¾ × 41½ in.). Collection of Karim Tabet, New York.

address.[67] Viewers are just as likely to blanch at the territorial display, the masculine posturing, and the wanton destruction of nature as they are to identify with an unfamiliar point of view. If we find ourselves sympathizing with the men in *Kings of the Hill*, we have Bartana's idiosyncratic form of anthropology to thank as much as we do her canny mimesis of Israeli journalism and Zionist propaganda films.[68] The latter tend to indulge in romantic excess, foster a strong sense of empathy between viewer and subject, and trade on longstanding myths that equate Jews with pioneers and confuse occupation with settlement. Such myths underwrite the ritual at Herzliya Pituach (a town named after the founder of the World Zionist Organization, Theodor Herzel), but Bartana does not disparage them. Rather, she seeks to counteract historical amnesia and denaturalize present-day customs by grounding them in the ideology and iconography of the past.

The Parafictional: In the context of contemporary Land Art, a commitment to investigation does not preclude a simultaneous commitment to fictionalizing and creative misinterpretation. For many of the artists in *Nobody's Property*, fact and artifice are inextricably intertwined.[69] Some choose to perform this condition, as Geyer does in *Spiral Lands/Chapter 1*, when she speaks through an avatar, while others, such as Lebanese artists Joana Hadjithomas and Khalil Joreige, make it the very basis of their work. Hadjithomas and Joreige leverage the porosity between documentation and fabrication at every opportunity, all the while maintaining a degree of plausibility that makes the confusion between what is real and what is not that much more acute. As such, they operate in what Carrie Lambert-Beatty has termed the *parafictional* mode. "Like a paramedic as opposed to a medical doctor," Lambert-Beatty writes, "a parafiction is related to but not quite a member of the category of fiction as established in literary and dramatic art. It remains a bit outside. It…has one foot in the field of the real. Unlike historical fiction's fact-based but imagined worlds, in parafiction real and/or imaginary personages and stories intersect with the world as it is being lived."[70]

Parafiction has proven indispensable to Lebanese artists, especially those still grappling with their country's protracted Civil War (1975–90).[71] That parafiction should dominate the work of artists determined to parse the effects and consequences of war is no surprise. After all, war and parafiction speak the same language, that of confusion, misdirection, and obfuscation. Nothing is certain in war. Propaganda and forced confessions compromise fact, while trauma confounds memory and violence undermines reality. Different speakers, each with his or her own agenda, narrate the same event in different ways.

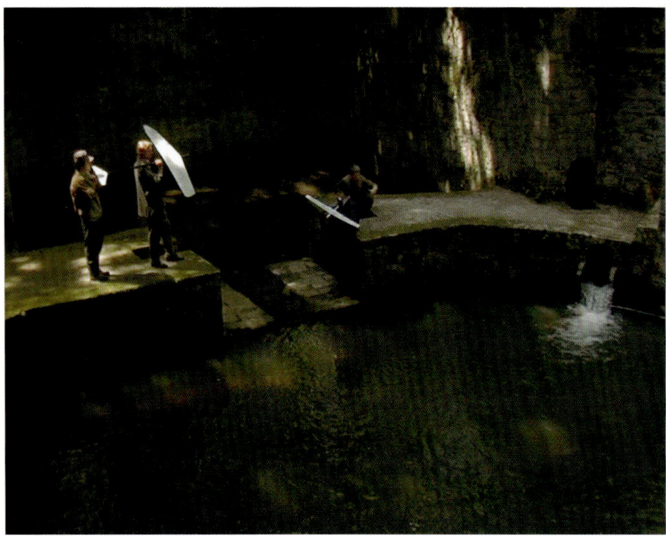

Emre Hüner. *Juggernaut*, still, 2009. Video, color with sound, 21:10 minutes. Courtesy of the artist and Rodeo Gallery, Istanbul.

Consensus about the Lebanese Civil War has proven particularly elusive, given the multiple fronts on which it was fought and the large number of factions involved. If the truth of war is a lie, then parafiction is the ideal vehicle for throwing this lie into high relief. Even when intended in the spirit of critique, though, parafiction provides little solace. It fills no gaps and offers no correctives for the ambiguities of war, no truer truths.[72] This is its strength but also its predicament; both are evident in Hadjithomas and Joreige's *Wonder Beirut: The Story of a Pyromaniac Photographer* (1998–2006).

Initially conceived as a project of archival reconstruction, *Wonder Beirut* consists of dozens of photographs based on postcards by Lebanese artist Abdallah Farah.[73] Farah's postcards, first published in 1968, depict Beirut in its heyday, when it was a glittering metropolis, a glamorous tourist destination attracting visitors from around the world. In 1975, to signal his dismay over the onset of the Civil War, Farah started to burn his negatives. The areas of blistered celluloid bear an uncanny resemblance to mortar fire, and they contrast abruptly with the original, blissful tableaux. Here, Beirut appears trapped between modernity and conflict, past and present. The negatives Farah damaged are the same ones later printed, with his permission, by Hadjithomas and Joreige. The only problem is this: Farah doesn't exist.[74] The postcards are real, likewise the

sense of despair they convey, but Farah is not.[75] As is typical of parafiction, fact and artifice mingle freely in *Wonder Beirut*.

If parafiction finds a place in Hadjithomas and Joreige's work, it is not only because conditions in post-war Beirut (including a controversial plan to modernize the city and eradicate any trace of war from its fabric) seem to demand it. Equally important is the artists' desire to introduce fiction to a country long constrained by the "hard fact of conflict."[76] For Hadjithomas and Joreige, fiction is a *right*, one normally reserved for the privileged. In *Wonder Beirut*, they claim this right for the Lebanese, who have been disenfranchised by the concept of victimhood and its evidentiary imperative as much as they have by three decades of civil war and their country's ongoing struggle with Israel. Here, parafiction operates on two different political registers simultaneously. It travesties the travesty of war, while redressing a longstanding inequity in the means and methods of representation.

In addition to war, trauma, and mnemonic instability, parafiction also enjoys a symbolic affinity with utopian wish fulfillment. What better way to figure the modern dreamscape — all those fantasies of military conquest and technological progress — than through parafiction? This is Turkish artist Emre Hüner's position, at least, and he puts it to excellent use in *Juggernaut* (2009), a video montage comprised of

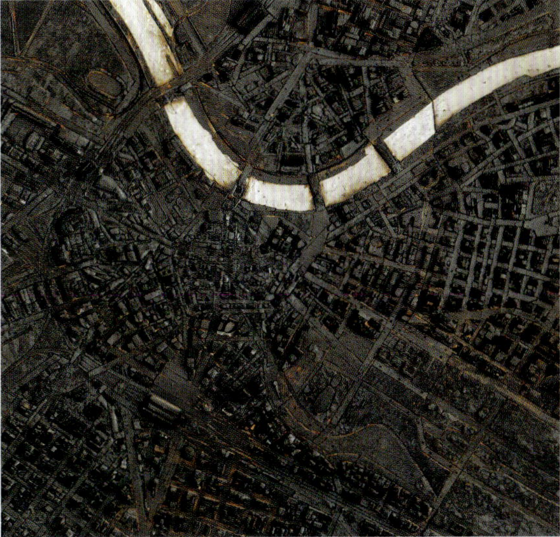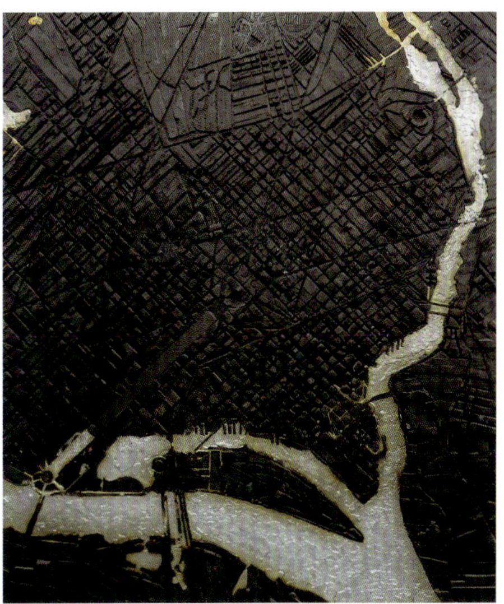

Matthew Day Jackson. *August 6th, 1945*, detail, 2010. Burnt wood and lead, 2.44 × 3.14 m (8 × 10 ft.). Princeton University Art Museum; Museum purchase, Fowler McCormick, Class of 1921, Fund. Courtesy of the artist and Peter Blum Gallery, New York. Photo credit: Bruce M. White.

Matthew Day Jackson. *August 6th, 1945*, 2009. Burnt wood and lead, 2.44 × 2.03 m (96 × 80 in.). Private collection, The Netherlands. Courtesy of the artist and Peter Blum Gallery, New York.

newsreels, documentaries, cartoon propaganda, and scenes of historical reenactment. All this material, whether staged by Hüner or sampled from the archives of NASA, General Motors, and Disney, treats the same subject: space. From it, the artist fashions an encyclopedia of sorts, a compendium of space as screen or fetish, one whose compass points include Bolshevik aviation clubs, the New York World's Fair of 1939–40, World War II, and the space race.

In the process of creating his anthology, Hüner subjects the categories of fact and fiction to immense pressure. These categories were never stable to begin with, though. Indeed, if the material in *Juggernaut* is any indication, the real is always shot through with fantasy, while the make-believe always answers to concrete, historically specific demands. Hüner is sensitive to these moments of collapse as well as their orchestration and instrumentalization by powerful interest groups, but he is also mindful of the aspirations that occasioned so much of the last century's dreamwork, in particular its spatial utopias. From this flawed and bankrupt dreamwork, might we salvage something for the present? What are the conditions of possibility for utopianism today? These are the questions Hüner poses from a critical, not cynical, point of view.

Matthew Day Jackson's approach, perspective, and frame of reference are similar to Hüner's. Like Hüner, Jackson tackles both the spatial politics of the 1940s and the contradictory impulses that animated that decade's attachment to progress and utopian dreamwork, but he does so using radically different means. *August 6th, 1945* (2010) is one in a series of assemblages comprised of melted lead and burnt pieces of wood. The series grew out of the artist's 2008–9 residency at the MIT List Visual Arts Center, where he researched the Apollo 11 space mission of 1969 as well as the scientific advances (flight, aerial mapping, and weapons technology) that made possible the nuclear attacks on Hiroshima and Nagasaki and the firebombing of Dresden in 1945.

The investigatory ethos is pronounced in *August 6th, 1945*, but it is by no means exhaustive. Much like *Juggernaut*, *Wonder Beirut*, and *Spiral Lands/Chapter 1*, Jackson's series performs a parafictional operation of its own. No matter which city each work represents (whether Hiroshima, Dresden, or Washington, D.C.), and no matter what act of devastation that work summons forth, its title identifies it and all the others with the same place on the same day: Hiroshima on August 6, 1945. Jackson's apparent mistake (Dresden was bombed in February of 1945, while the American capital escaped bombing altogether) cannot be reduced to a mere act of artistic license. For Jackson, this fiction, this deliberate prying apart of site, event, and history, signals an all-too-real fact: not just the

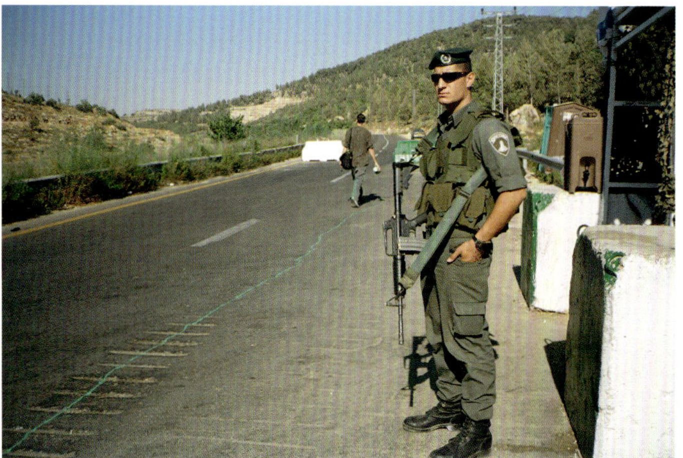

Francis Alÿs, *The Green Line: Some-times Doing Something Poetic Can Become Political and Sometimes Doing Something Political Can Become Poetic*, 2007. Video installation with various components. Dimensions variable. Collection of the Los Angeles County Museum of Art; Purchased with funds provided by The Bernard and Edith Lewin Collection of Mexican Art Deaccession Fund and the Michael and Dorothy Blankfort Bequest by exchange. Modified exhibition copy authorized by the Los Angeles County Museum of Art. Courtesy of the artist and David Zwirner Gallery, New York.

reciprocity of violence, a reciprocity that implicates victim and perpetrator alike, but the tragedy of return, the endless repetition of violence in ever new, supposedly more advanced forms.

**The Interrogative:** The works in the *interrogative* category are exploratory and probing. They problematize. They traffic in possibilities. They address highly charged issues without expecting to resolve them. Because it takes nothing for granted, because it disables habit and reorganizes perception, the interrogative mode is critical by nature. No work in *Nobody's Property* better exemplifies this mode than Francis Alÿs's *The Green Line: Sometimes Doing Something Poetic Can Become Political and Sometimes Doing Something Political Can Become Poetic*, from 2007.[77]

First and foremost, *The Green Line* is an event tailored to a specific historical and geopolitical context: the conflicted, contested city of Jerusalem. In June 2004, Alÿs walked a section of the Green Line, wandering past religious sites and historical landmarks, across roads and hills, through checkpoints, markets, and neighborhoods, leaving a trail of green paint in his wake.[78] The story of the line he recreated is a complicated affair. On November 30, 1948, as the Arab-Israeli War was drawing to a close, Israeli commander Moshe Dayan and Abdallah al-Tall,

commander of the Arab forces, signed a cease-fire accord. Each used a grease pencil (Dayan green and al-Tall red) to draw his army's armistice line on a map.[79] These lines quickly became the de facto borders separating Israel from the territories then occupied by Egypt and Jordan, territories roughly equivalent to Gaza and the West Bank today. The armistice lines also divided Jerusalem along a west-east axis, with the latter falling to Jordan.

The boundaries established during the cease-fire accord have since shifted in favor of the Israelis, who seized Gaza, the West Bank, East Jerusalem, and more in 1967 during the Six-Day War.[80] Prior to 1967, the Green Line was marked by mines, soldiers, concrete barriers, and barbed wire, at least in Jerusalem, but when the war ended and Israel "reunited" the city, many such obstacles were dismantled. (For the Palestinians who lived in and around East Jerusalem, of course, "reunification" essentially meant "occupation" — occupation by Israel instead of Jordan.) Given this set of historical circumstances, why would Alÿs have chosen to reconstitute in 2004 a political boundary that had been rendered all but obsolete in 1967?

Even though Israel occupied territories to the west of the Green Line after 1967, the boundary remained operative, both functionally and psychologically, well into the following decades, even more so after a series of Palestinian suicide bombings in 2000. Around this time, roadblocks and checkpoints started to proliferate once again along the Jerusalem portion of the Green Line, remilitarizing a partition whose very existence contradicted the myth of reunification. Soon thereafter, the gap between rhetoric and reality would be further widened by the West Bank Barrier. For all intents and purposes, the latter has replaced an inconvenient border (the Green Line) with one more amenable to Israeli ambitions, even if it has failed to unite the region's inhabitants.

Plans for a physical structure dividing Israel from the West Bank were initially proposed in 2000, and they gathered momentum over the following years. In April 2002, the Israeli Cabinet established a Seam Zone Administration and ordered the Israel Defense Forces to begin seizing and leveling land. A few months later, on June 23, 2002, construction on the Barrier commenced. From the beginning, the Israeli government intended to create an envelope around Jerusalem, effectively severing the eastern part of the city from the rest of the West Bank (and confining thousands of Palestinians on either side of a wall that can only be crossed through checkpoints, with permits). This is by no means the only instance in which the Barrier and the Green Line diverge: The Barrier strays from the Green Line into the West Bank at many points, largely in an effort to accommodate Israeli settlements. As of July 2009, 85 percent of the Barrier lies outside Israel proper, effectively annexing 9.5 percent of the West Bank.[81]

Over time, then, the identity and function of the Green Line have evolved both within Jerusalem and without: from an armistice line to a militarized border to a barrier that was acknowledged inconsistently — either enforced or disavowed depending on the dictates of security and ideology — to a partition preempted by another partition.[82] As its identity and function evolved, so too did its stake and meaning. For the Israeli government, the Green Line came to represent an untenable imposition on its sovereignty; for the Palestinian Authority, it came to represent the boundaries of a future Palestinian state and the key to its self-determination (or, at the very least, the foundation on which to begin negotiations with Israel).[83]

It is certainly no coincidence that Alÿs's project took place on June 4 and 5, 2004, almost two years to the day when construction on the Barrier began. It was at this very moment, by virtue of its gradual effacement, that the Green Line assumed renewed political importance. By the time Alÿs crossed through Jerusalem, moreover, humanitarian organizations had already begun to document the Barrier's disastrous consequences for Palestinians. Indeed, in February 2004, the

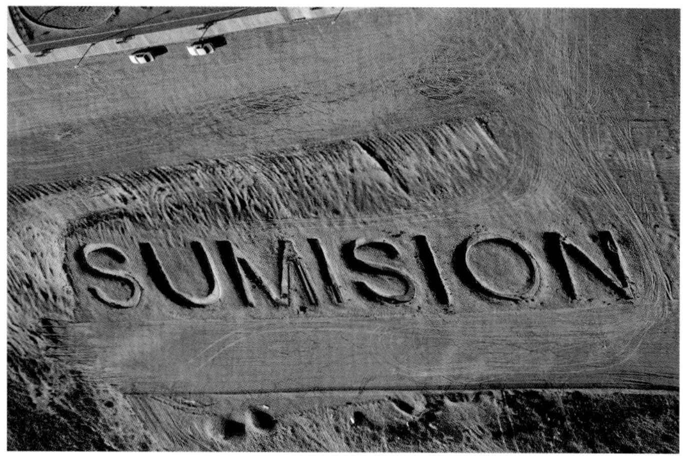



Santiago Sierra. *Submission (formerly Word of Fire)*, detail, October 2006/ March 2007. Documentation of an action, Anapra, Ciudad Juárez, Chihuahua, Mexico. Two-channel digital slide projection, black and white, silent,1:20 minutes (channel one), 78:20 minutes (channel two), looped. Courtesy of the artist and Lisson Gallery, London

International Court of Justice launched hearings about the Barrier's legality (it would eventually call for construction to cease and for those portions erected in the West Bank and East Jerusalem to be dismantled). By making legible an erratic, disputed perimeter, therefore, Alÿs's intervention underscored the bizarre acts of territorial calculus that had been, and were still being, performed in Israel and Palestine every day.[84] Re-creating the Green Line in June 2004 was not just a timely gesture, though; it was also a provocative one, something Alÿs seems to have recognized only after the fact. Although he initially claimed a neutral position vis-à-vis the Israeli-Palestinian conflict, he soon realized that to insist on the Green Line as he did, when he did — to insist on its facticity at the very moment Israel was challenging its validity and replacing it with a new, more generous border — was to take sides.[85]

*The Green Line* began as a series of questions — propositions, really — that concern the mechanics of art as well as the Israeli-Palestinian conflict.[86] What, Alÿs wondered, is the relationship between poetics and politics? Can poetics perform politically, and if so, how? Recreating the original Green Line allowed Alÿs to pose these questions by enacting them, by testing them against conditions on the ground. So, too, did his decision to discuss *The Green Line* with individuals from Palestine, Israel, and the United Kingdom, who parsed not only Alÿs's project but

the Green Line and the larger conflict to which it belongs.[87] The participants reached no consensus on the matter of poetics and politics, but Alÿs himself arrived at a provisional conclusion a few years later. "Poetic license," he said about *The Green Line* in a 2006 interview, "functions like a hiatus in the atrophy of a social, political, military or economic crisis. Through the gratuity or the absurdity of the poetic act, art provokes a moment of suspension of meaning, a brief sensation of sense-lessness that reveals the absurd [*sic*] of the situation and, through this act of transgression, makes you…revise your prior assumptions about this reality."[88]

**The Interruptive:** The artists who work in the *interruptive* mode bear a superficial resemblance to historical Land artists. In their work, material is manipulated and matter displaced, but these physical intrusions serve a larger purpose: to interrupt the operations of power, both symbolically and practically.[89] Take the case of Santiago Sierra. In 2007, Sierra hired a group of men to excavate the word *Sumisión* on a plot of land in Anapra, a small community a few miles west of Ciudad Juárez, on the United States-Mexico border. As with most of Sierra's sites, this one is not so much charged as it is overdetermined. If anything, Anapra suffers from *too much* meaning. Toxic waste, crime sprees, homeless immigrants, maquiladoras, border fences:

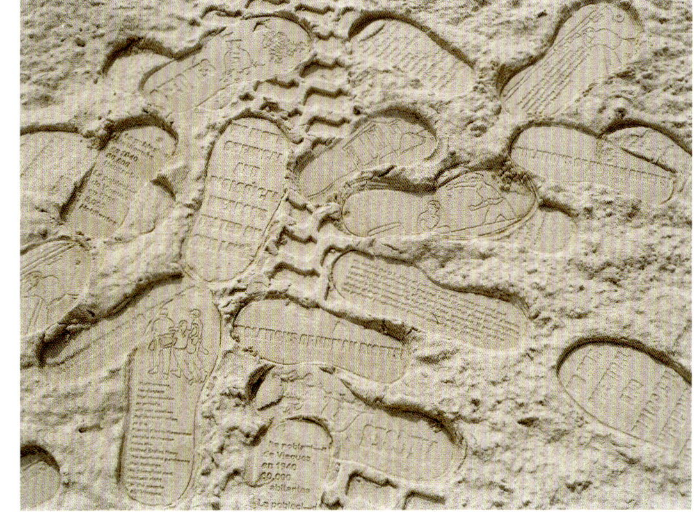

Jennifer Allora and Guillermo Calzadilla. *Land Mark (Foot Prints)*, detail, 2001–2. 12 digital C-prints, AP 1/3, each 46 × 60.5 cm (18⅛ × 23⅞ in.). Princeton University Art Museum; Museum purchase, Fowler McCormick, Class of 1921, Fund. Courtesy of the artists and Galerie Chantal Crousel, Paris.

These are the heady issues coalescing in this small stretch of desert.[90] For its part, Sierra's gesture carries the force of a demonstration. It disrupts by showing.[91] This is interruption in the declarative mode, and even though declarations — self-evident, categorical, and emphatic — tend to hinder dialogue, they also stave off complacency. If we were ever inclined to overlook the subjection of one hemisphere to another, to ignore the conditions of poverty that prevail in Mexico, to believe the rhetoric around NAFTA, the artist ensures that we do not.[92] Inscribing *Submission* into the Mexican desert also serves to interrogate the border, specifically the militarized border across which fluid, even, and symmetrical exchange ostensibly takes place.[93]

Ever the critical realist, Sierra goes no further than declaration and problematization.[94] Where he concludes, Jennifer Allora and Guillermo Calzadilla persist. On multiple occasions between 2001–2, Allora and Calzadilla infiltrated a United States Navy bombing range in Vieques, Puerto Rico with a group of activists. In addition to disrupting military operations for several hours, their intervention also left hundreds of footprints in the soft, pliable sand — footprints whose form and content, determined by specially designed soles, spoke to longstanding grievances against the American occupation.[95] If Sierra's approach is interruption as declaration, Allora and

Calzadilla's is interruption as civil disobedience campaign. Insofar as it conflates physical intervention with political intervention, moreover, *Land Mark (Foot Prints)* radicalizes the tradition of Earth Art.

The footprints that Allora, Calzadilla, and their collaborators planted on the beachside bombing range were gestures of resistance, to be sure, but they were also gestures of reclamation and reterritorialization. Furthermore, their intervention helped broker a future that actually came to pass: the departure of the United States military in 2003. Tragically, this otherwise auspicious event triggered yet another round of disputes, this time between the local population, corporations, real estate developers, and the Department of the Interior, which controls the land formerly occupied by the Navy. These second-generation conflicts and the second-order dispossessions they occasioned — dispossession by capital and administrative fiat — would occupy several of Allora and Calzadilla's later projects.[96]

There are as many different models of political speech at work in *Nobody's Property* as there are artistic typologies. Sierra's voice tends to be declamatory, even taunting, while Bartana's, Geyer's, Hüner's, and Hadjithomas and Joreige's are best described as diagnostic and expository.[97] For their part, Allora and Calzadilla exemplify a third model, one that embraces what Judith Butler has called "performative contradiction." According to Butler, "performative contradiction" involves taking a right that has not yet been granted and engendering that which does not yet exist, mainly social justice. This is political speech as "inducement, incitation, solicitation, as a kind of wager on a future," and *Land Mark* puts it to good use.[98] Alÿs's voice is the most elusive of all: neither declarative nor programmatic nor analytical, *The Green Line* leverages the imagination, the realm of possibility, liberating the future from the present, much like *Land Mark (Foot Prints)*. Insofar as it asks — what could be? — its tense is the future unreal conditional, the tense of utopian longing. Moreover, *The Green Line* is 'effective' only to the extent that it calls into doubt — deliberately and self-consciously — the political efficacy of art, preserving, even fueling, the dialectical tension between aesthetics and politics.

## RES NULLIUS

I first came across the phrase *res nullius* in 2009, in a *New Yorker* essay by Lawrence Wright. Latin for "nobody's thing" or "nobody's property," the term's use did not immediately seem to square with its meaning. In the context of the essay, *res nullius* signaled an act of dispossession — or, rather, the argument justifying an act of dispossession, specifically the occupation of Palestine by the British in 1917. According to Wright, the British

"considered Gaza *res nullius* — nobody's property," at least not the property of the individuals who resided there in 1917, individuals whose status as valid political subjects was essentially stripped by their designation as "nobody."[99] Indeed, to designate Palestine *res nullius* in 1917 was to declare it vacant, deserted, and available for the taking. But this is only one way — a rather cynical way — to understand *res nullius*. Besides a specious defense of imperialism, the concept also evokes the commons, a phenomenon addressed at the beginning of this essay.[100]

Along with appeals to new, more just ways of sharing space, the commons animates a great deal of philosophy today, thanks largely to the dominance of neoliberalism and privatization, as well as the ubiquity of war and violence.[101] In addition to Antonio Negri and Michael Hardt,[102] one thinks immediately of Judith Butler's recent writing, which addresses our ethical responsibility to one another and the relations that render subjectivity common.[103] Also relevant is Jacques Derrida's 1996 essay "On Cosmopolitanism," a call for the creation of "free cities."[104] Neither Butler nor Derrida harbor any illusions about the positions they espouse. Extending ethical consideration to others (others with whom we might have very different perspectives) is no easier than incorporating hospitality into public policy or rewriting laws to accommodate immigrants and refugees.

Insofar as Butler and Derrida admit to the arduous, contradictory task of achieving what they believe we have no choice
but to achieve, their efforts parallel those of the artists in
*Nobody's Property*. Neither simple, punctual solutions nor a
naive faith in the redemptive power of consensus will be found
here. For better or worse, conflict forms the basis of human
relations, and conflicted relations are precisely what the works
in this exhibition dramatize, even as a few imagine their miti-
gation or partial resolution. Where does antagonism manifest
itself today, in what land-sites and in what formations of space?
How do we live alongside others when we have as much "out of
common" as "in"? How do we negotiate coexistence in an era
of dwindling natural resources and burgeoning populations?[105]
How do we reconcile the practical and ethical demands of
solidarity with valid claims to self-determination? Last but not
least, what role might art play in all this? What is the nature of
its commitment to the dilemmas it addresses? To these questions and more, Allora and Calzadilla, Alÿs, Bartana, Geyer,
Hadjithomas and Joreige, Hüner, Jackson, Raven, and Sierra
provide provisional answers and illuminating insights.

Notes

1  Judith Butler, *Giving an Account of Oneself* (New York: Fordham University Press, 2005), 81.

2  The privatization (or enclosure) of public lands today follows a trend that began in England in the late fifteenth and early sixteenth centuries. The enclosure of communal land was a subject of great interest to Marx, who described it as an instance of "primitive accumulation." Enclosure involved the expropriation of land from peasant families. Upon being deprived of their means of sustenance as well as the ability to work for themselves, many migrated to urban centers, where they were eventually absorbed into a new, rapidly growing wage labor force. Systematic acts of enclosure radically altered social, economic, and property relations and, in so doing, laid the foundations for capitalism. See Karl Marx, "Capital, Volume 1," in *The Marx-Engels Reader*, ed. Robert C. Tucker, 2d ed. (New York: W. W. Norton, 1978), 431–38. For more information on primitive accumulation, both as it occurred in the past and as it operates today, see David Harvey's two books, *Spaces of Hope* (Edinburgh: Edinburgh University Press, 2000), 28, and *The New Imperialism* (Oxford: Oxford University Press, 2003), 144–47. For the members of Retort, a group of Bay Area writers and activists, the terms *enclosure* and *primitive accumulation* have great currency today. Retort uses them to describe acts of privatization as well as acts of dispossession, entrapment, and displacement (mostly of workers) upon which the global economy depends. See Retort, *Afflicted Powers: Capital and Spectacle in a New Age of War* (London: Verso, 2005), 10–12.

3  As Retort writes, "The great work of the past half-millennium was the cutting off of the world's natural and human resources from common use. Land, water, the fruits of the forest, the spaces of custom and communal negotiation, the mineral substrate, the life of rivers and oceans, the very airwaves — capitalism has depended, and still depends, on more and more of these shared properties being shared no longer, whatever the violence or absurdity involved in converting the stuff of humanity into this or that item for sale." Retort, *Afflicted Powers*, 193–94. Antoni Negri and Michael Hardt also comment on the enclosure of commonly held information, genetic material, and resources in *Multitude: War and Democracy in the Age of Empire* (New York: Penguin, 2004), 181–88. As these issues pertain to water specifically, see Irena Salina's 2008 documentary, *Flow: For Love of Water*.

4  A point about terminology: Some of the artists in this exhibition are concerned more with space than with land; for others it is the opposite. I will distinguish between land and space as much as possible, especially when describing specific projects. Also, land and space are by no means these artists' sole preoccupations, and the two topics figure in their different bodies of work with varying degrees of regularity.

5  Miwon Kwon, *One Place After Another: Site-Specific Art and Locational Identity* (Cambridge, Mass.: MIT Press, 2002), 29. James Meyer also explores the evolution of site-specific art in "The Functional Site; or, the Transformation of Site-Specificity," in *Space, Site, Intervention: Situating Installation Art*, ed. Erika Suderburg (Minneapolis: University of Minnesota Press, 2000), 23–37. Meyer contrasts the "literal site" (an "actual location" to which the work of art responds, either formally, logistically, or thematically) with the "functional site." According to Meyer, the functional site "may or may not incorporate a physical place.... Instead, it is a process, an operation occurring between sites, a mapping of institutional and textual filiations and the bodies that move between them (the artist's above all).... [The] functional work ... is a temporary thing, a movement, a chain of meaning and imbricated histories" (ibid., 25). The projects in this exhibition dovetail with functional site-specificity, but the artists insist on the simultaneous physical and discursive particularity of the sites they address.

6  As Henri Lefebvre wrote in 1974, "Social relations, which are concrete abstractions, have no real existence save in and through space. *Their underpinning is spatial*" (emphasis in original). Lefebvre, *The Production of Space*, trans. Donald Nicholson-Smith (Oxford: Blackwell Publishing, 1991), 404 (hereafter cited as *POS*). I will return to Lefebvre's work later in this essay.

7  There are many precedents for this exhibition, all of which have proven indispensable to my own project. That said, they tend to cover a slightly different set of issues and address different types of practices. Most focus on ecological welfare and environmental justice, and generally speaking, they privilege either the landscape tradition or ameliorative, design-based projects. A partial list would include *Human Nature: Artists Respond to a Changing Planet* (Museum of Contemporary Art, San Diego, 2009); *Badlands: New Horizons on Landscape* (Mass MoCA, 2008); *E.P.A.* (Exit Art, 2008); *Beyond Green: Toward a Sustainable Art* (iCI [Independent Curators International] Traveling Exhibition, 2005–9); *Groundworks: Environmental Collaboration in Contemporary Art* (Miller Gallery, Carnegie Mellon University, 2005); and *Fragile Ecologies: Contemporary Artists' Interpretations and Solutions* (Queens Museum of Art, 1992). Two other precedents are notable: *Experimental Geography* (iCI Traveling Exhibition, 2008–11) and *Territories: Islands, Camps, and Other States of Utopia* (KW Institute for Contemporary Art, Berlin, 2006). Besides a concern with space and spatiality, *Experimental Geography* shares very little with this exhibition, as my concerns here do not extend to alternative forms of mapmaking (although one of the works in *Nobody's Property*, Matthew Day Jackson's assemblage, draws from the tradition of aerial mapping). The focus of *Territories* is closest in spirit to *Nobody's Property*, but because it is trained almost exclusively on Israeli artists and architects, its point of view is significantly narrower. For more on the relationship between art and ecology, see Emily Apter, "The Aesthetics of Critical Habitats," *October* 99 (Winter 2002): 21–44, and Max Andrews, ed., *Land, Art: A Cultural Ecology Handbook* (London: Royal Society for the Encouragement of Arts, 2006). For a critical review of some of the efforts (both past and present) to align art with ecological and environmental ethics, see T. J. Demos, "The Politics of Sustainability: Art and Ecology," in *Radical Nature: Art and Architecture for a Changing Planet, 1969–2009*, ed. Jonathan Porritt (Cologne: Walther König; London; Barbican Art Gallery, 2009), 17–30. For Demos (who takes his cue in part from Yates McKee), the most successful of these practices trouble the self-evident status of the environment;

interrogate the rhetoric of sustainability; consider nature in the
context of larger social and political conditions; and examine the
asymmetrical risks and burdens
that both ecological despoilation
and green proposals carry for
different races, classes, communities, countries, and hemispheres.
In the process, these practices
also rely on irony and imagina-
tive play to simultaneously posit
other possibilities, other futures,
and to question the efficacy of any
purely pragmatic or ameliorative
approach to ecological devastation.
Although no one artist achieves
all of these goals, Nils Norman,
whose work ranges from the "critical realist" to the "ironic utopian,"
seems to come the closest, in
Demos's mind. See Demos's essay,
"The Cruel Dialectic: On the Work
of Nils Norman," *Grey Room* 13
(Fall 2003): 32–53.

8  See, for instance, Rosalind
Krauss, "Sculpture in the Expanded
Field," *October* 8 (Spring 1979):
33–44.

9  Other members of this new
generation, likewise their relationship to first generation Earth
artists, are addressed in a round
table convened by *Artforum* in
2005. See Tim Griffin, "Remote
Possibilities: A Roundtable
Discussion on Land Art's Changing
Terrain," *Artforum* 43:10 (Summer
2005): 288–95, 366, and Anne
Wagner's essay, "Being There:
Art and the Politics of Place" in
the same issue (265–69, 346).

10  One of the authors of a book on
Francis Alÿs's 2002 project, *When
Faith Moves Mountains*, summarizes
the relationship between contemporary Land artists and their
historical predecessors thus: "Land
Art has always been suspected of
romanticism, for it turns its back
on the city.... Beyond that, it posits
a quasi-metaphysical relationship
with landscape.... These works

were located well out of reach of
any public and safely removed from
the interference of modernization.
The Lima action [*When Faith Moves
Mountains*] wanted to *re-socialize*
Land Art. It wanted to *re-humanize*
it by turning sculpture into mass
experience, while referring to
the condition of landless people"
(emphasis added). Francis Alÿs and
Cuauhtémoc Medina, eds., *When
Faith Moves Mountains* (Madrid:
Turner, 2005), 98. This description is convincing up to a point, but
it has the effect of reducing historical Land Art to a stereotype, and it
ignores Robert Smithson's engagement with industrial and manmade
landscapes.

11  In a 1970 discussion with artists
Robert Smithson and Dennis
Oppenheim, and with *Avalanche*
editors Willoughby Sharp and Liza
Bear, Heizer couched his interest
in working outdoors exclusively in
terms of scale, the displacement
of mass, physical properties, and
raw matter. When asked about his
knowledge of archaeological excavations and their possible impact
on his work, Heizer more or less
brushed the notion aside. He then
continued: "My personal associa-
tions with dirt are very real. I really
like it, I really like to lie in the dirt. I
don't feel close to it in the farmer's
sense.... And I've transcended the
mechanical, which was difficult."
See *Robert Smithson: The Collected
Writings*, ed. Jack Flam (Berkeley
and Los Angeles: University of
California Press, 1996), 248, 245,
251. Yates McKee complicates
my reading of Heizer's work in a
thoughtful essay that appears in
this catalogue.

12  Smithson assiduously strove
to deromanticize, despiritualize,
deidealize, deaestheticize, and
even denaturalize nature. For
him, nature was inextricably tied
not only to geological and physical systems but also to social and
symbolic ones. Instead of an inert,

static object, nature was always
contradictory and incomplete.
History, Smithson believed, bore
as heavily on nature as entropy,
and it bore on it in much the
same way, furthering its decay
and decomposition. Smithson's
approach to landscape is
manifested in his attraction to
"stressed" sites—sites under
pressure from either natural
or manmade forces, such as
quarries, mines, suburbs, post-
industrial ruins, and the Great
Salt Lake. See his "A Tour of the
Monuments of Passaic, New
Jersey" (1967), "A Sedimentation
of the Mind: Earth Projects" (1968),
and "Cultural Confinement" (1972)
in *Smithson: Collected Writings*.
Perhaps the most important of
Smithson's essays in this respect
is "Frederick Law Olmsted and
the Dialectical Landscape" (1973),
also in the *Collected Writings*
volume. For Smithson, a dialectical approach to landscape
involved "seeing things in a mani-
fold of relations, not as isolated
objects. Nature for the dialecti-
cian is *indifferent* to any formal
ideal." What he says of Central
Park, moreover, applies to many of
the sites he investigated and transformed over his career: "Olmsted's
parks...remain carriers of the
unexpected and of contradiction
on all levels of human activity,
be it social, political, or natural"
(ibid., 160). For additional information on historical Earth Art,
see Jeffrey Kastner, ed., *Land
and Environmental Art* (London:
Phaidon, 1998); Suzaan Boettger,
*Earthworks: Art and the Landscape
of the Sixties* (Berkeley and Los
Angeles: University of California
Press, 2002); and Eugenie Tsai,
ed., *Robert Smithson* (Los Angeles:
Museum of Contemporary Art;
Berkeley and Los Angeles: University of California Press, 2004).

13  Similar to historical Earth
artists, artists today anticipate their
work's textualization, mediatization,

and dissemination. As this pertains
to Smithson, see his "Incidents of
Mirror-Travel in the Yucátan" (1969)
in *Smithson: Collected Writings*.
Besides Yates McKee, whose
essay appears in this volume,
Jane McFadden is one of the first
art historians to analyze in any
sustained fashion Earth Art's critical
engagement with media and
mediation—with the issue, in other
words, of how and where Land
Art "appears" in the public realm.
Her subject is Walter de Maria,
for whom a *site* might constitute
a location in the desert, a film,
or a photo-essay in an art magazine. See her "Toward Site," *Grey
Room* 27 (Spring 2007): 36–57, and
"Earthquakes, Photoworks, and Oz:
Walter de Maria's Conceptual Art,"
*Art Journal* 68 (Fall 2009): 68–87.

14  Sierra is the one artist in
*Nobody's Property* whose cross-
professional collaborations are as
asymmetrical as those of historical
artists. These collaborations, which
involve outsourcing labor and
construction, are purely economic
and contractual. In Sierra's case,
though, such relationships are
pursued deliberately and self-
consciously, and their disparity
is folded back into the subject of
the work. Insofar as collaboration is the subtext of many of the
projects in this exhibition, it dovetails with relational or collaborative
aesthetics (sometimes referred to
as "community-based art" or "new
genre public art"). The latter is a
very diverse body of artistic production that solicits the participation
of viewers and creates platforms
for communicative exchange. For
more information, see Hal Foster,
"The Artist as Ethnographer," in
*The Return of the Real* (Cambridge,
Mass.: MIT Press, 1996), 171–203;
Nicholas Bourriaud, *Relational
Aesthetics* (Dijon, France: Les
Presses du réel, 2002); Grant H.
Kester, *Conversation Pieces:
Community and Communication
in Modern Art* (Berkeley and Los

Angeles: University of California Press, 2004); Jessica Morgan, *Commonwealth* (London: Tate Publishing, 2003); Claire Bishop, "Antagonism and Relational Aesthetics," *October* 110 (Fall 2004): 51–79, and "The Social Turn: Collaboration and Its Discontents," *Artforum* 44:6 (Feb. 2006): 178–83; Kester, "Crowds and Connoisseurs: Art and the Public Sphere in America," in *A Companion to Contemporary Art since 1945*, ed. Amelia Jones (Oxford: Blackwell Publishers, 2006), 249–68; and Bishop, ed., *Participation* (London: Whitechapel; Cambridge, Mass.: MIT Press, 2006).

15 "Earthwords" is Smithson's own term, and he uses it in the context of a discussion of Edgar Allan Poe's 1838 novel *The Narrative of Arthur Gordon Pym.* Poe's "descriptions of chasms and holes," Smithson writes, "verge on proposals for 'earthwords.' The shapes of the chasms themselves become 'verbal roots' that spell out the difference between darkness and light." Smithson picks up the textual metaphor again later in the essay when he says, "The strata of the Earth is a jumbled museum. Embedded in the sentiment is a text that contains the limits and boundaries which evade the rational order." "A Sedimentation of the Mind: Earth Projects" (1968), in *Smithson: Collected Writings*, 108, 110. For more on the place of text and language in Smithson's work, and on the collision Smithson effected between the visual and the verbal, see Craig Owens, "Earthwords," *October* 10 (Fall 1979): 121–30.

16 In this respect, Smithson anticipates artists today. Nonetheless, I would argue that contemporary artists' understanding of the ways in which land and space are implicated in larger social, political, economic, and representational systems — in particular, the myriad ways in which land and space serve as weapons in civil and transnational conflict — is far more complex and nuanced than Smithson's.

17 Smithson himself demonstrated no lack of interest in fiction. See his "Strata: A Geophotographic Fiction" (1970), in *Smithson: Collected Writings*, and Owens, "Earthwords."

18 Lefebvre, "Space: Social Product and Use Value" (1979), in *State, Space, World*, ed. Neil Brenner and Stuart Elden (Minneapolis: University of Minnesota Press, 2009), 187. Special thanks to Jill Dawsey for her comments on this section of the essay.

19 Ibid., 186. Lefebvre adds: "From this [the spatialization of the economy] follows an important consequence: the planning of the modern economy tends to become spatial planning" (ibid.). As the economy becomes spatialized, moreover, space (which includes everything from the city, roads, and ports to air, light, and natural resources) comes to function as a means of production (187–88). See also *POS*, 85, 347.

20 "Spatial practice in its entirety," Lefebvre writes, has "saved capitalism from extinction" (*POS*, 346). Indeed, capitalism has "demonstrated that [its] survival depends on [its] being able to extend [its] reach to space in its entirety: to the *land* (in the process of absorbing the towns and agriculture . . .); to the *underground* resources lying deep in the earth and beneath the sea-bed — energy, raw materials, and so on; and lastly to what might be called the above-ground sphere, i.e. to volumes or constructions considered in terms of their height, to the space of mountains and even of the planets. . . . once integrated into capitalism, [space] only gains in strength as a specific element or function in capitalism's expansion" (325). See also "Space: Social Practice," 186, and the chapter "Social Space" in *POS*, 68–168.

21 See Lefebvre, "Space: Social Practice," 187; "The Worldwide and the Planetary," in *State, Space, World*, 201; and *POS*, 378.

22 Space serves in a specifically political capacity insofar as the relations it produces and reproduces are those of power and exploitation (*POS*, 228).

23 This is not to say that space was ever asocial, only that today the "social character of space — those relations that it implies, contains, and dissimulates — has begun *visibly* to dominate" (*POS*, 83). See also *POS*, 26, 347, and "Space: Social Practice," 186–87.

24 *POS*, 143, 201, 319–20. Lefebvre gives the examples of gates, the replacement of parks by roads, the creation of enclaves for the wealthy, and the segregation of minorities and workers, all of which prohibit communication between people in general and across classes and ethnicities more specifically.

25 *POS*, 11, 289. Lefebvre elaborates: "Space is becoming the principle stake of goal-directed actions and struggles. It has of course always been the reservoir of resources, and the medium in which strategies are applied, but it has now become something more than the theatre, the disinterested stage or setting, of action. . . . space can no longer be looked upon as an 'essence,' as an object distinct from the point of view of . . . 'subjects.' . . . Nor can it be treated as a result or resultant, as an empirically verifiable effect of a past, a history of a society. Is space indeed a medium? A milieu? An intermediary? It is doubtless all of these, but its role is less and less neutral, more and more active, both as instrument and goal, as means and as end" (*POS*, 410–11). See also Lefebvre, "Space and Mode of Production," in *State, Space, World*, 212.

26 Hannah Arendt, *The Origins of Totalitarianism* (1951; repr., New York: Harcourt Brace Jovanovich, 1973), 232. Nation-states, which began to emerge in Europe after the French Revolution, matured over the course of the nineteenth century. According to Arendt, nations followed on the heels of states, which evolved many years earlier out of other forms of government, including the "monarchy and enlightened despotism" (ibid., 230). The development of nations is inextricably tied to their recognition of a common homeland, one rooted in the soil. Arendt writes, "Nations entered the scene of history and were emancipated when peoples had acquired a consciousness of themselves as cultural and historical entities, and of their territory as a permanent home, where history had left its visible traces, whose cultivation was the product of the common labor of their ancestors and whose future would depend upon the course of a common civilization. Wherever nation-states came into being, migrations came to and end" (229). For a more recent and extremely nuanced interpretation of the coming of age of nations, see Benedict Anderson, *Imagined Communities: Reflections on the Origin and Spread of Nationalism*, rev. ed. (London; New York: Verso, 2006). According to Anderson, many factors helped trigger the national imagination (both popular and official, Western and postcolonial) over the course of the nineteenth and twentieth centuries, among them print media, language, education, capitalism, maps, and, in the European colonies, colonialism itself. Even if they

share a common model, though, nations develop out of local and historically specific conditions, so they always assume unique forms. More so than Arendt, moreover, Anderson emphasizes the largely arbitrary nature of territorial divisions.

**27** For more on the case of Diego Garcia, see the review of David Vine's 2009 book, *Island of Shame: The Secret History of the U.S. Military Base on Diego Garcia*: Jonathan Freedland, "A Black and Disgraceful Site," *New York Review of Books*, May 28, 2009. In the early 1970s, after almost two decades of negotiations, Great Britain leased Diego Garcia to the United States, which demanded that the indigenous population be removed from the island. The Chagossians and their descendants are currently pursuing legal action against Britain in an effort to return home. On extra-territorial camps, see too An Architektur, "Extra-Territorial Spaces and Camps: Judicial and Political Spaces in the 'War on Terrorism,'" in *Territories: Camps, Islands, and Other States of Utopia*, ed. Anselm Franke, Rafi Segal, and Eyal Weizman (Berlin: KW Institute for Contemporary Art, 2003), 23–28. This essay is indebted to the work of philosopher Giorgio Agamben, specifically his writing on "bare life" and the "state of exception." See Agamben's own essay on camps in *Means Without Ends: Notes on Politics* (Minneapolis: University of Minnesota Press, 2000), 36–44.

**28** See "The Political Emancipation of the Bourgeoisie" (123–57), "Continental Imperialism: the Pan-Movements" (222–66) and "The Decline of the Nation-State and the End of the Rights of Man" (267–302) in Arendt's *Origins of Totalitarianism*. Overseas expansion, in particular, stands in pointed contrast to many of the founding principles of the nation-state, such as popular sovereignty and territorial limits (ibid., 131). Such expansion also admits into the body politic a mass of heterogeneous elements, whose inability or unwillingness to assimilate makes the cultural and linguistic homogeneity on which nation-states rely even more difficult to sustain (125, 128). In the 1880s, expansion helped restore the stagnant economies and faltering institutions of Europe's nation-states, but it ultimately weakened the very thing it was intended to reproduce (147–53). For its part, the crisis of statelessness threw into high relief a constitutional bias that has plagued the nation-state since its inception, rendering it impotent when faced with hundreds of thousands of refugees. Contrary to its claims to universality, the nation-state allows only nationals to be citizens, and it guarantees rights and legal protection to citizens alone (230, 275, 280, 286, 290–91, 293). For Arendt, the nation-state is a deeply flawed political model. It is not only ill-equipped to meet the demands of the twentieth century; it is also ill-suited to the vast majority of European peoples and communities, which lack the requisite demographic uniformity and territorial stability to form proper nation-states (231–2, 269–70). Worse yet, Arendt argues, nation-states are structurally inclined to create statelessness (290). Arendt proposed various solutions to the problems posed by the nation-state in general and by Israel in particular. In the 1940s, she advocated for a federated Jewish nation, uncoupled from the state and territory alike, while in the 1960s, she argued for a federated Jewish-Arab state. Arendt explored these issues in essays now collected in *The Jewish Writings*, ed. Jerome Kohn and Ron H. Feldman (New York: Schocken Books, 2007). See Judith Butler's review, "'I merely belong to them,'" *London Review of Books*, May 10, 2007. Arjun Appadurai also discusses the gradual disintegration of the nation-state-territory nexus in *Modernity at Large: Cultural Dimensions of Globalization* (Minneapolis: University of Minnesota Press, 1996). According to Appadurai, this nexus shows signs of weakness on multiple fronts. We can no longer assume that states represent a single nation or that every nation sees itself adequately represented in its corresponding state. Nations are battling states, while states are struggling to control and standardize nations. If the isomorphism of the nation-state has declined, it is due largely to globalization. More than ever before, people, and the ethnic and national identities they embrace, are being dispersed across territorial boundaries. Solidarity and belonging are now figured on a transnational basis— they exceed the nation-state at both the political and the spatial level, frustrating its attempts to maintain national homogeneity (ibid., 147, 157–77, 188–93). See also Daniel Heller-Roazen, *The Enemy of All: Piracy and the Law of Nations* (New York: Zone Books, 2009), especially chapters 11, 12, and 14. Here, Heller-Roazen discusses the ways in which changes to warfare (the introduction of the "partisan") and military technology (specifically the submarine) stressed the nation-state-territory nexus. Many thanks to Hal Foster for introducing me to this fascinating book.

**29** This is the crux of Appadurai's *Modernity at Large*. The author focuses in particular on the deterritorialization of ethnic and national identity (ibid., 48–49, 158–77, 188–93). As he writes, "One major fact that accounts for strains in the union of nation and state is that the nationalist genie, never perfectly contained in the bottle of the territorial state, is now itself diasporic. Carried in the repertoires of increasingly mobile populations of refugees, tourists, guest workers, transnational intellectuals, scientists, and illegal aliens, it is increasingly unrestrained by ideas of spatial boundary and territorial sovereignty.... Where soil and place were once the key to the linkage of territorial affiliation with state monopoly of the means of violence, key identities and identifications now only partially revolve around the realities and images of place" (161). Much of Appadurai's book is devoted to sketching the parameters of transnational and postnational forms of identity and solidarity at the close of the twentieth century.

**30** For an excellent discussion of (mostly activist) NGOs, see Michel Feher, ed., *Nongovernmental Politics*, with Gaëlle Krikorian and Yates McKee (New York: Zone Books, 2007), especially Feher's introduction (12–27). McKee addresses the artistic implications of NGOs, as well as the artistic strategies they employ, in two essays, "'Eyes and Ears': Aesthetics, Visual Culture, and the Claims of Nongovernmental Politics" (327–55) and "Art and the Ends of Environmentalism: From Biosphere to the Right to Survival" (538–83). McKee makes two important points. The first regards art's role in environmental activism. "The task of the new environmental art," he writes, is "to unsettle the self-evidence of 'environment' itself, addressing it as a contingent assemblage of biological, technological, economic, and governmental concerns whose boundaries and agencies are perpetually exposed to conflict" (ibid., 557). The second point is more general, addressing the relationship between art and activism. Taking his cue from Michel Foucault and Jacques Rancière, McKee argues that art serves not merely to visualize information, frame political objectives, and fashion modes of address, but also to allow previously silenced voices to be heard (329).

**31** For a fascinating discussion of delocalized, transnational conflicts as figured in contemporary art, see T. J. Demos, *Zones of Conflict* (New York: Pratt Manhattan Gallery, 2008). See also Faisal Devji's excellent book, *Landscapes of the Jihad: Militancy, Morality, Modernity* (London: Hurst, 2005). According to Devji, jihad is exemplary of global conflict (the most prevalent type of conflict today) in that it has been uncoupled from the nation-state and its corresponding legal system; it has become unmoored in time and place; it advances no specific political agenda (such as freedom and autonomy for a specific group); it expresses no desire for territorial control; and it finds its most perfect expression in the mediasphere. The global character of jihad can also be discerned in the makeup of its participants—who come from many different backgrounds and profess beliefs often at odds with one another—and in its abandonment of a "politics of intentionality," in which means and ends are synchronized (ibid., 73). Precisely because it frames "social relations outside of the language of the state and citizenship," jihad encapsulates many of the characteristics of globalization and global conflict today (76). Extraterritorial and transnational conflicts also have a long history, although they have become more pronounced during the last fifty years. See Heller-Roazen, *Enemy of All*, especially ch. 12.

**32** Appadurai speculates that territorial claims might very well play a lesser role in the context of demands for independence and sovereignty than first assumed. See *Modernity at Large*, 165–66.

**33** On the devastating effects of weapons testing on the people, animals, and environment of the American West, an area the Pentagon has designated a "national sacrifice zone," see Mike Davis, "The Dead West: Ecocide in Marlboro Country," *New Left Review* 1:200 (July–Aug. 1993).

**34** Michael Pollan, *The Omnivore's Dilemma: A Natural History of Four Meals* (New York: Penguin, 2007), 38. My comment is not meant to suggest that the landscape of nineteenth-century Iowa was any more "natural" or "authentic" than the landscape of present-day Iowa, but rather to underscore the radical changes that this area (and, indeed, the world as a whole) has undergone in just the last century and a half. Rather than nostalgia for an earlier moment, I wish to express apprehension about the negative impact such changes have had or might yet have on the environment and on human beings, especially those already disenfranchised because of race, ethnicity, and class.

**35** On the Three Gorges Dam, see Jim Yardley, "Chinese Dam Projects Criticized for Their Human Cost," *New York Times*, Nov. 19, 2007 (hereafter cited as *NYT*). According to a report issued in 2000, the Three Gorges Dam is only one among 45,000 large dams constructed over the past one hundred years. These have generated much needed energy and water, but they have also displaced millions of people, most of them poor; threatened species and ecosystems; inundated towns; and destroyed areas of cultural and historical significance. See Tom Zeller, "Ideas & Trends: Ebb and Flow of Opinion: Big Dam Projects," *NYT*, Nov. 19, 2000. On dam construction in India, see Harvey, *New Imperialism*, 177–78.

**36** Were we to extend our timeline to the period between 1870 and 1925, these changes would become even more drastic. According to Harvey, the majority of national boundaries were drawn between 1870 and 1925. The Africa of today, for instance, was largely configured by the British and French in 1885. Harvey, *Spaces of Hope*, 34.

**37** I say "Palestine" and "Transjordan" even though the original British Mandate of Palestine made no distinction between them. It was not until *after* the mandate was approved in June 1922 that the territory was divided into two distinct administrative entities: one east of the Jordan River (Transjordan), the other west (Palestine). Only Palestine was opened to Jewish settlement. Transjordan began to establish its independence from Britain by the late 1920s, two decades before the mandate officially ended in 1946. The original French mandate applied to what was then Syria and Lebanon. The latter was gradually established as an independent entity over the course of the 1920s, 1930s, and 1940s. Both the French and British mandates served to formalize occupations dating back to 1917–18.

**38** Many factors have facilitated urban development, including excess capital, lax environmental laws, and a migrant work force with few rights and little ability to organize. The megalopolises of Dubai, Shanghai, and Bejiing, which are being made with capital, are also being transformed into its very image—that is, into global centers attractive to both tourists and transnational corporations. Nor is this phenomenon exclusive to the East or Middle East, as the same imperative governs the growth of cities such as New York and Berlin. The building boom in Dubai has slowed considerably since the beginning of the economic downturn in 2007, and many of the laborers who immigrated with the hope of finding jobs in construction, industry, or the service sector are now out of work and have been forced to return home. On the building booms in China and the Persian Gulf, see Nicolai Ouroussoff, "The New, New City," *NYT*, June 8, 2008. On Shenzhen, see Howard W. French, "Chinese Success Story Chokes on Its Own Growth," *NYT*, Dec. 19, 2006. On Shanghai, which some say is literally sinking under the weight of the 4000 skyscrapers built on the island between 1978 and 2008, see "Race for Skyscrapers," *China Daily*, Dec. 1, 2008, and Howard W. French, "Shanghai's Boom: A Building Frenzy," *NYT*, Apr. 13, 2006. On the relationship between Shanghai's frenzied growth and the 2010 World Expo, which will showcase the city in much the same way the 2008 Olympics did Beijing, see David Barboza, "Shanghai Buys Itself a Makeover," *NYT*, May 30, 2009. On China's building boom, see Christopher Hawthorne, "China Pulls Up the Drawbridge," *NYT*, Sept. 19, 2004; Barboza, "China Builds Its Dreams, and Some Fear a Bubble," *NYT*, Oct. 18, 2005; Arthur Lubow, "The China Syndrome," *NYT*, May 21, 2006; Barboza, "China Builds Its Large-Scale Future," *NYT*, May 1, 2008; and Ouroussoff, "In Changing Face of Beijing, a Look at the New China," *NYT*, July 13, 2008. Upon assuming office, French President Nicolas Sarkozy asked a group of prominent architects to devise a new "blueprint" for Paris, one whose rhetoric (or so it seems to me) is deeply ethnophobic and steeped in the language of dirt and hygiene. See Ouroussoff, "Remaking Paris," *NYT*, June 8, 2009. A building boom in one place tends to have collateral effects elsewhere, as in Indonesia, which lost several islands in its archipelago to sand mining. Sand is a key ingredient in cement, the material that facilitated the building boom in Singapore much as steel facilitated Beijing's. See Wayne Arnold and Thomas Fuller, "Neighbor Leaves Singapore Short of Sand," *NYT*, Mar. 16, 2007. This same dialectic is at play at the local level, where growth and development proceed at the expense of historic neighborhoods and lower- and working-class communities. When it comes to land and space, there is no creation without destruction, no gain without loss. For an especially optimistic and even triumphant response to the modernization of cities in East and Southeast Asia, see Hou Hanru and Hans Ulrich Obrist's 1999 essay "Cities on the Move," written for a traveling exhibition by the same name. Thanks to a dynamic exchange between East and West, these cities have become hubs in a global network and their residents the epitome of the global citizen: mobile, flexible, hybridized, technologically savvy, politically conservative, and predominantly middle-class. For Hanru and Obrist, every change triggered by modernization, no matter how severe or dramatic, is cause for excitement. They describe even the disappearance of historical landmarks, the increase in conflict, traffic, and pollution, the further immiseration of the poor, and the adoption of Western patterns of consumption with apparent blithe indifference. See Fiona Bradley, ed., *Cities on the Move: Urban Chaos and Global Change, East Asian Art, Architecture, and Film Now* (London: Hayward Gallery, 1999).

39  Seth Mydans, "Singapore Prepares to Gobble Up Its Last Village," *NYT*, Jan. 3, 2009.

40  Singapore has increased its land area from 224 to 299 square miles over the last several decades (ibid.).

41  See Ian Parker, "The Mirage," *New Yorker*, Oct. 17, 2005. See also Mike Davis, "Fear and Money in Dubai," *New Left Review* 41 (Sept.–Oct. 2006). In November 2009, Dubai's bubble burst, and Dubai World, its investment arm, was forced to seek relief from its

creditors. Aid from Abu Dhabi (in the form of a $10 billion bailout) arrived a few weeks later. For a synopsis, see Landon Thomas Jr., "Abu Dhabi Tightens Its Grip as It Offers Help to Dubai," *NYT*, Dec. 14, 2009.

42  See Katharine Q. Seelye, "Sacramento and Its Riverside Tent City," *NYT*, Mar. 11, 2009, and Jesse McKinley, "Cities Deal with a Surge in Shantytowns," *NYT*, Mar. 25, 2009. These tent cities have their corollaries in the trailers (built with toxic materials) that were distributed to New Orleans residents after Hurricane Katrina, and in the refugee camps created for those fleeing conflicts in Africa, the Middle East, and elsewhere. For a sophisticated reading of the multiple interests that converge in the debate over housing in post-Katrina New Orleans, see Yates McKee, "Haunted Housing: Eco-Vanguardism, Eviction, and the Biopolitics of Sustainability in New Orleans," *Grey Room* 30 (Winter 2008): 84–113. McKee draws attention to the lacunae and biases that plague many of the extant proposals to rebuild New Orleans — proposals that focus almost exclusively on sustainability and fail to consider the role that race and class play in the demographic organization of the city.

43  Arendt, *Origins of Totalitarianism*, 232.

44  Many examples could be cited in the United States alone, among them the recent (and still unresolved) debates over immigration legislation; the premiere, in January 2009, of a new reality television program, *Homeland Security USA* (canceled soon thereafter); the founding of the Minuteman Project in 2005; and the passing of the Secure Fence Act that same year. As of April 16, 2009, 613 miles of a 1000-plus mile fence separating

Mexico from the United States have been constructed. See April Reese, "U.S.-Mexico Fence Building Continues Despite Obama's Promise to Review Effects," *NYT*, Apr. 16, 2009.

45  I take the idea of the local as spectacle — that is, the local as figured for consumption by local and global audiences alike — from Lee Weng Choy, "Just What Is It That Makes the Term 'Global-Local' So Widely Cited, Yet So Annoying," in *Over Here: International Perspectives on Art and Culture*, ed. Gerardo Mosquera and Jean Fisher (New York: New Museum of Contemporary Art; Cambridge, Mass.: MIT Press, 2004), 16.

46  Lefebvre's writing is crucial to consider here; see my discussion earlier in this essay. Lefebvre also offers an extended analysis of some of the contradictions and characteristics (among them homogeneity, fragmentation, and hierarchization) inherent to capitalist space. See "From the Contradictions of Space to Differential Space," *POS*, 352–400. Like Lefebvre, Harvey too has devoted a great deal of research to understanding how capitalism — specifically global capitalism — has reshaped space and built its own geography. As he writes, "If . . . 'globalization' signifies anything about our recent historical geography, it is mostly likely to be a new phase of exactly this same process of the capitalist production of space." Harvey, *Spaces of Hope*, 54. See too Appadurai's discussion of the complex, disjunctive characteristics of globalization, which play out on registers at once spatial, discursive, and political, in *Modernity at Large*, 32–37, 46–47.

47  See John Bellamy Foster, "Contradictions in the Universalization of Capitalism," *Monthly Review*, Apr. 1999.

48  David Harvey's work on the geography of capitalism is important to consider here. According to Harvey (and Marx and Engels before him), capitalism is beset by internal contradictions, which lead, in turn, to crises such as the over-accumulation of capital and labor. In response, he argues, capitalism has engineered a number of "spatial fixes." Harvey, *New Imperialism*, 87–89, 109–24. Put simply, capitalism resolves the crises it generates by expanding geographically toward new resources, new markets, and new investment possibilities. Expansion across once-closed national borders allows capitalism to identify potential outlets for surplus capital as well as a cheaper work force and a larger pool of consumers. Capitalism eliminates barriers to this expansion in numerous ways, which have ramifications for how land is used and space is organized. It invests in transportation and communication, for instance, which reduces the "friction of distance" and allows ideas, raw goods, and commodities to flow more quickly. Harvey, *Spaces of Hope*, 59–60. Insofar as it involves finding a productive outlet for surplus capital, one that fixes capital literally "in and on the land," investment in infrastructure is itself a spatial fix (*New Imperialism*, 115). Expansion is as creative as it is destructive, however, and the reorganization of space always has consequences for pre-existing social, political, ecological, and property relations. On an earlier phase of economic and political expansion, see Arendt, "The Political Emancipation of the Bourgeoisie," in *Origins of Totalitarianism*, 123–57.

49  On the push-pull between deterritorialization and reterritorialization, see Harvey, *Spaces of Hope*, 60, 65–66. According to Harvey, the labor of reterritorialization falls mainly to the state,

regional trading blocs, and supra-national organizations.

**50**  Glossing Gilles Deleuze and Félix Guattari, philosopher Alain Badiou described the reterritorialization of identity as follows: "There is nothing more captive, so far as commercial investment is concerned . . . than a community and its territory or territories. . . . What inexhaustible potential for mercantile investment in this upsurge . . . of women, homosexuals, the disabled, Arabs! And these infinite combinations of predicative traits, what a godsend! Black homosexuals, disabled Serbs, Catholic pedophiles, moderate Muslims, married priests, ecologist yuppies, the submissive unemployed, prematurely aged youth! Deleuze put it perfectly: capitalist deterritorialization requires a constant reterritorialization . . . a permanent creation of subjective and territorial identities." Alain Badiou, *Saint Paul: The Foundation of Universalism*, trans. Ray Brassier (Stanford, Calif.: Stanford University Press, 2003), 11.

**51**  See Harvey, *New Imperialism*, 142–45, and Retort, *Afflicted Powers*, 10–12, 193–94. Primitive accumulation, these authors insist, is still operative today, most recently in places like China, India, and Mexico, but this is not to suggest that it always goes uncontested. See Harvey, *New Imperialism*, 154, 160. In August 2008, for instance, 40,000 farmers in Singur, India, convened in front of the Nano automobile plant to protest the confiscation of their land. See Agence France-Presse, "Tens of Thousands Protest Site of Auto Plant in India," *NYT*, Aug. 24, 2008. Not all forms of primitive accumulation involve the expropriation of land. To these extraterritorial acts of accumulation Harvey gives the name "accumulation by dispossession." They include the credit system, finance capital,

and speculation; the licensing of genetic material; the expansion of intellectual property rights; the "commodification of cultural forms, histories, and . . . creativity," and the "corporatization" of "public assets" and utilities. See Harvey, *New Imperialism*, 146–48. According to Harvey, some forms of accumulation portend positive developments (ibid., 162–64, 177–79).

**52**  Weizman was one of Alÿs's interlocutors in *The Green Line* (the project featured in this exhibition), and excerpts from his response were incorporated into the video's soundtrack.

**53**  *Hollow Land* was preceded by two exhibitions, both organized by Weizman and Rafi Segal, a partner in Weizman's architectural firm. The first, *A Civilian Occupation*, included the work of Israeli architects, historians, photographers, and journalists, and it explored the relationship between Zionism, architecture, and urban planning. This project was supposed to have appeared in the 2002 UIA (International Union of Architects) Berlin Architectural Congress, but it proved too polemical for the Israeli Association of Architects, which banned it and destroyed all 5000 copies of the catalogue. In the end, the Storefront Gallery for Art and Architecture in New York hosted the exhibition. *A Civilian Occupation* was followed by *Territories: Islands, Camps, and Other States of Utopia*, co-curated with Anselm Franke for the KW Institute for Contemporary Art in Berlin in 2003. *Territories* featured one of the artists in this exhibition, Yael Bartana, and its catalogue includes a wealth of insight and information on the politics of space, including W. J. T. Mitchell's essay "Space, Place, and Landscape" (which features his important "theses on landscape" as well as a nuanced description of the relationship between imperialism and landscape). See Franke,

Segal, and Weizman, *Territories: Islands, Camps*.

**54**  On the settlements, see too Tony Judt, "Fictions on the Ground," *NYT*, June 22, 2009. Judt, director of the Remarque Foundation at New York University, writes that "the settler myth has been transposed . . . to the Palestinian lands seized in war in 1967 and occupied illegally ever since," even though many settlements consist of quite large and very modern communities. According to Judt, "there are about 120 official Israeli settlements in the occupied territories of the West Bank. In addition, there are 'unofficial' settlements whose number is estimated variously from 80 to 100. Under international law, there is no difference between these two categories; both are contraventions of Article 47 of the Fourth Geneva Convention, which explicitly prohibits the annexation of land consequent to the use of force, a principle re-stated in Article 2(4) of the United Nations Charter" (ibid.).

**55**  On the use of the bulldozer as a weapon in the Israeli-Palestinian conflict, see Stephen Graham, "Lessons in Urbicide," *New Left Review* 19 (Jan.-Feb. 2003). Graham describes the myriad ways in which the Israeli government and military deploy the bulldozer as part of a larger strategy to undermine Palestinian modernity, the Palestinian economy, and the proto-Palestinian state. Thanks to Paul Chan for bringing this essay to my attention.

**56**  See, for instance, Ethan Bronner and Isabel Kershner, "Parks Fortify Israel's Claim to Jerusalem," *NYT*, May 10, 2009. This article also describes the highly politicized discipline of archaeology and the role it plays in the Israeli-Palestinian conflict. The discovery of archaeological material is often used to justify Israeli

control over areas occupied illegally since 1967. See Eyal Weizman, *Hollow Land: Israel's Architecture of Occupation* (London: Verso, 2007), 39–42. The United Nations Security Council Resolution 242, from 1967, describes the Israeli seizure of land during the Six Day War as "inadmissible" and calls for the withdrawal of Israeli forces from the occupied territories; see http://www.un.org/documents/sc/res/1967/scres67.htm. In addition to parks and archaeological digs, I could have added the example of signs. In September 2009, Yisrael Katz, Israel's transport minister, announced plans to strip the country's directional signs of Arabic and English and designate the country's cities, airports, roads, and landmarks by their Hebrew names alone. Whether or not this plan has been (or will be) implemented is unclear. See Jerrold Kessel and Pierre Klochendler, "By Any Other Name," *NYT*, Sept. 9, 2009. Thanks to Jaleh Mansoor for drawing my attention to this op-ed piece.

**57**  Weizman's reading of the role that land and space play in the Israeli occupation of Gaza and the West Bank is informed by Lefebvre's consideration of the relationship between space, power, and the State. Indeed, Lefebvre could have been describing the situation in Palestine and Israel when he wrote, "State action is . . . not limited to the management of the social and 'private' life of millions of people . . . by institutional and administrative means. It proceeds in a more indirect but no less effective way by making use of this privileged instrument — space" ("Space and the State," 240). See also *POS*, 281, 358. For a discussion of landscape and geography in the Israeli-Palestinian conflict, see W. J. T. Mitchell, "Holy Landscape: Israel, Palestine, and the American Wilderness," in *Landscape and Power*, ed. Mitchell (Chicago: University of Chicago Press, 2002),

261–89, and Edward W. Said, "Invention, Memory, and Place" in the same volume (241–59). For Mitchell, *landscape* is understood as representations of land (what he calls "idols"), all with varying degrees of ideological potency and truth-value. As in most landscapes, depictions of the Holy Land are always politically motivated, and they often have a tenuous connection to the real places, experiences, and memories they claim to illustrate.

**58**  In June 2006, Hamas militants crossed into Israel using one of the tunnels, injured two Israeli soldiers, killed two others, and captured a third, whom they still hold as of Dec. 12, 2009. For more information on the tunnels, see Abigail Hauslohner, "In the Tunnels: Gaza's Underground Economy," *Time*, Oct. 13, 2009. On the status of Gaza since summer 2006, when Hamas won parliamentary elections and its most recent violent conflagration with Israel began, see Lawrence Wright, "Letter from Gaza: Captives," *New Yorker*, Nov. 9, 2009, 46–61.

**59**  Weizman, *Hollow Land*, 84. The artistic and philosophical tradition informing Israeli strategy is important to consider here. On the reading list of the Israeli Defense Force (IDF), for instance, is a wide variety of radical, postcolonial, and poststructuralist theory, including texts by Gilles Deleuze, Félix Guattari, Guy Debord, Georges Bataille, and Bernard Tschumi, while the work of Gordon Matta-Clark appears in a section of an IDF training manual devoted to urban warfare (ibid., 187, 209).

**60**  Weizman uses the analogy of a "prosthetic" to describe the relationship between power and space (ibid., 145). Besides the example of the Israeli-Palestinian conflict, we might cite the Chinese government's decision to raze and then reconstruct as a simulacrum much of the ancient town of Kashgar, once an important destination along the Silk Route. Doing so would involve uprooting the town's residents, some 13,000 members of an ethnic minority called the Uighurs (Muslims of Turkish descent), and relocating them to nearby housing developments. The government claims that Kashgar's ancient buildings are prone to collapse in the event of an earthquake, but given that a small but vocal group of Uighur separatists also reside in Kashgar, displacing residents and destroying their cultural heritage might also be intended to control and administer an unruly population. See Michael Wines, "To Protect an Ancient City, China Moves to Raze It," *NYT*, May 27, 2009.

**61**  *POS*, 287.

**62**  Mitchell understands landscape (as opposed to land) is similar terms. He writes, "Landscape is a medium not only for expressing value, but also for expressing meaning, for communication between persons — most radically, for communication between the human and the non-human." Here Mitchell stresses landscape's role in constructing relations between human beings and the natural world. Instead of a human relation made concrete, moreover, landscape is for him a kind of communicative device, a "body of symbolic forms," that enables exchange. See "Space, Place, and Landscape," in Franke, Segal, and Weizman, *Territories: Islands, Camps*, 171, 174. My description of space as the concrete expression of immaterial relations also derives from Lefebvre. Much like the commodity, he writes, space is "both *abstract* and *concrete* in character: abstract inasmuch as it has no existence save by virtue of the exchangeability of all its component parts, and concrete inasmuch as it is socially real and as such localized." *POS*, 342.

**63**  Unlike a conventional typology, the one I have developed for this exhibition is more elastic than rigid, and its goal is to bring clarity to an emerging development without presuming to exhaust the projects to which it applies. In choosing the specific components of this typology, I followed the lead of the works themselves. As will become clear in the following notes, this typology has relevance beyond contemporary Earth Art.

**64**  The investigative aesthetic has its roots in conceptual art and institutional critique of the late 1960s and early 1970s, specifically the polemical, idiosyncratic form of "investigative journalism" practiced by Hans Haacke and members of the Art Workers Coalition. See Julia Bryan-Wilson, *Art Workers: Radical Practice in the Vietnam War Era* (Berkeley and Los Angeles: University of California Press, 2009), 173–213. There are many other contemporary artists and artist collectives whose primary concern is land and space and whose work partakes of the investigatory ethos, including Ursula Biemann, Farmlab, Land Arts of the American West, the Center for Land Use Interpretation (CLUI), Rirkrit Tiravanija and Kamin Lertchaiprasert (specifically their project the Land), and Trevor Paglen (Paglen's work often partakes of the parafictional as well, a topic I will address shortly). Mel Chin's *Revival Field* might be included in this group, although it tends towards the scientific rather than the archival. Works that operate in the investigatory mode also dovetail with broader trends in contemporary art, in particular the current interest in the documentary tradition; the archive as medium, subject, and source; history and historical representation; and the relationship between past and present. See Hal Foster, "An Archival Impulse," *October* 110 (Fall 2004): 3–22; Charles Merewether, ed., *The Archive* (London: Whitechapel; Cambridge, Mass.: MIT Press, 2006); Nato Thompson, ed., *Ahistoric Occasion: Artists Making History* (North Adams, Mass.: MASS MoCA, 2006); Mark Godfrey, "The Artist as Historian," *October* 120 (Spring 2007): 140–72; and Okwui Enwezor, *Archive Fever: Uses of the Document in Contemporary Art* (New York: International Center of Photography, 2008).

**65**  Raven's digital film is reminiscent of Steve McQueen's films *Western Deep* (2002) and *Gravesend* (2007), both of which explore the relationship between mining operations in Africa and consumption in the West, likewise the effect this asymmetrical relationship has on African miners. For more information on McQueen, see T. J. Demos, "The Art of Darkness," *October* 114 (Fall 2005): 61–89, and "Moving Images of Globalization," *Grey Room* 37 (Fall 2009): 6–29.

**66**  Galit Eilat, "A Conversation with Yael Bartana," in *Yael Bartana: Videos and Photographs*, ed. Charles Esche and Esra Sarigekik Öktem (Eindhoven: Van Abbemuseum, 2006), 41–42, and "Klaus Biesenbach Interviews Yael Bartana," *Yael Bartana: Short Memory*, ed. Sergio Edelsztein and Klaus Biesenbach (Tel Aviv: Center for Contemporary Art; New York: P.S.1 Contemporary Art Center, 2008), 137.

**67**  Moshe Ninio identifies the site as Herzliya Pituach, a suburb north of Tel Aviv on the Mediterranean coast. See her essay "On *Kings of the Hill* and Some Other Videos by Yael Bartana," in *Yael Bartana*, ed. Yilmaz Dziewior (Ostfildern: Hatje Cantz Verlag, 2006), 26. Bartana describes the ritual as a kind of occupation, one that aligns it symbolically with the state of Israel. The drivers of the jeeps and trucks, she says, remind her of "reserve soldiers on their tour of duty…[It is] a very macho kind of pastime," one that symbolizes "militarism and nationalism," but it is very "playful" as well, "funny on the verge of stupidity." Edelsztein and Biesenbach, *Yael Bartana: Short Memory*, 137, 138.

68  On Bartana and the Israeli media, see Eilat, "A Conversation with Yael Bartana," 36. On Bartana's reference to and appropriation of Zionist propaganda films, which is also apparent in her 2007 video installation *Summer Camp*, see Eilat, "Non-Zionist Propaganda," in *Yael Bartana: Short Memory*, 105–9, as well as video documentation of Bartana's presentation at the 2009 Creative Time Summit: Revolutions in Public Practice, held in New York in October 2009, at http://www.youtube.com/watch?v=PrhwdcMe5Bc.

69  Indeed, many of the texts cited in the previous footnote on history, archives, and contemporary art are relevant here as well. On the parafictional aspects of Pierre Huyghe's *A Journey That Wasn't* (a work that could have been featured in this exhibition, given the important role it accords to land and space), see Mark Godfrey, "Pierre Huyghe's Double Spectacle," *Grey Room* 32 (Summer 2008): 38–61. On the confusion of fact and fiction in contemporary avatars and "navigational art," see David Joselit, "Navigating the New Territory," *Artforum* 43 (Summer 2005): 276–79. T. J. Demos uses the term "fictional documentaries" to describe the work of artists such as Steve McQueen, the Otolith Group, and Hito Steyerl. According to Demos, fictional documentaries tend to resist the imperative to represent their subjects with absolute certainty, to render them fully

visible. The documentaries' political efficacy, moreover, resides in their engagement with subjects as images. Political contestation occurs in such work, according to Demos, through the recalibration of images, through the reorganization of what is seen, which serves to activate the creative and critical faculties of viewers. See Demos, "Moving Images of Globalization."

70  Carrie Lambert-Beatty, "Make Believe: Parafiction and Plausibility," *October* 129 (Summer 2009): 51–84. Although Hadjithomas and Joreige most certainly operate in the parafictional mode, their motivations do not necessarily correlate with those Lambert-Beatty describes. According to Lambert-Beatty, the parafictioneer's primary task is to produce epistemological doubt and heighten the critical capacities of viewers. Hadjithomas and Joreige, on the other hand, seem more concerned with identifying an appropriate and compelling aesthetic equivalent for the experience of war and its aftermath. Special thanks to Hal Foster and the students in our Fall 2009 contemporary art seminar at Princeton University for helping me sort through the different iterations of parafiction.

71  For more on the mixing of imaginary and archival modes in contemporary Lebanese art, see Demos, *Zones of Conflict*; Suzanne Cotter's and Kaelen Wilson-Goldie's essays in *Out of Beirut*, ed. Cotter (Oxford: Modern Art Oxford, 2006); and the Summer 2007 issue of *Art Journal* (66:2). Other artists whose preoccupations tend towards land, space, and the parafictional are Joachim Koester, Matthew Buckingham, and Walid Ra'ad.

72  See Tim O'Brien's 1990 short story, "How to Tell a True War Story," in *Postmodern American Fiction: A Norton Anthology*, ed. Paula Geyh et

al. (New York: W. W. Norton, 1998), 174–83. Many thanks to Chris Reitz for introducing me to this essay.

73  *Wonder Beirut* also supplies a provisional answer to the following question: What is the most appropriate way to represent a city in the aftermath of war? See the interview with Jean Charles Massera in *Fundamentalisms of the New Order* (Copenhagen, 2002). Downloaded from CRG Gallery website, http://www.crggallery.com/artists/joana-hadjithomas-and-khalil-joreige/press/?article=8.

74  Hadjithomas and Joreige maintain this fiction in press releases, on their website, and in the essays they write about the project. See their "The Story of a Pyromaniac Photographer," *Cabinet* no. 16 (Winter 2004–5): 37–38, and "Wonder Beirut," in *Out of Beirut*, 77, as well as the material on their website, http://www.hadjithomas-joreige.com.

75  When I describe the postcards as "real," I mean they predate the artists. They are actual postcards, in other words, and not the invention of Hadjithomas and Joreige. This does not mean, however, that the Beirut they depict is somehow more "real" than the Beirut of 1975 or 2009. Clearly, the city represented in the postcards is as much a spectacle or phantasmatic projection as it is a material fact. In this respect, the postcards appropriated by the artists are already implicated in the parafictional.

76  In this, Hadjithomas and Joreige were inspired by a comment filmmaker Jean-Luc Godard made about Palestinians in 2004. Since 1948, Godard argues, "Palestinians have been a 'documentary,' defined by their conflict with Israel and unable to develop other concepts of individual and national identity. Jews, by contrast, have been the stuff of fiction, free

to create diverse understandings of self and community." Godard's remarks are summarized by Joshua Mack in "Art and Politics in the Gulf and the Middle East," *Art Review* (July 2007). Downloaded from CRG Gallery website, http://www.crggallery.com/artists/joana-hadjithomas-and-khalil-joreige/press/?article=2. Godard's comment postdates the beginning of *Wonder Beirut* by eight years, but the project continued until 2006, and it is reasonable to assume that Hadjithomas and Joreige mentioned Godard in the first place because they already felt sympathy with his position.

77  Ayreen Anastas and Rene Gabri's project, *Camp Campaign*, merges the conventions of the investigative and the interrogative. See their website, http://www.campcampaign.info/about.htm.

78  The video documenting Alÿs's intervention identifies many of the landmarks and neighborhoods he passed through, including the Ein Yaël checkpoint; Beit Safafa, an Arab neighborhood in southeastern Jerusalem, home to many Israeli settlements; No Man's Land, the former demilitarized zone separating the Israeli and Jordanian parts of the city; Abu Tor, a neighborhood originally divided by the Green Line; Mount Zion; the Old City; the Jaffa Gate; City Hall; the Damascus Gate; Mandelbaum House (site of the only crossing point between the Arab and Israeli portions of the city between 1949 and 1967); Route 1; Kiryat Aryeh (Aryeh); Sanhedrya (Sanhedria), home to an Orthodox community; Ramot (Ramat) Eshkol, a former Arab neighborhood whose land was expropriated by the Israelis in 1967 and transformed into one of the first Jewish quarters in East Jerusalem; and the Ramot (Ramat) checkpoint, site of a 1995 suicide bombing. On Ramat Eshkol, see Bernard Wasserstein, *Divided*

*Jerusalem: The Struggle for the Holy City*, 3rd ed. (New Haven: Yale University Press, 2008), 218.

79  Like Alÿs's, Dayan's too is a performative gesture, a symbolic act that brings into being that which it represents. For more information on the original Green Line, see Corinne Diserens, "Borders and Subway Exits," in Alÿs and Medina, *When Faith Moves Mountains*, 164. The borders established by the Green Line — specifically the borders separating Israel from Gaza and the West Bank — roughly correspond to those established in the 1947 United Nations partition plan, which aimed to divide Palestine into two states, one Arab, the other Jewish. Thanks to gains made in 1949 and again in 1967 (some of which were later reversed), Israel now controls a far greater portion of the territory than originally allotted to it, but it does so in contravention of international law and at the expense of Palestinians, more than 750,000 of which have been displaced and dispossessed.

80  Even though Palestinians were granted partial administrative control of Gaza and the West Bank in 1993, in the wake of the Oslo Accords, and even though Israel disengaged from Gaza in 2005 and dismantled its settlements, both Gaza and the West Bank are still considered "occupied" by the United Nations.

81  These percentages are even higher in the case of Jerusalem: as of July 2009, only 3 percent of the Barrier corresponds to the Green Line. For more information on the history, progress, and parameters of the West Bank Barrier as well as its negative impact on Palestinians, see Weizman, *Hollow Lands*, 161–82, and the July 2009 report issued by the United Nations Office for the Coordination of Humanitarian Affairs (OCHA):

"Five Years after the International Court of Justice Advisory Opinion: A Summary of the Humanitarin Impact of the Barrier," http://www. ochaopt.org/documents/ocha_opt_ barrier_report_july_2009_english_ low_res.pdf. For information on the "Jerusalem envelope," that portion of the Barrier that surrounds Jerusalem, see http://www.btselem .org/english/Separation_Barrier/ Jerusalem.asp. Thanks to Juliana Ochs for leading me to this website.

82  See Wasserstein, *Divided Jerusalem*, esp. chap. 5 and 6, as well as the interviews that appear in Francis Alÿs, *Sometimes Doing Something Poetic Can Become Political and Sometimes Doing Something Political Can Become Poetic: The Green Line (Jerusalem 2004–2005)* (New York: David Zwirner, 2007), n.p.

83  Israeli and Palestinian positions on the Green Line, the Barrier Wall, and the conflict as a whole are by no means consistent. Points of view differ from person to person, group to group, and party to party. For the purposes of better understanding Alÿs's project, though, I have tried to summarize the general perspective of the two primary administrative entities involved.

84  Much like Santiago Sierra, Emily Jacir, and Christian Philipp Müller, Alÿs captures something essential about the ontological state of borders, the curious way they induce separation and proximity, exclusion and belonging, at the same time. Patrick Ffrench describes the border thus: "The border is always double. It is not a single line of separation or transgression that one steps over … but a line facing two sides, a double line.… And the two sides of the border are tied in with each other in a complex and irreducible relation of tension." See his essay, "Passage Barré: Port Bou, September 26, 1940," in Franke,

Segal, and Weizman, *Territories: Islands, Camps*, 232. Port Bou is the Spanish border town in which Walter Benjamin committed suicide in 1940 while trying to flee the Nazis.

85  See Alÿs's interviews with Eyal Weizman and Jean Fisher in Alÿs, *Sometimes Doing Something Poetic.*

86  Ibid. For more information on *The Green Line*, see Mark Godfrey, "Walking the Line," *Artforum* 44 (May 2006): 260–68.

87  The respondents' comments are likewise published in Alÿs, *Sometimes Doing Something Poetic.*

88  Cuauhtémoc Medina, Russell Ferguson, and Jean Fisher, *Francis Alÿs* (London: Phaidon, 2007), 40.

89  The interruptive mode does not necessarily require a physical component. Sometimes it operates on the legal, symbolic, or administrative level alone, as in Amy Balkin's *This Is the Public Domain* (2003–present) and Christoph Büchel and Gianni Motti's *Guantánamo Initiative* (2004). In the case of the latter, the artists proposed to lease Guantánamo Bay from Cuba and transform it into a creative laboratory, closing the current detention center and supplanting the longstanding American lease, which the Castro government disputes and which international law (were it to be enforced) would consider illegal. A Yes Men intervention, in which one of the artists impersonated a representative from HUD (the U.S. Department of Housing and Urban Development) at an August 2008 housing conference in New Orleans, also operated in the interruptive mode. See http:// theyesmen.org/hijinks/hud.

90  See Pilar Villela Mascaró, "Not in My Name: Reality and Ethics in the Work of Santiago Sierra," in

*Santiago Sierra: 7 Trabajos/7 Works* (Cologne: Walther König, 2007), 13–14, 38 n. 8. The source of the toxic waste that poisoned hundreds was ASARCO (American Smelting and Refining Company), a foundry owned by Meyer Guggenheim that operated in El Paso, Texas, directly across the border from Ciudad Juárez, from 1887 to 1999. Sierra includes a photograph of an ASARCO smokestack in the slide show documenting his intervention. For Sierra's description of *Submission*, see ibid., 146.

91  Sierra uses similar language to describe his projects. See *Santiago Sierra* (Málaga: Centro de Arte Contemporáneo de Málaga, 2006), 1:19, 2:13, 2:17. During a conversation with the students in our contemporary art seminar at Princeton University in Fall 2009, Hal Foster suggested we understand Sierra's gesture as one of accusation (directed, apparently, at the United States), while Joe Scanlan interpreted "submission" as a description of the relationship between the artist and the workers he hired to excavate the letters. Because it is focused on production instead of reception, my discussion of *Submission* bypasses a very promising avenue of interpretation suggested by Grant Kester, one that would take as its point of departure the complex "relay of identifications and misidentifications" between artist, critic, and viewer that Sierra's work orchestrates. See Mick Wilson, "Autonomy, Agonism, and Activist Art: An Interview with Grant Kester," *Art Journal* 66:3 (Fall 2007): 116.

92  Curator Mariana David, who commissioned *Submission* for the public art festival Proyecto Juárez, writes: "Fourteen years after … NAFTA came into effect, the speeches on equality and progress contradict reality: between 1994 and 2000 poverty in Mexico shifted

from affecting 51% of the population to affect 70%.... [The] income of the poorest 20% of the population diminished from 3.6% to 2.9% of the national average, while in the case of the richest 10% it increased from 44% to 50%" *Santiago Sierra: 7 Trabajos/7 Works*, 143.

**93** *Submission* is by no means an anomaly in the context of Sierra's broader career. Over the last decade, the artist has consistently addressed issues around borders, nationality, and immigration, often staging his work in extra-institutional arenas. What links these investigations is an overarching interest in space and power — or, rather, in the spatialization of power. Sierra's work is typically subsumed under the rubric "relational aesthetics" (and for good reason), but the persistence of this label has eclipsed other readings of his practice. Indeed, until I began to read more about Sierra for this exhibition, even I was unaware of the extent of his commitment to a spatial (as opposed to a purely relational) pratice. As a precursor to *Submission*, we might consider the many physical obstacles Sierra has erected that serve to reiterate existing borders or create new ones. These obstacles are sometimes intended to shock and unbalance viewers, but they are also designed to prohibit exchange and polarize an already polarized audience along (un- or under-acknowledged) class, racial, and national lines. For more information, see Rosa Martínez, "Merchandise and Death," in *Santiago Sierra: Spanish Pavilion, 50th Venice Biennale* (Madrid: Turner, 2003), 23–25. In Martínez's interview with Sierra in the same catalogue, he says that "walls, whether visible or not, set on either side of a social relationship...are an allusion to vertically arranged impositions, to compartments of order.... [As] with borders...we are prevented from gaining access to a hierarchically

superior reality" (ibid., 153). Medina says in his catalogue essay, titled "Customs," that "Sierra's work...[blows] the whistle on the fraud that prevails in the history of emancipation," a history which promised freedom of movement only to have it strictly curtailed in the 20th century" (233).

**94** Sierra does not identify as an activist, nor does he claim the high road or attempt to change that which he decries. For him, there is no "outside" to capitalism, no comfortable, innocent, or triumphant perspective from which to survey the havoc wreaked by a system that creates and feeds on inequality. That said, Sierra's work most certainly strives to disarm, discomfort, and implicate viewers (especially art viewers) in relations they might otherwise believe themselves to rise above. As the artist says, "I do indeed aspire to the 'ideological placement of the political unconscious,' if you will excuse this outlandish expression. I feel that the moments of tension set up by some works spawn minimal political animals, by which the individual's mindset is laid bare" (ibid., 189). For more on Sierra's positions on activism and social change, see his comments in *Santiago Sierra: Spanish Pavilion* (207, 211), as well as the interviews in vol. 2 of *Santiago Sierra*, the Málaga exhibition catalogue cited above.

**95** The men and women who infiltrated the bombing range wore customized shoe soles imprinted with words and images chosen by the person wearing them. For detailed information, see Margo Handwerker's essay, as well as my own supplemental essay in this catalogue.

**96** For a social history of Vieques and a review of all the projects from the *Land Mark* series (whose overarching goal was to explore the myriad ways in which the island

was "marked" by competing social, historical, and economic interests), see Jennifer Allora and Guillermo Calzadilla, *Land Mark* (Paris: Palais de Tokyo, Paris Musées, 2006). See also McKee, "Art and the Ends of Environmentalism"; Sofía Hernández Chong Cuy, ed., *Puerto Rican Light: Jennifer Allora and Guillermo Calzadilla* (New York: Americas Society, 2003); Allora and Calzadilla, "1000 Words," *Artforum* 43:7 (Mar. 2005): 205; McKee and Jaleh Mansoor, "The Sediment of History: An Interview with Allora and Calzadilla," *Parkett*, no. 80 (2007): 42–48; and Hannah Feldman, "Sound Tracks," *Artforum* 45:9 (May 2007): 337–96. A dynamic similar to the one on Vieques is currently playing itself out in the Mau Forest, in Kenya, where development, conservation, and environmental sustainability are coming into conflict with indigenous land rights. See Jeffrey Gettleman, "Forest People May Lose Home in Kenyan Plan," *NYT*, Nov. 14, 2009.

**97** I borrow the concept of "taunt" from Abigail Solomon-Godeau, who describes it as one of two "tactics of enunciation" utilized by women artists of color, the other being "to haunt." About taunting, Solomon-Godeau writes that it "operates on the register of what everybody knows, the totally available and altogether familiar manifestations of sexism, racism, domination, and aggression. Its mode is aggressive, confrontational." Art in the taunting mode most often relies on mimetic parody and inversion. I believe Solomon-Godeau's terms apply to a much wider range of artistic practices than she discusses here. See her "Taunting and Haunting: Critical Tactics in a 'Minor' Mode," in *Women Artists at the Millennium*, ed. Carol Armstrong and Catherine de Zegher (Cambridge, Mass.: MIT Press, 2006), 371–401.

**98** Judith Butler and Gayatri Chakravorty Spivak, *Who Sings the*

*Nation State? Language, Politics, Belonging* (New York: Seagull Books, 2007), 55, 66, 68.

**99** Wright, "Letter from Gaza: Captives," 51. By "Gaza," I take Wright to mean "Palestine" (of which it is a part), instead of Gaza City or the Gaza Strip. The latter is a designation that, as far as I understand, emerged after the 1917 British occupation of Palestine — territory currently comprised of Israel, Palestine (Gaza and the West Bank), and Jordan.

**100** *Res nullius* is a phrase with origins in ancient Roman law. According to Daniel Heller-Roazen, the Romans assiduously categorized things according to the rights of ownership that did and did not apply to them, a kind of inventory of property types as well as property rights (both positive and negative). This inventory amounts to a "fully articulated account of the legal 'thing,' in the totality of its relations to the rights of which it may be made an object." Heller-Roazen, *Enemy of All*, 59. *Res nullius* is one such thing, and it stands alongside divine things (*res divini iuris*), which fall under the purview of the gods; public things (*res publicae*), things claimed by the state on behalf of its people; and common things (*res communis omnium*). The latter include naturally occurring entities such as air, seas, and shores; because they defy borders, these entities are in excess of ownership, and they belong to neither human law nor divine law. *Res nullius* not only occupies a curious position in relation to these other legal things; it also designates a curious position on the continuum of property rights — a position both provisional and precarious. Strictly speaking, *res nullius* is a thing that is not *yet* property. Rather than a thing that belongs to no one in perpetuity, in other words, it is a thing on which a claim of ownership has not *yet* been made. Heller-Roazen compares *res nullius* to a wild animal: Both are free, but only until they have been captured (ibid., 62–65). Clearly, my use of *res nullius* in the body of my essay does not quite square with its original definition. In fact, *res communis omnium* is probably closer to the word (and the spirit) I seek. Nonetheless, I have decided to retain *res nullius*, since its English translation has an emphatic, declarative quality that belies the provisional, precarious status of the things it corresponds to, and both have a corollary in the works of art and land-sites under discussion here.

**101**  The commons is also the subject of research by economists such as Elinor Ostrom, who shared the 2009 Nobel Memorial Prize in Economic Sciences with Oliver Williamson. Ostrom's work demonstrated the viability of the commons as a model of social, economic, and even ecological relations. See Louis Uchitelle, "Two Americans Are Awarded Nobel in Economics," *NYT*, Oct. 12, 2009. For a brief disquisition on the resurgence of interest in the commons and its demonization by writers such as Garrett Hardin in the late 1960s, see Tom McDonough, "Fictions of the Dismal Theorem," *October* 123 (Winter 2008): 107–9. In April of 2009, Midnight Notes Collective, along with some unidentified "friends," published a text titled "Promissory Notes: From Crisis to Commons," which sketches a history of the current economic crisis as well as past, present, and future responses to it, responses in which "communing" plays an important role. See http://www.midnightnotes.org/mnpub-articles.html (accessed Feb. 22, 2010). Finally, for a history of the commons as embodied in the Magna Carta and its Forest Charter, see Peter Linebaugh's fascinating *The Magna Carta*

*Manifesto: Liberties and Commons for All* (Berkeley and Los Angeles: University of California Press, 2008). Among other things, these two documents guaranteed right of access to common land, and in so doing, they established a link between communing and civil rights, a link that has been alternately preserved, betrayed, and altered by later legal bodies. Historically, when the commons are curtailed, liberty and economic security have been restricted as well. Thanks to Hal Foster for drawing my attention to this book.

**102**  In their 2004 book *Multitude*, Negri and Hardt introduce a variant of the term commons — the singular *common*, broadly understood as anything one might share with another. For Negri and Hardt, the common is the key to realizing a true democracy. It is "produced," they argue, through acts of communication, cooperation, and collaboration. These acts and the common store of knowledge they generate are the conditions of possibility for the multitude, that heterogeneous assembly of "singularities" that constitute Empire's primary enemy.

**103**  Judith Butler, *Precarious Life: The Powers of Mourning and Violence* (London: Verso, 2004) and *Giving an Account of Oneself*. See also Adriana Cavarero, "The Necessary Other," in *Relating Narratives: Storytelling and Selfhood*, trans. Paul A. Kottman (New York: Routledge, 2000), 81–92.

**104**  In their introduction to *On Cosmopolitanism and Forgiveness*, Simon Critchley and Richard Kearney summarize Derrida's argument. On the one hand, they write, we have the "unconditional purity" of the concepts Derrida invokes — hospitality and forgiveness — while on the other, we have the "pragmatic conditions,

at once historical, legal, political, and quotidian" in which these concepts must be put into action. "Just political action," Critchley and Kearney assert, "requires active respect for both poles of this tension." "Preface," in Jacques Derrida, *On Cosmopolitanism and Forgiveness*, trans. Mark Dooley and Michael Hughes (New York: Routledge, 2001), xi–xii. For an excellent discussion of Derrida's essay and its philosophical context, see Gene Ray's "Installing a 'New Cosmopolitics': Derrida, the Writers, and the Cities of Asylum," in Franke, Segal, and Weizman, *Territories: Islands, Camps*, 286–92. Giorgio Agamben addresses the status of the refugee in an essay from 1993. According to Agamben (who takes his cue from Arendt), the refugee is a "limit-concept that at once brings a radical crisis to the principles of the nation-state and clears the way for a renewal of categories that can no longer be delayed." Agamben, *Means without Ends*, 22. The categories Agamben has in mind are those of the paradigmatic political subject (the citizen) and international relations founded on strict notions of territoriality.

**105**  The urgency of this question, which opens out onto issues of social justice, civil rights, and economic parity, grows every day. It is the stake, for instance, of debates around "agro-imperialism," a recent trend in which wealthy countries, many of them Middle Eastern, lease "empty" land in poorer countries like Africa and use it to grow crops to feed their own populations. See Andrew Rice, "Is There Such a Thing as Agro-Imperialism?" *NYT*, Nov. 22, 2009.

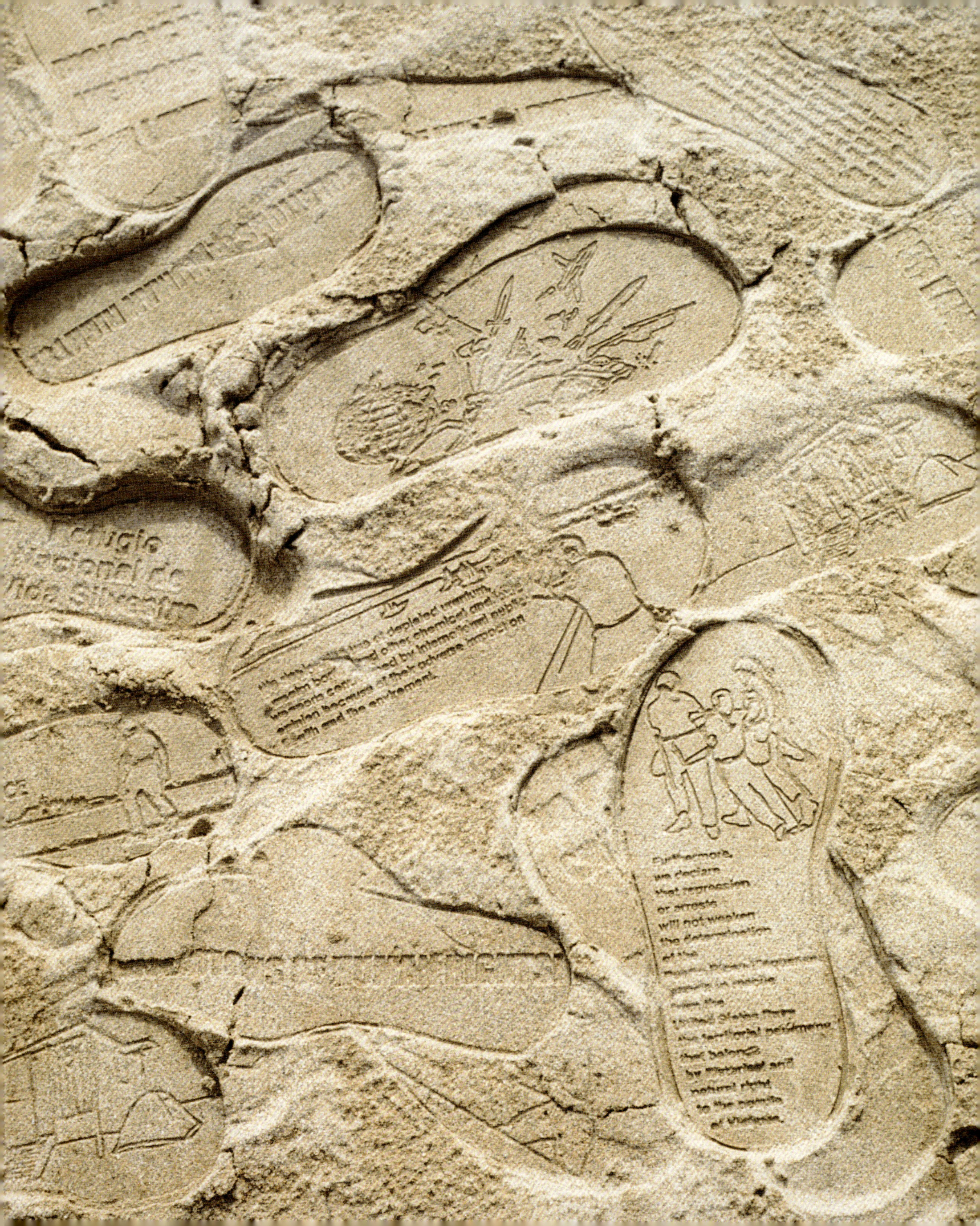
Refugio
Nacional de
Vida Silvestre
use of depleted uranium
and other chemical and
by international rights
law because of their adverse impact on
civilians and the environment
Furthermore,
we declare
that repression
or arrests
will not weaken
the determination
of the
United States from
its territorial neighbors
who belongs
by historical and
natural right
to the people
of Vietnam

# Land Art in Parallax: Media, Violence, Political Ecology
Yates McKee

*The authentic artist cannot turn his back on the*
*contradictions that inhabit our landscapes.*
　　　　　　　　　　　—Robert Smithson[1]

1. Much of the most compelling art made over the past decade
has been marked by a distinctive geographical turn. This turn
is inflected to varying degrees with a concern for the intersection between the topographical formations and deformations
of land, on the one hand, and the territorial determination of
such formations in political, economic, and cultural terms, on
the other. Emerging from a number of critical problem sets
developed in the late 1990s and early 2000s (site-specificity, the
archival impulse, the parafictional), this turn is evident in a wide
spectrum of practices, ranging from the oblique spatial poetics
of Francis Alÿs and Matthew Buckingham, to the experimental
geographical research of the Center for Land Use Interpretation
and Trevor Paglen, to the counter-memorial landscape investigations of Jennifer Allora and Guillermo Calzadilla, Ayreen
Anastas and Rene Gabri, and Andrea Geyer, to the activist
program of "tactical cartography" put forth by the Institute
for Applied Autonomy.[2] These internally variegated practices
constitute neither a rejective break with nor a simple revival
of "historical" Land Art, which has sometimes functioned as a
perfunctory reference point in assessments of contemporary art
that deals with landscape and land use.[3] With varying degrees
of historical self-consciousness and polemical intent, contemporary practices are involved in a kind of art-historical parallax.
As described by Hal Foster, parallax "involves the apparent

displacement of an object caused by the actual movement of
its observer. This figure underscores both that our framings of
the past depend on our positions in the present, and that these
positions are always defined through such framings."[4]

In the essay that follows, I will not be explicitly addressing
contemporary practices. Rather, I will reconsider several
important moments in the emergence of Land Art in light of
the historical events and pressing conceptual problems to
which contemporary spatial practices demand that we respond.
Present-day Land artists are concerned with the imbrications
of media technologies and terrestrial matter, the mnemonic,
economic, and political inscription of territory, and the crises
and conflicts surrounding ecological life-support systems at
local and planetary scales. Their work simultaneously illu-
minates and interrogates certain questions inhering in the
legacies of historical Land Art, which have often been down-
played, if not ignored altogether.

2. Historical Land Art has frequently been posited as the quin-
tessence of site-specificity. Radicalizing the phenomenological
here-and-now of, say, Robert Morris's 1964 Green Gallery
installation in New York (often cited as a landmark of Minimalism), works of Land Art are said to epitomize the grounded
actuality of place and the irreducible physicality of land as

a "raw" material or process. They do so in opposition to two other models: first, the disembodied viewing subject posited by high modernism, and second, the contemporaneous project of conceptualist dematerialization. Though Land Art per se is curiously marginal to Miwon Kwon's canonical discussion of site-specificity, her primary allusions to Land art (metonymized by "the Nevada desert") place it firmly within an approach to site as "something grounded, bound to the laws of physics… an actual location, a tangible reality, its identity composed of a unique combination of constituent physical elements."[5] This "classical" approach to site-specificity functions as a foil for Kwon's account of the gradual "crisis" and "unhinging" of site, which she links to endogenous developments within artistic practice and to the cultural, political, and economic dynamics of capitalist globalization. Kwon's narrative is avowedly heuristic, and she stresses that her phases of site-specificity (phenomenological, institutional-critique, and discursive) do not necessarily proceed in a linear fashion and may indeed overlap. Nonetheless, Kwon leaves the distinct impression that Land Art was concerned primarily with the "actuality of place," and thus anterior to the problematic of "deterritorialization" — the inscription of the physical terrain of the earth into expanded networks of media technologies, policy regimes, and political economies that constitute all sites as nodal points of historically uneven and politically contested exchanges, flows, and displacements.[6]

More recent research, however, has demonstrated that from its inception historical Land Art was engaged with issues of deterritorialization in ways that were variously symptomatic, critical, and, most frequently, ambivalent. Authors such as Jane McFadden point to the central role played by media technologies in the conception and realization of works of Land Art, a role that goes beyond the problem of simply documenting a site-specific work that would otherwise exist independent of its mediatic displacement, archival inscription, and public circulation.[7]

Indeed, the moniker "Land Art" first came into being as the title of a 1969 German public television program produced by Gerry Schum. The program featured a spectrum of sculptural and performative works by artists such as Walter De Maria, Michael Heizer, Richard Long, Robert Smithson, Dennis Oppenheim, and Jan Dibbets, addressed self-consciously to the film-camera and broadcast audience. Describing what he (correctly) perceived as a paradoxical or ironic structure emergent within the discourse of site-specificity, Dibbets remarked, "the whole thing is specially constructed for TV, so on the moment people are looking at this project on TV they have (during that time) an original artwork by Dibbets in their room."[8]

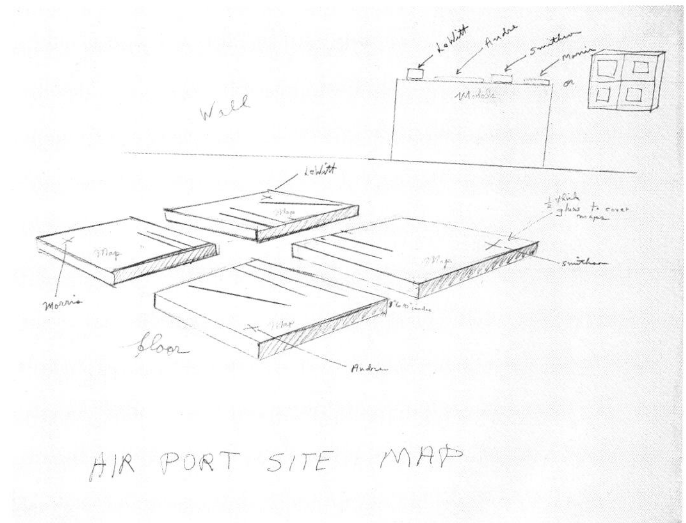

Robert Smithson. *Airport Site Map*,
1967. Pencil on paper, 48.3 × 61 cm
(19 × 24 in.). © Estate of Robert
Smithson, Courtesy of James Cohan
Gallery, New York. Collection of the
Modern Art Museum of Fort Worth,
Gift of the Estate of Robert Smithson.
Licensed by VAGA, New York, N.Y.

Such questions had already been broached in what is arguably the foundational document of Land Art: Robert Smithson's 1966 essay, "Towards the Development of an Air Terminal Site," which was written in response to a commission extended by Tippetts-Abbett-McCarthy-Stratton, an engineering and architecture firm then working on a plan for the Dallas-Fort Worth Airport. Smithson was acutely interested in the airport as a construction site, especially the computational surveying techniques used by engineers to scale between abstract models and actual building processes on the ground. Smithson's exposure to the working methods of surveyors led to his realization that "all air and land is locked into a vast crystalline lattice" of cartographic technologies, electronic media networks, and aerial positioning systems, including those based on nascent satellite-imaging techniques.[9] Invoking a history of planetary telecommunications bookended by Alexander Graham Bell and Buckminster Fuller, Smithson recognized the irreducibly mediated character of space, whether by maps, diagrams, cameras, clocks, screens, or some combination thereof. In particular, he was intrigued by two interrelated artistic possibilities for the airport: that artworks might address an audience traveling thousands of feet above the surface of the earth, and that the construction of such works might be recorded and broadcast via television cameras to passengers waiting in the terminal.[10] Smithson praised the "aesthetic potential" of "aerial photography and air transportation," which "brings into view the surface features of this shifting world of perspectives," transforming the landscape from a "rustic garden" into "a three-dimensional map."[11]

Smithson took the airport commission as an opportunity to extend a set of secondary commissions to three colleagues. In critical dialogue with the surveys, borings, excavations, clearings, fillings, and gradings involved in the airport's construction process, Robert Morris proposed an "earth mound" and a series of asphalt pavements, inspiring Smithson's remark that "Morris would like to use a bulldozer rather than a paintbrush." Sol LeWitt planned an iteration of his ironically non-visual 1968 project, *Buried Cube Containing an Object of Importance but Little Value*. For his part, Smithson suggested a large-scale version of his 1968 sculpture *Gyrostasis*, unfolded flat against the ground as an articulation of triangular pavements whose crystalline structure would be legible from an aerial perspective. (This prefiguration of *Spiral Jetty* retrospectively suggests the centrality of the helicopter-camera assemblage to his later work.) Whereas Morris, LeWitt, and Smithson's proposals, though heterodox, would in principle have been plausible for the (ultimately unrealized) airport project, Carl Andre adopted a more sardonic tone. As recorded by Smithson in his 1969 article "Aerial Art," Andre called for "A crater formed by a one-ton bomb dropped from 10,000 feet/or/An acre of blue-bonnets (state flower of Texas)."[12]

Andre's project links the technologically enabled aesthetic shifts associated with Smithson's "three-dimensional" map to a politics of terrestrial destruction.[13] Aerial photography and air transportation are here associated not only with the increasingly ubiquitous perceptual reorientation of the airline passenger (to whom the emergent genre of "earthworks" might be addressed), but also with the airborne bombardier testing nuclear weapons in the Southwestern desert or flying sorties over Vietnamese villages. The second part of Andre's proposal—an acre of bluebonnets—evokes state iconographies linking geographical territory, biological life, and supposed regional character.

3. Andre's ironic "proposal," with its hyperbolic extremes of military obliteration and nostalgic preservation, was unique in early discussions of Land Art for its polemical insistence that the production and perception of landscape is bound up with historically specific forms of political control, technological deployment, and ideological overdetermination.[14] His proposal thus provides an urgent contemporary counterpoint to the emergent landscape imaginary of Michael Heizer, which was itself marked by a certain dialectics of extremity shadowed by military violence.

To describe Heizer's work in terms of a "landscape imaginary" complicates the artist's obstinate appeal to the raw phenomenology of land, as in his famous axiom that "place is the material, and the material is the place."[15] Through Heizer's various procedures of displacement, excavation, subtraction, and incision, the status of place is decentered. The viewer is thus forced to encounter traditional sculptural problems of scale and perspective, volume and mass, figure and ground, line and color in terms of a fundamental void in the spatio-temporal coordinates of perception and consciousness.[16] It is important to note, however, that the logic of negativity operative in Heizer's work was sublated by the artist and many of his critical advocates into a set of highly problematic narratives, fantasies, and anxieties concerning the space of the desert. These narratives closely resonate with colonial-*cum*-primitivist discourses operative in art history specifically, and in social history more generally.

Heizer framed the Southwest desert as a space free of the European influences he still considered to be dominant in New York; it was thus the site of an authentically American art. For Heizer, like Jackson Pollock before him, America needed to be understood in terms of its archaic, pre-Columbian essence, which he associated with a primordial intimacy with materials, sites, and environmental processes. In Heizer's words, "I think earth is the material with the most potential because it is the original source material. It brought up all kinds of things about the prehistorical or preliterate past, and referred to traditions about art that were more interesting than looking at works in the Louvre or the Metropolitan."[17] Heizer's appeal to pre-Columbian origins was directly related to his experience as a teenager accompanying his father, a prominent archaeologist, on site visits throughout North and South America, especially in the Nevada desert. Indeed, Heizer identified as something of a "native" himself vis-à-vis Nevada. His father, a descendant of the region's nineteenth-century European settlers, grew up in the state. Significantly, both of Heizer's grandfathers worked as professionals in the mining industry, one as a geologist and the other as an engineer.

Appealing to this biographical background, Heizer imagined his work as a synthesis of the grandeur of what he (ethnocentrically) called "preliterate or prehistorical" mark-making and building practices (the Nazca Lines incised into the Peruvian desert, the petroglyphs found throughout North America, the Mayan city of Chichen Itza on the Yucatán Peninsula) with the large-scale physical transformations of the earth enabled by new technologies of surveying and extraction. Among these technologies were explosives, whether for military or industrial purposes, which Heizer famously used in blasting out the first excavations for *Double Negative* (1969–70), the massive "cut" incised across a canyon that itself cuts between two mesas in Nevada.

For Heizer, then, the Southwestern desert was a Janus-faced realm suspended between historical extremes. "We live in a world that's technological and primordial simultaneously," he explained to an interviewer in 1984. "I guess my art starts from this premise."[18] Alluding to weapons testing in the Great Basin, Heizer told the same interviwer, "The H-Bomb, that's the ulti-mate sculpture; the world is going to be pounded into the Stone Age, and what kind of art will be made after that?"[19] Heizer's remark merges a rhetoric of what David E. Nye has called "the American technological sublime" with a kind of apocalyptic primitivism, an extreme iteration of the end-of-art narratives that proliferated, with varying ideological inflections, through-out the twentieth century.[20] For Heizer, this end of art — "the ultimate sculpture" — is also the end of humanity as we know it, a sublime act of technological self-destruction that would return the world to a Stone Age akin to the "prehistoric, prelit-erate" cultures from which he claims to take inspiration.[21] To be clear, Heizer does not simply celebrate the hydrogen bomb in the Futurist fashion of war-glorification diagnosed by Walter Benjamin in 1936. In Benjamin's scenario, the artist "expects war to supply the artistic gratification of a sense perception that has been changed by technology," so that humanity "can experience its own destruction as an aesthetic pleasure of the highest order."[22]

However, Benjamin's citation of the Futurist slogan "Fiat ars — pereat mundus" (Let art be created — let the world perish) does resonate uncannily with Heizer's remark, which seems to grimly anticipate an unprecedented aesthetic opportunity in the self-induced reprimitivization of humanity. Indeed, Heizer would shift during the mid-1970s from the subtractive procedures and ephemeral temporality of a work such as *Nine Nevada Depressions* (1968) to the ongoing production of a sculpture-edifice constructed from locally derived concrete entitled *Complex* (begun in 1972). Inspired by the ritual architectures of pre-Columbian cultures, *Complex* is a monumental "blast shield" erected on Heizer's private tract of land in the Great Basin in response to a nearby nuclear testing site. When asked by an interviewer in 1984 about the relation between these sites, Heizer responded, "Yes, it's a highly charged area, but I am reluctant to discuss it that much.... Part of my art is based on an awareness that we live in a nuclear era. We're probably living at the end of civilization."[23]

Unlike the performative irony of Andre's proposal for the Dallas-Fort Worth Airport, which aimed to warn the would-be land artist about the historical entanglements and complicities involved in engaging new scales and technologies, Heizer's evocation of bombing has a tone of deadly serious survivalism that transcends any such transitory political concerns. Heizer imagines the desert as a sublime emptiness that testifies to the ends of civilization (vanished pre-Columbian mark-makers, soon-to-be-vanished advanced technological society) and to the rebirth of art, "re-immersing [it] in the aura and sacrality of the archaic ritual typical of Mesoamerican religious cultures."[24] In such a fantasy scenario, Heizer *qua* artist would emerge as a post-historical demiurge, reestablishing civilization on the basis of an elementary affinity with the materiality of the earth itself.

In his approach to the desert as an exemplary site, "technological and primordial simultaneously," Heizer dehistoricizes the Southwestern landscape. He calls for us to read the landscape only in terms of its prehistorical origins and post-historical desolation, an eschatlogical master-narrative that effaces the contested histories of land use inscribed in the putatively empty sites in which Heizer made his interventions and onto which he projected his Janus-faced fantasies. These histories implicate Heizer's own ancestors in the development

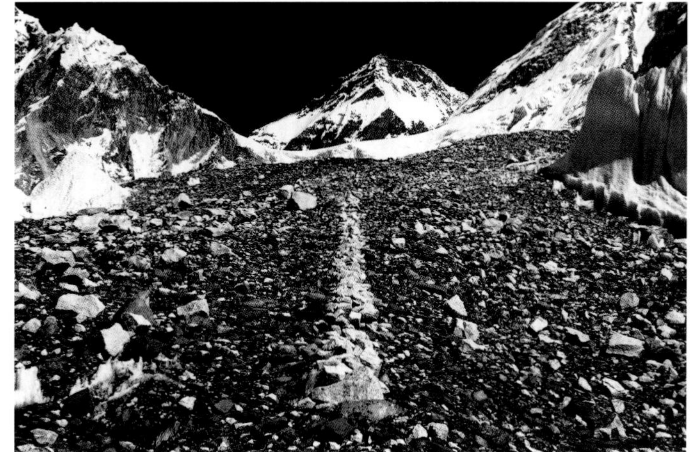

Richard Long. *A Line in the Himalayas*, 1975. Silver gelatin print, 88 × 124 cm (34 ⅝ × 48 ¾ in.). Sanders Collection, Amsterdam. © 2010 Richard Long/ Artists Rights Society (ARS), New York/ DACS, London. Courtesy of James Cohan Gallery, New York/Haunch of Venison, London.

of geological surveying, resource extraction, and even archaeological research in the region, all of which were intimately bound to the territorial expropriation of indigenous peoples by the United States government in the second half of the nineteenth century and beyond. Such events are obliquely inscribed in Heizer's apparently remote sites, such as Massacre Dry Lake, named for an 1863 attack by displaced Shoshone on a caravan of Euro-American settlers whose bodies were reportedly buried in a unmarked mass grave.[25]

4. The landscape imaginary of Heizer finds a counterintuitive echo in the work of Richard Long. The English artist has loudly proclaimed his distance from American practitioners of Land Art, whom he accused of adopting a technologically domineering, possessive, and ultimately destructive relation to the landscape. Against the use of giant earth-moving machines and the purchasing of sites for the realization of their works, Long claimed to tread lightly on the earth, using simple gestures of marking (sticks, small stones, footprints) to leave ephemeral trails across the grounds over which he passed on his walking exercises, which were then preserved as spare photographic documents. While sometimes deriving his routes from, or in relation to, ready-made road maps, in general Long has treated the supposedly natural landscape as a neutral surface for

the projection of a universal phenomenological exploration of time, space, and embodiment. Though his work is formulated in dialogue with Minimalism and Conceptualism, Long has supplemented the latter's concerns with material processes and automatic programs with a neo-Romantic desire for spiritual reconnection between a tragically alienated humanity and the primordial "being" of the earth. His subtle formal interest in inscription and erasure, presence and absence, appearance and disappearance notwithstanding, Long has arguably been complicit with a sense of the landscape and humanity alike as *unmarked* terms that somehow precede or transcend the violent histories inscribed into them. Consequently, he evades the ethical and political responsibilities that an avowal of such histories would entail. This becomes especially evident in his walking projects in locations such as the Saharan desert and the Himalayan mountains, which he treats as either "empty" sites of the non-human sublime, or as realms of a primitive ontological reciprocity between indigenous social groups and their physical environments.[26] In so doing, however, Long falls prey to what Johan Fabian famously diagnosed in his *Time and the Other: How Anthropology Makes its Object* (1983) as the "denial of coevalness" on the part of traditional anthropology — the tendency to situate cultural systems that are geographically remote as somehow existing in a static, prehistorical era.[27]

While opposed at one level, artists such as Heizer and Long share an approach that proclaims an affinity with indigenous site-marking practices while participating in the erasure of the entangled, modern histories of existing landscapes.

In her canonical 1979 account of "sculpture in the expanded field," Rosalind Krauss disarticulated work such as Heizer's and Long's from humanist art-historical master-narratives understood on the scale of "millennia rather than decades. Stonehenge, the Nazca lines, Toltec ball courts, Indian burial mounds — anything at all could be hauled into court to bear witness to this work's connection to history and thereby to legitimize its status as sculpture."[28] Against the transhistorical horizons of these accounts, Krauss insisted that such work needed to be understood in terms of a logical permutation of a set of culturally specific terms — sculpture, architecture, landscape — as elaborated in Western art history since the eighteenth century. Krauss's point remains methodologically irrefutable in terms of the structural and historical conditions of possibility for the emergence of post-Minimalism. Her dismissal of any relation to ancient or non-European practices of building and marking, however, fails to address the inconvenient fact that many of the artists she addresses did indeed express an intense interest in such phenomena, though with varying degrees of critical awareness. The danger of taking such an interest at face value is evident in Lucy Lippard's remarkable but highly flawed work *Overlay: Contemporary Art and the Art of Prehistory* (1983), which rehearses exactly the kind of transhistoricizing humanism that Krauss warned against five years earlier. The question for us today is: What would it mean to take seriously the question of indigeneity that haunts historical Land Art, and how would we then evaluate the various legacies of Land Art in contemporary work concerned with land, territory, and space?[29]

**5.** Dennis Oppenheim's site-specific interventions in the Southwestern desert and elsewhere during the 1970s provide a provocative entry point to this set of questions. Rather than apocalyptic endgames (Heizer) or tread-lightly idealism (Long), Oppenheim articulated a more complicated understanding of the relay between technology, land, and territory. Along with Smithson, Oppenheim was arguably the only artist of his generation to acknowledge the irreducible mediation of any land whatsoever in terms of its technical and administrative inscription *qua* territory, no matter how apparently remote or desolate the site. In *Timeline* (1968), for instance, Oppenheim used a running snowmobile to inscribe an ephemeral cut through the middle of the frozen St. Johns River. The work marked the invisible latitudinal boundary between the United States

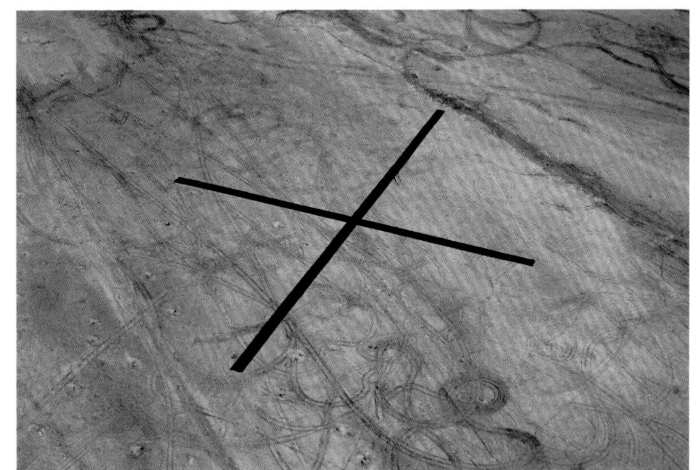

Dennis Oppenheim. *Relocated Burial Ground*, 1978. El Mirage Dry Lake, Southern California. Asphalt primer, 2000 square foot intersection. Courtesy of the artist.

and Canada, as well as the vertically oriented international line demarcating the Eastern and Central time zones. Oppenheim's incision was preserved as a photographic document and displayed in a kind of pin-up archival arrangement alongside a cartographic representation of the site and a photograph of an actual state-sanctioned boundary marker.

From the late 1960s through the late 1970s, Oppenheim created a series of works that combined terrestrial, photographic, and cartographic site-marking, thereby complicating any appeal to "actual location," as Kwon describes it in her history of site-specificity. The most resonant piece for our purposes is one of Oppenheim's last earthworks, *Relocated Burial Ground* (1978). Here, the artist inscribed an enormous letter *X* in asphalt primer in the middle of the dry El Mirage Lake in California. With each arm of the *X* measuring 610 feet, the complete work was only visible from an aerial viewpoint, as imagined by Smithson in his 1969 essay "Aerial Art." The *X* serves both to indicate or point to the spot, and to negate or cancel it, simultaneously preserving it for memory and consigning it to oblivion. Marking the spot as the target of a future attack or a past violation, *Relocated Burial Ground* questions the site's spatiotemporal identity and our relation to it. This sense of site-insecurity is compounded by the title of the work, which evokes the cultural sacrality of the burial ground

*qua* place while suggesting its profane dislocation, uprooting, or disinterring. *Relocated Burial Ground* does not overtly comment on the specific histories of the region, but it does imply that every square inch of the American Southwest is the "scene of a crime" (to paraphrase Walter Benjamin).[30] Such a forensics of territory reads "site" as a traditional resting place of the people who once lived there at the same time that it evokes their violent displacement and effacement.

*Relocated Burial Ground* can thus be seen as a counter-monument informed by a post-Minimalist concern with entropy as well as an ethical concern, however oblique, with bearing witness to the absent traces and marks of others in the landscape. As one critic described it, "the asphalt primer would not have left an indelible mark on the landscape; instead, it disappeared in the same way that ancient burial sites may have been erased or buried as the forces of nature erase man-made markings on the land."[31] Rather than posit a transhistorical affinity—whether apocalyptic or nostalgic—between the post-minimalist marked site and the site-markings of the original inhabitants of the American Southwest, the mnemonic play between appearance and disappearance, inscription and effacement, indication and negation at work in *Relocated Burial Ground* stages a kind of ambivalent violence, implicating us in a scenario of profane disinterment and sacred witness-bearing.

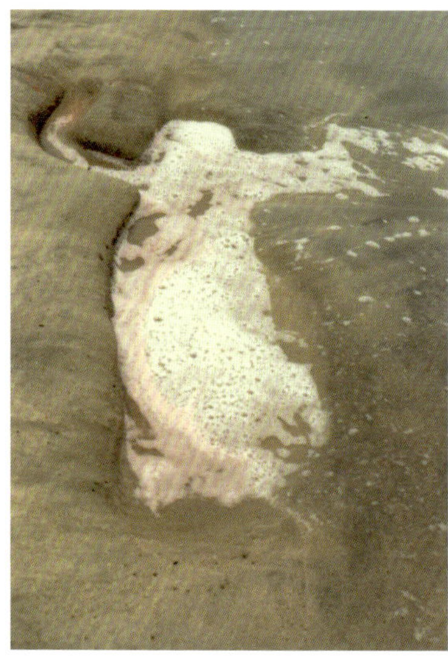

Ana Mendieta. *Untitled (Silueta Series)*, July 1976. 1 of 9 chromogenic prints, each 33.7 × 50.5 cm (13¼ × 19⅞ in.). © The Estate of Ana Mendieta Collection. Courtesy of Galerie Lelong, New York.

With these questions of media, witnessing, and violence in mind, a final figure to consider with respect to the contemporary genealogy of historical Land Art would be Ana Mendieta. In her famous *Silueta* series (1973–80), Mendieta impressed her own body into the ground of various unspecified "natural" landscapes (beaches, swamps, meadows), then photographed the ephemeral aftermath of this indexical process: outlines or traces of a body that was no longer present.[32] Mendieta has often been assimilated to a primitivist ideal of ecofeminism that would posit an essential affinity between the supposed maternal generativity of the female body and the bounteous plenitude of Mother Earth, defined over and against the alienating forces of technological modernity.[33] Mendieta herself often appealed to certain primitivizing tropes in both her own words and in her frequent, if oblique, incorporation of feminine iconographic forms evocative of prehistoric or non-European goddess worship (the Venus of Willendorf, for instance, or pre-Columbian and Afro-diasporic deities drawn from her own Cuban heritage).

Mendieta's primitivist inclinations, however, were constantly checked by her interest in the indexical sign, examples of which include stains, shadows, footprints, wakes from boats, ashes, and smoke. Distinguished from a symbolic representation by the "absoluteness of its physical genesis" and bearing a "causal relation to its referent," according to Rosalind Krauss, the indexical sign testifies to a "trauma of signification" that speaks to an irrecoverable absence or loss rather than to any spiritual vitality.[34] Mendieta doubled this sense of absence or loss by insisting on a dialogue with the double indexicality of the photograph. In other words, her work consists of indexical marks (photographic traces of light bouncing off physical surfaces onto light-sensitive film) of indexical marks (bodily impressions in the earth) otherwise destined to oblivion or effacement. Rather than original bodily events centered on the physical site of their enactment, Mendieta's *Siluetas* were media events in their very conception. Structured by and addressed to the camera, the *Siluetas* "leave their site," as Benjamin might put it, anticipating their own mediatic dislocation, public circulation, and archival accumulation beyond the auratic here-and-now of the indexical impression itself.[35]

Indeed, Mendieta's interest in the indexical sign in the *Silueta* series is arguably marked by a forensic impulse first indicated in *Untitled (Rape Piece)* of 1972.[36] Responding to a newspaper report concerning a rape at the University of Iowa, where Mendieta was then studying, the artist issued an open-ended invitation to attend a performance at her home. Entering the room, viewers encountered Mendieta unclothed and bent over a table with what appeared to be blood running down her thighs and legs, as if she had just been sexually violated. This media event thus functioned as a kind of performative supplement to the cursory media coverage of the actual rapes that had been occurring at the university, suggesting the inadequacy of typical forms of publicity in the face of the ongoing reality of sexual violence.[37]

Without effacing the irreducible specificity of rape as a criminal act, it is possible to extend the general forensic concern of *Untitled (Rape Piece)* to the overall interrogation of landscape in Mendieta's *Siluetas*. Like Oppenheim's *Relocated Burial Ground,* Mendieta's work extends beyond its local instantiation to frame every square inch of the earth as the scene of a crime in which we are implicated as viewers or witnesses. While problematic in its essentialism, Mendieta's feminist appeal to the alterity of "non-Western" mark-making systems — and her attention to the simultaneous effacement and preservation of those systems via technical reproducibility — resonates with what Craig Owens famously called the "discourse of others" in his 1983 critique of the ethnocentricism and androcentricism of Western art criticism.[38]

6. The counter-memorial forensic ethos at work in Oppenheim's *Relocated Burial Ground* and Mendieta's *Siluetas* indirectly relates to a remarkable text by Robert Morris entitled "Art and/as Land Reclamation." Delivered at a meeting of the King County Arts Commission in Washington State in 1979 and later published in the journal *October*, Morris's statement programmatically aims to open the formal concerns and procedures of post-minimalist Land Art to questions of ecological remediation and environmental justice. In so doing, it extends the anti-idealist model of ecology put forth in Smithson's 1973 account of the "dialectical landscape" of Central Park. Constituted by geological and biological processes as well as socio-economic histories and technologies of mapping, photographic surveying, and infrastructural maintenance, Central Park served as the foundation of Smithson's critique of what he called ecological "spiritualism."[39] In contradistinction to the latter, which posited nature as something preceding or transcending the realm of human activity to then be "preserved," Smithson called for an ecological art that would acknowledge the immanent mediation, artificiality, and impurity of any landscape whatsoever. He himself presented a series of proposals for large-scale sculptural remediation projects to mining companies in Utah and Ohio towards the end of his life. While he was never able to realize them, he gave visual form to their underlying concerns in his Pop-Surrealist collage *King Kong Meets the Gem of Egypt* (1972). Here a giant earthmoving machine (GEM) at work in a strip mine in Ohio's Egypt Valley is juxtaposed with the robotic ape "Mechani-Kong" from the post-Hiroshima Japanese

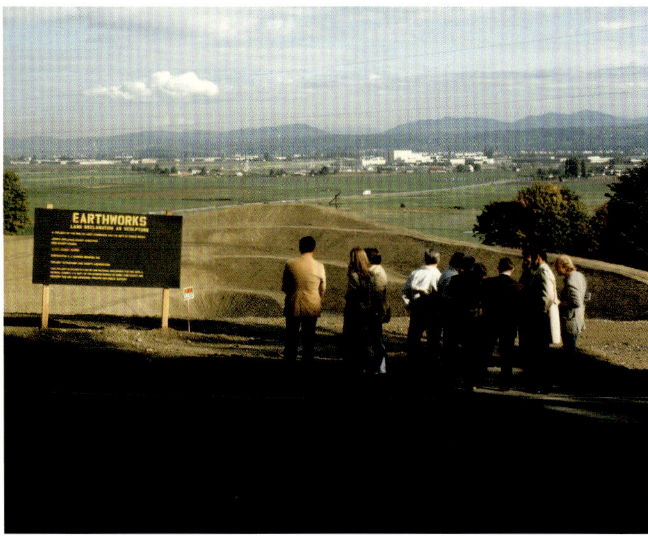

Robert Morris. *Untitled Reclamation Project*, 1979. Kent, Washington. Photographed in 1979 by Greg Skinner. © 2010 Robert Morris/Artists Rights Society (ARS), New York.

remake *King Kong Escapes* (1967).[40] Critically ironizing the rhetoric of the "American technological sublime" that Heizer had taken as the deadly-serious horizon of his own practice, Smithson's collage suggests his ambivalent desire to engage the material and psychic aftermath of monstrous-*cum*-monumental environmental destruction.

At once extending and complicating his late friend's project (Smithson died in a plane crash in 1973), Morris's statement ruminates on the possibility that art concerned with ecological remediation could very well become an aestheticizing alibi for the very forces it claimed to oppose. In other words, earthworks could end up performing a clean-up operation for environmentally destructive corporations and government agencies. By suggesting the viability of "healing" the landscape on a site-by-site basis, earthworks might work to legitimize further harmful activities instead of questioning the socioeconomic structures that gave rise to the destruction in the first place.

Morris opens the article by calling for close attention to the multiple agencies and forces at work in the discourse of land reclamation: "The issue of art's potential involvement in land reclamation can only be focused through a perspective on the history, conflicts, and confusions involved in that admittedly broad cluster of topics related to land abuse: technology, mining, governmental policy and regulations, ecological

concerns, and public opinion."[41] Morris goes on to perform an inventory of the environmental impacts of various forms of mining, along with statements by mining companies concerning their supposed commitment to pursuing reclamation programs.

Morris focuses on the work of Peabody Coal, a transnational energy company that "began operations at Black Mesa, Arizona in the 1960s. Leased from the Navajo and Hopi Indian tribes, 400 acres a year are to be mined for 35 years."[42] The artist cites a claim by then-CEO Edwin J. Phelps to "make the land more useful than it was originally" through nutrient-intensive revegetation of exhausted mining sites. As a counterpoint to Phelps's statement of corporate benevolence, Morris invokes the following testimony by Ted Yazzie, an indigenous resident of the region: "It's terrible when they work. Since they started, people began to change. The air began to change. It is something we have not known before. The plants seem to have no life. When the wind blows our way, the coal dust covers the whole ground, the food, the animals, the hogans, the water. The dust is dirty, it is black. The sun rises, it is gray. The sun sets, yet it is still gray. I imagine the night is gray."[43]

Morris proceeds to relate Yazzie's testimony concerning the deleterious effects of coal mining in Black Mesa to broader networks of energy production and its toxic byproducts, linking this specific site to an overall ecological crisis in the

United States and beyond. Citing Hans Magnus Enzenberger's prescient 1974 article "A Critique of Political Ecology," Morris lists among the "unintentional side effects of the industrial process" not only air and water pollution, but also "changes in climate, irreversible changes to rivers and lakes, and oceanographic changes." Countering accounts of ecology that would take as their ethical horizon the so-called purification of the natural environment over and against the activities of a generic Man, Enzenberger calls for a political analysis that would link ecological crises to capitalist resource extraction, military-industrial activity, and social inequalities (such as the disproportionate levels of environmental risk to which indigenous groups are exposed).[44]

What role could art play in relation to such political-ecological entanglements, other than superficially restoring devastated landscapes and neutralizing the marks of destruction left behind by corporations and governments? For Morris, a critical art of land reclamation would need to highlight the violent history of the landscapes in question. He himself only undertook one such project, which involved the sodding and concentric terracing of a nearly four-acre (1.6 hectare) abandoned gravel-pit in Kent, Washington. In this way, the extracted site was transformed into a phenomenologically dynamic amphitheater suspended between the naturally occurring topography and the mechanically determined contours of the quarry, deranging any traditional sense of scale, horizon, and ground as dictated by the history of Western landscape aesthetics. Though this project does little to commemorate the specific social, economic, and political dimensions of the site in question, Morris's insistence on preserving the perceptually jarring crater-like depression of the industrial quarry — rather than smoothing it over in favor of a spuriously original topography — reads as an ambivalent compromise of his provocative suggestion that "such aesthetic efforts are incapable of signaling any protest against the escalating use of nonrenewable minerals and energy sources." Citing one of the world's largest man-made excavations, the Bingham Canyon Mine in Utah (managed by Kennecott Utah Copper), Morris asks: "What, one wonders, could be done for the Kennecott-Bingham site, the ultimate site-specific work of such raging, ambiguous energy, so redolent with formal power and social threat, that no existing earthwork should even be compared to it? It should stand unregenerate as a powerful monument to a one-day nonexistent resource."[45]

In this passage, Morris seems to take a certain masochistic pleasure in the sublime environmental scale and devastating ecological footprint of the mine. However, as with Smithson's *King Kong Meets the Gem of Egypt*, we should heed the

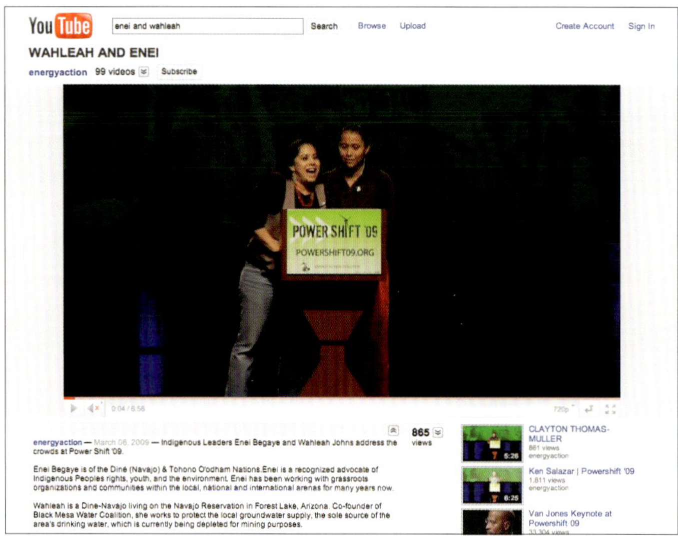

Enei Begaye, indigenous peoples' rights advocate, and Wahleah Johns, co-founder of the Black Mesa Water Coalition, speaking at Power Shift '09, March 6, 2009. Screen shot from video posted on YouTube (http://www.you tube.com/watch?v=o2f1nzY6_ro).

aggressively ironic tone marking his appeal to catastrophic monumentality, and place it in relation to his earlier evocation of the voice of Black Mesa resident and activist Ted Yazzie.

While Yazzie's voice plays only an incidental role in Morris's overall article, it can be read as a testimonial trace of the contemporary subaltern populations that unevenly bear the brunt of ecological risk from past and present capitalist land use. This trace significantly reorients the problem of indigeneity that haunted discourses of historical Land Art, as represented by the work of Heizer, Long, Oppenheim, and indeed Morris himself, whose slightly later essay "Aligned With Nazca" (1975) participated in a primitivizing fantasy about the supposed formal affinity between the Peruvian Nazca Lines and mini-malist understandings of space.[46] Rather than frame the desert as an apocalyptic wasteland (Heizer), a realm of primordial reciprocity with nature (Long), or even a site of cryptic violence (Oppenheim, Mendieta), Yazzie's voice reminds us of the deep integration of the Southwestern desert in contemporary political economies and ongoing conflicts over the territorial expropria-tion of indigenous landscapes and resource bases (including air, water, and soil).[47] Indeed, Peabody Coal's Black Mesa operation continues to be a major nodal point in indigenous struggles concerning land claims and human rights. In recent years, activists have begun to advocate for a broader vision of a post-carbon energy economy, one that mitigates global warming and provides development opportunities for low-income areas and communities (including, for instance, tapping into the poten-tial wind-power resources of many reservations). Black Mesa activists have come to articulate their demands for ecological remediation in terms of "climate justice," linking their site-specific grievances to those of other subaltern groups around the world suffering from the adverse effects of global warming and the regimes of resource extraction and consumption that lie behind it.[48]

7. Historical Land Art has traditionally been associated with "actual location" (as Kwon calls it in her heuristic account), over and against both the sitelessness of modernist art and the nomadic networks of global biennial culture. The thesis of the present text has been that Land Art was never simply grounded in actuality. Rather, it was always already involved (with varying degrees of historical self-consciousness) with questions of media, violence, and political ecology that extend far beyond either the phenomenological investigations of perception or the structuralist mapping of the expanded field put forth by Krauss. This essay also represents a departure from Lucy Lippard's position, as expressed in her book *Overlay*. Lippard's ecological primitivism and New Age mysticism tended

to idealize rather than interrogate the political, environmental, and territorial concerns running through the altered landscapes of historical Land Art. Indeed, it is arguably because of the "nostalgic" tendency of Lippard's writing (as later diagnosed by Kwon) that many of the post-Land Art practitioners whom she advocated, including Agnes Denes, Helen and Newton Harrison, and Alan Sonfist, largely fell outside the purview of advanced critical writing in the 1980s and 1990s — as did their ecological concerns.[49] Indeed, such work and the criticism surrounding it often fetishized nature as pure exterior or ideal, thus disavowing — if not programmatically resisting — the postmodern insight that "nature," in Frederic Jameson's words, "is gone for good."[50] Rather than proposing an apocalyptic endgame, however, Jameson was simply pointing out that every square inch of the earth has long been marked by the forces of global-capitalist resource use, and that any appeal to something or somewhere untainted by its constituent dynamics and conflicts would be highly irresponsible in ethical, political, and ecological terms. The intensive displacements, crises, and conflicts concerning territories and life-support systems under post-Cold War globalization have brought this long-existent condition into relief. The realization that "there is no outside"[51] retroactively reframes our sense of the problems and stakes involved in historical Land Art in terms of an "aesthetics of

critical habitat" (as formulated by Emily Apter), in which "media and environment are increasingly difficult to disentangle as a semiotic system."[52] The best contemporary art concerned with space, land, and territory — by Jennifer Allora and Guillermo Calzadilla, Andrea Geyer, Eyal Weizman, the Center for Land Use Interpretation, and others — offers crucial insights into this project of reframing. In turn, art-historical research can itself become a resource for the future extension and radicalization of contemporary practice.

Notes

1  Robert Smithson, "Frederick Law Olmstead and the Dialectical Landscape," (1973) in *Smithson: Collected Writings*, 164.

2  For general statements on the spatial turn in contemporary art, see Nato Thompson, *Experimental Geography* and Institute for Applied Autonomy, "Tactical Cartographies," in *An Atlas of Radical Cartography*, ed. Lize Mogel and Alexis Baghat (Los Angeles: Journal of Aesthetics and Protest Press, 2007), 29–36. On the archival impulse, see Foster "An Archival Impulse," and on the parafictional, see Carrie Lambert-Beatty, "Make Believe: Parafiction and Plausability." On Alÿs and Buckingham respectively, see Godfrey, "Walking the Line" and "The Artist as Historian." On the Center for Land Use Interpretation, see Sarah Kanouse, "Touring the Archive, Archiving the Tour: Image, Text, and Experience with the Center for Land Use Interpretation," *Art Journal* 64:2 (Summer 2005): 78–87, and Matthew Coolidge and Sarah Simons, eds., *Overlook: Exploring the Internal Fringes of America with The Center for Land Use Interpretation* (New York: Metropolis Books/Distributed Art Publishers, 2005). On Trevor Paglen, see Karen Beckman, "Telescopes, Torture, Transparency: Trevor Paglen and the Politics of Exposure," *Art Journal* 66:3 (Fall 2007): 62–67. On Anastas and Gabri, see T. J. Demos, "Means Without End: Camp Campaign," *October* 126 (Fall 2008): 69–90. On Andrea Geyer, see Geyer, *Spiral Lands*. On Allora and Calzadilla, see Yates McKee, "Wake, Vestige, Survival: Political Ecology and Sustainability in Allora/Calzadilla's *Landmark*," *October* 133 (Summer 2010).

3  See, for instance, Jeffrey Kastner, "There, Now: From Robert Smithson to Guantánamo," in Andrews, *Land, Art: A Cultural Ecology Handbook*, 22–31. While cursory statements such as Kastner's are crucial in their linking of past and present practices in light of contemporary political concerns, they forego a certain dimension of art-historical analysis that would shed light on the often contradictory and ambivalent relations between different generations of artists. That said, Kastner's overall work has been foundational for much contemporary practice concerned with the politics of and landscape, as exemplified by his ground-breaking survey, *Land and Environmental Art*. See especially Brian Wallis's "Survey," 18–43. The tendency to emphasize historical continuity rather than disjunction is rectified to some degree in the special issue of *Artforum* (Summer 2005) entitled "Inside Out: Land Art's New Territory," especially the roundtable convened by Tim Griffin with critics Pamela Lee and Claire Bishop, among others (Griffin et al., "Remote Possibilities").

4  Hal Foster, *Return of the Real*, xii. Foster relates this nonlinear temporality to the psychoanalytic notion of "deferred action" in which "one event is only registered through another that recodes it."

5  Miwon Kwon, "One Place After Another: Notes on Site-Specificity," *October* 80 (Spring 1997): 85.

6  "Deterritorialization" is the term famously coined by Gilles Deleuze and Felix Guattari in their 1980 book *Milles plateaux*. See Deleuze and Guattari, *A Thousand Plateaus*, trans. Brian Massumi (London: Continuum, 2004). Among the most influential applications of the term in the humanities and social sciences has been Arjun Appadurai's discussion of the unmooring of cultural systems and geographical locations in "Disjuncture and Difference in the Global Cultural Economy" (1990) in *Modernity at Large*, 27–47. David Joselit invokes Appadurai's typology of "scapes" — mediascape, financescape, ethnoscape, and so forth — in "Navigating the New Terrain."

7  See Jane McFadden's "Toward Site," which discusses Walter de Maria's *Mile Long Drawing* in relation to both the dematerialized event-scores of Fluxus and Gerry Schum's interest in televisual broadcast.

8  Jan Dibbets, cited in Michael Lailach, *Land Art* (Cologne: Taschen, 2007), 6. On the paradoxical spatiotemporal suspension of television between sites of production, transmission, and reception, see Samuel Weber, "Television: Set and Screen," in *Mass Mediauras: Form, Technics, Media* (Stanford, Calif.: Stanford University Press, 1996), 108–28.

9  Robert Smithson, "Towards the Development of an Air Terminal Site" (1966), in *Smithson: Collected Writings*, 54.

10  In "Aerial Art," Smithson writes that "the terminal complex might include a gallery (or aerial museum) that would provide visual information about where these aerial sites are situated. Diagrams, maps, photographs and movies of the projects under construction could be exhibited — thus the terminal complex and its entire airfield site would expand its meaning from the central spaces of the terminal itself to the edges of the airfields." "Aerial Art" (1969), in *Smithson: Collected Writings*, 117. In the earlier text, "Towards the Development of an Air Terminal Site," Smithson had suggested that "remote places such as the Pine Barrens of New Jersey and the frozen wastes of the North and South poles could be coordinated by art forms that would use the actual land as a medium. Television could transmit such activity all over the world" (ibid., 56).

11  Smithson, "Aerial Art," (1969), 116. Smithson's work on the airport project provides a crucial background not only to his insistence on the tripartite non-site structure of *Spiral Jetty* as a sculpture, text, and film, but also his later theorization of Central Park as a "dialectical landscape" suspended between earthen materiality and media technologies. See "Frederick Law Olmsted and the Dialectical Landscape."

12  Smithson, "Aerial Art," 117.

13  Smithson, "Towards the Development of an Air Terminal Site," 52–62.

14  The authoritative theorization of landscape along these lines is Mitchell, *Landscape and Power*.

15  Cited in Germano Celant, *Michael Heizer* (Milan: Fondazione Prada, 1997), xxvii.

16  See Rosalind Krauss's canonical phenomenological reading of *Double Negative* in Krauss, *Passages in Modern Sculpture* (Cambridge, Mass.: MIT Press, 1977), and Mark C. Taylor's deconstructive analysis in "Rend(er)ing," in Heizer and Taylor, *Michael Heizer: Double Negative* (Los Angeles: Museum of Contemporary Art; New York: Rizzoli, 1991). In Taylor's words, "The play of figure and ground staged in *Double Negative* creates a clearing that allows disappearance to appear.

The appearance of disappearance occurs not only in the *between* created by the walls of the cut but also transpires in the midst of the empty center between which the two tears on either side of the canyon are suspended. The deeper one digs, the more negation proliferates" (ibid., 17–18).

17 Cited in Celant, *Michael Heizer*, 60.

18 Julia Brown and Michael Heizer, "Interview," in *Michael Heizer: Sculpture in Reverse*, ed. Julia Brown (Los Angeles: Museum of Contemporary Art, 1984), 8.

19 See Alessandra Ponte's discussion of Heizer in relation to nuclear testing in "Desert Testing," in *Architecture and the Sciences: Exchanging Metaphors*, ed. Ponte and Antoine Picon (New York: Princeton Architectural Press; Princeton, N.J.: Princeton University School of Architecture, 2003), 81–115.

20 See David E. Nye, "Atomic Bomb and Apollo XI: New Forms of the Dynamic Sublime," in *American Technological Sublime* (Cambridge, Mass.: MIT Press, 1994), 224–56. On the "ends" repeatedly announced by artists and critics alike in twentieth-century art, see Hal Foster, "This Funeral is for the Wrong Corpse," in *Design and Crime: And Other Diatribes* (London: Verso, 2002): 123–43. On the dialectic of apocalyptic self-annihilation and redemptive self-realization on the part of a universalized "Man," see Jacques Derrida, "The Ends of Man" (1968), in *Writing and Difference*, trans. Alan Bass (Chicago: University of Chicago Press, 1978), 109–36.

21 Further, Heizer's choice of the phrase "pounded into the Stone Age" echoes the infamous remark by U.S. general Curtis

Lemay during the early years of the Vietnam War: "My solution to the problem [of North Vietnam] would be to tell them frankly that they've got to draw in their horns and stop their aggression, or we're going to bomb them back into the Stone Age. And we would shove them back into the Stone Age with Air power or Naval power — not with ground forces." Lemay, *Mission With Lemay: My Story* (New York: Doubleday, 1965), 565.

22 Walter Benjamin, "The Work of Art in the Age of Its Technological Reproducibility: Second Version" (1936), in Walter *Benjamin: Selected Writings: Volume 3: 1935–1938*, ed. Howard Eiland and Michael W. Jennings (Cambridge, Mass.: Belknap Press of Harvard University Press, 2008), 122.

23 Brown and Heizer, "Interview," 11. Cited in Ponte, "Desert Testing," 99–100.

24 Celant, *Michael Heizer*, xx.

25 See Margaret M. Bryant, "Nevada Names," *American Speech* 49 (Aug.–Winter 1974): 288. Bryant, writing as a pre-postcolonialist cultural historian, did not address the ideological implications of the term "massacre," which mainstream American historians had traditionally reserved to denote the savage violence of Indians as opposed to the supposed civilizing march of Manifest Destiny. For an important redress of such problems in the study of American art and visual culture, see the chapters "Native Americans in the Popular Press: *Harper's Weekly* and the Washita Massacre" and "The End of the Ghost Dance" in Frances K. Pohl's magisterial textbook, *Framing America: A Social History of American Art* (New York: Thames and Hudson, 2008), 236–37. On photographic landscape surveys and the politics of settler-colonial site-naming,

see Alan Trachtenberg, "Naming the View," in *Reading American Photographs: Images as History, Mathew Brady to Walker Evans* (New York: Farrar, Strauss, Giroux, 1990), 119–63. Here it is important to consider Matthew Buckingham's *The Six Grandfathers, Paha Sapa, in the Year 502,002 C.E.* (2002), which investigates the colonial violence of place-marking at the site known in settler-nationalist parlance as Mount Rushmore, formerly a site sacred to local indigenous people. Consulting with geologists, Buckingham juxtaposes the predicted state of decay to which the monumental presidential portraits of Mount Rushmore will have succumbed in a half-million years with a timeline detailing conflicts between indigenous people and settler-colonialists over the site's naming, control, and usage. See Godfrey, "The Artist as Historian" and Buckingham, "Muhheakantuck — Everything Has a Name," *October* 120 (Spring 2007): 173–81.

26 Referring to Long's procedure of "brushing" locally specific footpaths in the Himalayas so as to "unveil" their status as indexes of a primordial encounter between the human body and the Being of the natural landscape, Herman Rappaport asks "if in lifting the veil by brushing the path in Nepal Richard Long does not walk in the footsteps of others in order to forget beings? The photograph by Long, like the vast majority of his photographs, is devoid of people. And no doubt because of this, his photographs are also devoid of nightmare, hallucination, and phantoms. It is as if in detaching us from beings by an attentiveness to the erasure of the trace, Long has cleared the way for a return of the aesthetic in the persistence of that which has withdrawn from the human." Rappaport, "Brushed Path, Slate Line, Stone Circle: On Martin Heidegger, Richard

Long, and Jacques Derrida," in *Deconstruction and the Visual Arts*, ed. Peter Brunette and David Wills (Cambridge: Cambridge University Press, 1994), 164–65.

27 Hal Foster cites Fabian in "The Artist as Ethnographer," but his primary point of reference is the model of 1990s "fieldwork research" by post-conceptualist artists such as Mark Dion and Renée Green rather than the naive — and often pernicious — invocation of cultural alterity by artists such as Long and Heizer. See Foster, *Return of the Real*, 177.

28 Rosalind Krauss, "Sculpture in the Expanded Field," in *Originality of the Avant-Garde and Other Modernist Myths* (Cambridge, Mass.: MIT Press, 1985), 279.

29 Lucy Lippard, *Overlay: Contemporary Art and the Art of Prehistory* (New York: New Press, 1983).

30 See Anthony Vidler, "X Marks the Spot: The Exhaustion of Space at the Scene of the Crime," in *Warped Space: Art, Architecture, and Anxiety in Modern Culture* (Cambridge, Mass.: MIT Press, 2002), 123–32.

31 Unattributed image caption in Kastner, *Land and Environmental Art*, 78.

32 For a crucial revisionist reading of Mendieta that foregrounds questions of loss and absence, see Miwon Kwon, "Bloody Valentines: Afterimages by Ana Mendieta," in *Inside the Visible: An Elliptical Traverse of Twentieth Century Art in, of, and from the Feminine*, ed. Catherine de Zegher (Cambridge, Mass.: MIT Press, 1996), 164–71. For a reading of Mendieta that emphasizes photographic mediation and displacement — rather than self-evident somatic presence — see Kelly Baum, "Shapely

Shapelessness: Ana Mendieta's *Untitled (Glass on Body Imprints — Face)*, 1972," in *More than One: Photographs in Sequence*, ed. Joel Smith (New Haven: Yale University Press; Princeton, N.J.. Princeton University Art Museum, 2008), 80–93.

33  See Lippard's discussion of Mendieta in *Overlay*, 49–50.

34  Rosalind Krauss, "Notes on the Index, Part 1" (1979), in *Originality of the Avant-Garde*, 196–209.

35  "Technological reproduction can place the copy of the original in situations which the original itself cannot attain.... The cathedral leaves its site to be received in the studio of an art lover.... These changed circumstances... devalue the here-and-now of the artwork." Benjamin, "The Work of Art in the Age of Its Technological Reproducibility," 103.

36  On the forensic impulse, see Ralph Rugoff, ed., *Scene of the Crime* (Cambridge, Mass.: MIT Press, 1997).

37  For an account of *(Untitled) Rape Piece*, see Julia P. Herzberg, "Ana Mendieta's Iowa Years: 1970–1980," in *Ana Mendieta: Earth Body: Sculpture and Performance, 1972–1985*, ed. Olga B. Viso (Washington, D.C.: Hirshhorn Museum and Sculpture Garden; Ostfildern-Ruit, Germany: Hatje Cantz, 2004), 155–56. Herzberg discusses another "forensic" tableau by Mendieta entitled *Clinton Piece: Dead on Street* (1973). As the audience of this performance-event exited the auditorium, "they discovered Mendieta lying motionless in a pool of blood as though she were an accident or crime-scene victim. She asked a fellow performer to stand over her taking pictures with a camera, as would a police or tabloid photographer at the scene of an accident" (156).

38  Craig Owens, "The Discourse of Others: Feminists and Postmodernism," in *The Anti-Aesthetic: Essays on Postmodern Culture*, ed. Hal Foster (Port Townsend, Wash.: Bay Press, 1983): 57–82.

39  Smithson, "Frederick Law Olmstead and the Dialectical Landscape," 164.

40  Taking as our starting point Smithson's remark that Olmsted's "before" photograph of Central Park "reminds me of the strip-mining regions I saw last year in southeastern Ohio...a man-made wasteland" (ibid., 158), Matthew Friday and I are currently developing a Critical Regionalism Initiative at Ohio University that will explore the local, national, and global legacies of coal mining in the Appalachia. See McKee, "Ohio University School of Art Critical Regionalism Initiative: Political Ecology Research Sites," in ...*In a Most Dangerous Manner*, ed. Steven Lam and Sarah Rogers (Cleveland: SPACES Gallery, 2010).

41  Robert Morris, "Art as/and Land Reclamation," *October* 12 (Spring 1980): 87.

42  Ibid., 90.

43  Ibid., 94.

44  Ibid., 94–95.

45  Ibid., 99. See http://www.kennecott.com/ for the company's current self-presentation as an innovator of environmental remediation. Thanks to Jane E. Boyd for this reference.

46  See Robert Morris, "Aligned With Nazca," *Artforum* 14:2 (October 1975), reprinted in Morris, *Continuous Project Altered Daily: The Writings of Robert Morris* (Cambridge, Mass.: MIT Press, 1994), 142–72, and Gayatri Spivak's

critique thereof in *A Critique of Postcolonial Reason* (Cambridge, Mass.: Harvard University Press, 1999), 347–51.

47  Janet Catherine Berlo provides the following information concerning the Black Mesa region, drawn from historian John Redhouse: "From the colonial Ternary of Guadalupe Hidalgo to the Navajo Hopi Land Settlement Act, the United States of America has repeatedly violated the human rights and territorial integrity of the Navajo and Hopi people living on Black Mesa and throughout the former Joint Use Area. The executive, legislative, and judicial branches of the American state have separately and in concert aided and abetted this process by robbing the two tribes of their sovereign status and dispossessing them of their aboriginal land base. Seeking to divide and conquer, a coalition of special interests ranging from government-paid claims attorneys to multinational energy corporations have succeeded to a fine legal degree in alienating the two peoples and ending their joint tenure of the shared soil. Failing to resolve the dispute it helped create, the U.S. government through its Relocation Commission is now bent on clearing the land for large-scale mineral and water expropriation that will follow Indian removal in the late 1980s." Berlo, "'Libraries of Meaning and of History': *Spiral Lands* and Indigenous American Lands," in Geyer, *Spiral Lands*, n. 66, 131.

48  See the website of the Black Mesa Indigenous Support Group at http://blackmesais.org and the Black Mesa Water Coalition at www.blackmesawatercoalition .org. On the theory and practice of post-colonial environmental justice in the United States and beyond, see Robert Bullard, ed., *The Quest for Environmental Justice:*

*Human Rights and the Politics of Pollution* (San Francisco: Sierra Club Books, 2005), especially Al Gedicks, "Resource Wars Against Native Peoples," 168–187. See too Van Jones, *The Green Collar Economy: How One Solution Can Fix Our Two Biggest Problems* (New York: HarperOne, 2008).

49  For Kwon's critique of Lippard's appeal to the "lure of the local" in the mid-1990s, see *One Place After Another*, 157–60. It is important to note, however, that in *On the Beaten Track: Art, Tourism, and Place*, Lippard devotes much attention to the work of contemporary Native American artists involved in a postcolonial critique of precisely the type of landscape primitivism informing her own writing in *Overlay*.

50  Frederic Jameson, *Postmodernism, or The Cultural Logic of Late Capitalism* (Durham, N.C.: Duke University Press, 1991), xi. For an exemplary misreading and rejection of such a "postmodern" position that ends up reaffirming the harmonious equilibrium of "nature" as the ideal foundation of ecological art, see Eleanor Heartney, "Ecopolitics/Ecopoetry: Helen and Newton Harrison's Environmental Talking Cure," in *But is it Art? The Spirit of Art as Activism*, ed. Nina Felshin (Seattle: Bay Press, 1995), 140–64. As Heartney defensively puts it, "postmodern theory relegates nature to the junk heap of outmoded concepts" (ibid., 140). The crucial counterpoint to such an anti-postmodern stance is Mark Dion, whose work explores the culturally and economically contested status of "nature" as a horizon for thought and action under conditions of capitalist globalization. On more recent developments in the relation between art and ecology, see McKee, "Art and the Ends of Environmentalism" and "Wake, Vestige, Survival."

51 Paraphrasing Derrida's famous axiom that "there is no outside the text," Michael Hardt and Antonio Negri posit that "any postmodern liberation must be achived within this world, on the plane of imma- nence, with no possibility of any even utopian outside." Hardt and Negri, *Empire* (Cambridge, Mass.: Harvard University Press, 2000), 65.

52 Emily Apter, "Aesthetics of Critical Habitat," *October* 101 (Spring 2002): 21–44.

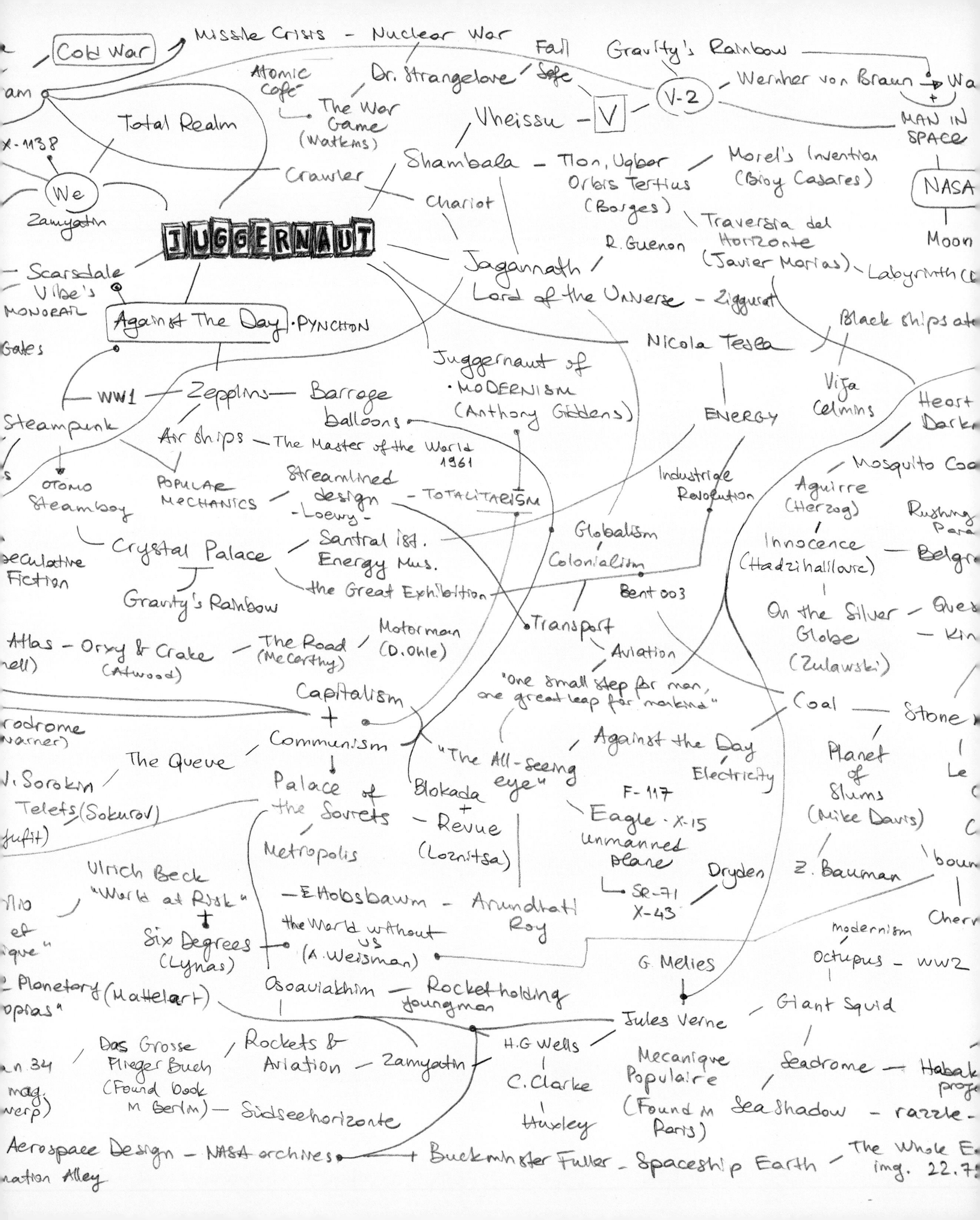

Cold War — Missile Crisis — Nuclear War    Fall    Gravity's Rainbow

...am    Atomic Café    Dr. Strangelove / Safe    V-2 — Werner von Braun → Wa...

Total Realm    The War Game (Watkins)    Vheissu — V    MAN IN SPACE

X-1138    Crawler    Shambala — Tlon, Uqbar    Morel's Invention (Bioy Casares)    NASA

We    Chariot    Orbis Tertius (Borges)    Traversía del Horizonte (Javier Marías)    Moon

Zamyatin

JUGGERNAUT    Jagannath    R. Guenon    Labyrinth (...

— Scarsdale Vibe's    Lord of the Universe — Ziggurat

MONORAIL    Against The Day · PYNCHON    Nicola Tesla    Black Ships at...

Gates    Juggernaut of    Vija Celmins

— WW1 — Zeppelins — Barrage    · MODERNISM (Anthony Giddens)    ENERGY    Heart Dark...

Steampunk    balloons    Industrial Revolution

Air Ships — The Master of the World 1961    Mosquito Coa...

OTOMO Steamboy    Streamlined    — TOTALITARISM    Aguirre (Herzog)    Rushing Para...

POPULAR MECHANICS    design    Globalism    Innocence (Hadzihalilovic) — Belgr...

Crystal Palace    -Loewy-    Colonialism    Bent 003

...eculative Fiction    Santral Ist. Energy Mus.    On the Silver — Ques...

Gravity's Rainbow    the Great Exhibition    Transport    Globe (Zulawski)

Motorman (D. Ohle)    Aviation    Coal — Stone...

Atlas — Oryx & Crake — The Road (McCarthy)    "one small step for man,    Planet of Slums (Mike Davis)

...ell)    (Atwood)    one great leap for mankind"

...rodrome    Capitalism    Against the Day

(...rner)    +    "The All-Seeing    Electricity

The Queue    Communism    eye"    F-117

V. Sorokin    Palace of    Blokada    Eagle · X-15    Dryden    Z. Bauman

Telets (Sokurov)    the Soviets    +    unmanned

...fit)    — Revue (Loznitsa)    plane    SR-71    modernism

Metropolis    X-43    Octupus — WW2

Ulrich Beck    "World at Risk"    —E Hobsbawm — Arundhati Roy    Cherr...

...io    +    the World without US (A. Weisman)    G. Melies    Giant Squid

...f    Six Degrees (Lynas)    Jules Verne

...que"    Osoaviakhim — Rocket holding    H.G Wells    Mecanique Populaire

Planetary (Mattelart)    Youngman    C. Clarke    (Found in Paris)    Seadrome — Habak...

...pras"    Rockets & Aviation — Zamyatin    Sea Shadow — razzle...

...n. 34    Das Grosse    Huxley

mag.    Flieger Buch (Found book in Berlin) — Südseehorizonte

...werp)

Aerospace Design — NASA archives — Buckminster Fuller · Spaceship Earth — The Whole E... img. 22.7...

...ation Alley

# In Conversation: Land, Space, Territory

Uriel Abulof, Kelly Baum (moderator), Rachael Z. DeLue, and Jonathan Levy

Roundtable discussion
Princeton, New Jersey
May 5, 2009

Kelly Baum (KB): We're here to discuss some of the issues raised by the exhibition *Nobody's Property*. Because the question of land belongs to so many disciplines, because it intersects with subjects that are simultaneously aesthetic, political, and economic in nature, this seemed like an especially opportune moment to assemble a roundtable comprised of scholars from disparate fields.

Rachael, Jon and Uriel: Each of you has a unique perspective on land, one shaped by the various disciplines in which you work. As a way to introduce you to one another and also to the reader of this transcript, I thought we could start by discussing land as it pertains to your specific areas of research and study.

Jonathan Levy (JL): I work on the history of capitalism, specifically in the United States, and I investigate issues of risk, security, and speculation. So where land figures in for me is the nineteenth-century commodification of land. In the early nineteenth century, land was an economic bulwark of security. Land offered some means of subsistence — quite literally, subsistence crops — apart from the fluctuations of the market. And what happens over the nineteenth century, up until the middle of the twentieth century, is that land becomes a commodity. Like any other kind of commodity, it's measured, it's traded, it's fungible, and therefore land enters into capitalist streams of speculation and exchange, and then other forms of security crop up, ending with, most notoriously, the welfare state. So for me, the trajectory is a sense of loss, where land is really central to identity and autonomy in the economic sense. With capitalist transformation, land enters into other kinds of streams of meaning and economic exchange.

KB: I read an article you wrote in 2006 on the development of futures trading in the last decades of the nineteenth century, and it seems like — from what I remember of the essay — the increasing abstraction or commodification of land was met with resistance, especially from farmers, from the people who worked on the land.

JL: Yes, well, there is a real epistemological register in which the debate occurs, in which you're taking something that's real, palpable — and what's more real, palpable, than land? — and you're turning it into a complete abstraction. In a larger sense, the economic abstraction of land is crucial for understanding political claims of self-determination, which are equally abstract and also tied to land.

Rachael DeLue (RD): Because I'm an historian of art and visual culture, I tend primarily to think about land in the abstract. By which I mean my interest is not so much in land as such but in landscape, meaning in the representation of land, or nature, or wilderness, or space. I'm curious if we may at some point think about the meanings of these various terms and try to imagine where something like nature fits in or how this exhibition figures out the relationship between land and nature.

But, more to the point, I spend a lot of time thinking about the representation of land, which means I think of land more as an idea than as a concrete thing and as an idea that is invented for a variety of reasons — social, economic, political, historical, mythic, phantasmatic. And one of the things I have realized in the course of thinking about this representational abstraction of landscape is that, increasingly, over the course of the nineteenth and twentieth centuries, our relationship to land has become one of estrangement, and I think that's interesting given what you said about loss. It might be useful to think a little bit about estrangement and also to think about, with the increasing estrangement or loss from land as such, how simultaneously the idea of landscape has had to perform more and more duties and has had to assume even more mythic and phantasmatic proportions. So there's a simultaneous estrangement and abundance of access when it comes to land, one in terms of actuality and one in terms of representation.

JL:  So the loss of land as a concrete form leads to an embrace of nature as an ideal?

RD:  An ideal at times, yes, but at base an idea, one that is used to shore up fantasies of identity. When I say fantasies of identity, I mean that identity in many instances is no longer a matter of an actual relationship to land, but land as an imaginary still figures in the formation of identity, in constructions of self or nation.

Uriel Abulof (UA):  From my political international relations perspective, land is both resource and source. A resource that mainly manifests itself in the form of nation-states. Land as mainly borders, as allocating the resources to the various nations and peoples. And a source, as an area of contestation, of conflict. As a space in which one must find a way to move to from battleground to middle-ground or perhaps to common ground for the aspirations of communities too often contesting one another.

There is a deep symbolic level to all conflicts, which revolves inevitably around land, but there is also a very strong tangible component to that. We live on land, so as much as we imagine land in all its various symbolic forms, this is where we reside. I guess that's perhaps because of my stronger inclination to Hebrew than English. When I speak of land in Hebrew, the name is *adamah*. The roots of the word are also that of *adam*, which is that of man or women, and *dam*, which is blood. So I guess that in many ways this is the triangle in which I deal in my work.

KB:  There's something you wrote in a recent essay, "Two Rights Make a Wrong: Self-Determination in Kosovo and Georgia," that I found interesting: "Reconciling self-determination with territorial integrity is an ongoing task of modern diplomacy." You seem to be arguing that an over-investment in territory can precipitate violence, and this violence might be in the name of self-determination, but it can lead in dangerous directions. You also argue that the concept of self-determination itself can be misused.

UA:  Right, because self-determination is really the pinnacle of political ethics, but it has been deeply distorted, misinterpreted, misused, and even abused in global politics. The issue of territorial integrity is interesting in that sense, because it basically boils down to what is referred to as the beginning of international relations, where states, rather than city communities, for example, became the prime actor in global politics, and the ruler was given, in theory at least, complete control over a certain territory.

From the onset of self-determination as a principle, from about the mid-nineteenth century, an almost inevitable tension arose between the principle of the territorial integrity of the state, or of the ruler of that state, and the self-determination of peoples. So, it's not that self-determination is not about land — it's still about land — but now the land is not that of the ruler but that of the people, and the tension between the two is an ongoing one in international relations. Unsolvable. And as we've seen in the recent crises in Kosovo and Georgia, it will continue to haunt us.

JL:  So land belonging to the state versus land belonging to the nation, they work together, but . . .

UA:  The way I see it, land is the place where the nexus between liberty and responsibility, where the political claim actually manifests itself, and the question becomes to what extent that nexus should be held by the community or by its authority. From the Peace of Westphalia, in 1648, up until two centuries later, in the Spring of Nations, 1848 [the European Revolutions], it was an area in which the authority, mainly that of despots, was the prime focus of global politics. The understanding of political legitimacy was through the prism of these specific authorities, which sometimes derived their creed from the belief that God bestowed that authority on them. From the mid-nineteenth century onwards, in Europe and Latin America, and then all over the world, the issue of popular sovereignty gained much more stride, and we can begin to talk about a true international system rather than an inter-state system. That's the basic tension—who holds the territory? States or nations?

RD: Given what you've just said, it might be useful, at least for me, to think about one of the questions that Kelly raised—well, a series of questions, as follows: "What is the role that land or territory is playing in present-day wars and conflicts? These wars and conflicts are often described as transnational or extraterritorial—is this an accurate description?" And my first thought would be: Not really. How is it possible that these wars and conflicts could even be conceived of as extraterritorial? Because it sounds as if, from what you're saying, that territory or terrain or land or space or whatever we want to call it is absolutely central to the ways in which people or nations negotiate the questions of sovereignty and self-determination.

UA: Yes, there is no way to transcend land, this is where we fight. [*laughter*]

JL: This is fighting space.

KB: I agree. I have also found the emphasis on extraterritorial conflict to be odd, given everything we know and read about…

UA: But transnational…?

KB: Transnational is different. Conflict is also described as increasingly spectacular.

It occurs over and in images, and in the media sphere, and I think that's true.

RD: "Shock and awe" is a good example of that.

KB: I think there's something to the idea that conflict is now transnational. In many respects, we can no longer understand conflict as being between two distinct states or even confined to a specific area. Power too transcends national borders, as in the case of the extraterritorial prisons run by the United States. Territory as a kind of bounded entity matters less to the exercise of power now than it did in the past, perhaps.

RD: So there would be two ways to understand *extraterritorial*. The answer to your question [is conflict extraterritorial?] would be no, if war is imagined as something having to do with land and fights over land. But the answer would be yes, if one imagines that the battles fought spectacularly or materially are in a sense global, and are no longer delimited by any kind of national boundaries. That makes sense.

JL: It used to be that in wars, if you could capture particular places, or put boots on the ground, the war was simply over. Or if you could somehow capture an enemy's capital, well, that was it. There was no other way you could fight. Certainly that's now no longer the case.

UA: I wonder…of course there is much literature that deals with the processes of globalization as an indication of the erosion of the nation-state and the transformation that comes along with it, for example, in the battlefield. So there has been much discussion about the need for

modern armies nowadays to combat also on the symbolic level, but often that means for many that the main battle is on the symbolic level. Which makes it, in a way, I think, a post-modern warfare. And it has many limitations, because even in those examples that we use to refer to it, eventually the battle was won on the ground.

For me, as an Israeli, the demonstration of that was the second Lebanese war, in 2006, in which it was very clear that in the eyes of those who designed the war on the Israeli side, the symbolic level was perhaps even more prominent than the actual one on the ground. Just to give you one example: There was a very famous speech by Hassan Nasrallah, the head of Hezbollah, in 2000, just after Israel withdrew from southern Lebanon. In that speech, he depicted Israel as a cobweb state, so fragile that if you blow on it hard enough, it will simply collapse. It became a prime metaphor in public discourse in Israel, something that really haunted both the masses and the elites. This speech was given in the town of Bint Jbeil, in southern Lebanon. Now there was no reason, in 2006, strategically speaking, for Israel to try to invade this township, other than it was where Hassan Nasrallah made that famous cobweb speech. So Israel invaded that town, with high casualties for its soldiers. On the symbolic level, the whole operation was called "Steelweb."

KB: "Steelweb"?

UA: A web made of steel. The end result of the war, and this is where we close the circle, was that it was perceived as a failure, and the reason was that it was perceived to be conducted really more on the symbolic level, fatally so, than on the ground, combating those units of the

Hezbollah, trying to win and capture more land and driving away those forces. This shift from a kind of modern land-based warfare to a purely symbolic conflict is interesting and, as you can probably tell, has important ramifications.

JL: Self-determination and popular sovereignty have to be at stake here too. In the famous example, the British Empire in the nineteenth century controlled the territory of India with something like 40,000 British troops. There are mutinies and conflicts for sure, but it works. And for some time, much of the Indian population felt like, well, this is the way the world works. The Mughals had come down from the north, and now here come the British.

But something happens in the nineteenth and twentieth centuries, through these ideas of self-determination and popular sovereignty, where you simply can't hold territory without putting an enormous number of boots on the ground. And even if you do that, that might not be successful, because so-called issues of hearts and minds have to somehow work into the equation. We're seeing that now in the Middle East, right? With the war in Lebanon, where military power cannot create the kind of effect, either desired or required, for the kind of project. No?

UA: Possibly. Take the case of India. If we trace the ideals of self-determination with Gandhi, here it was called *Swaraj*, the notion that the Indian people, not Hindu, but Indian in the sense of the whole community on the territory…here perhaps we should make the problematic distinction between blood-based community and land-based community.

KB: Between what?

UA: Blood-based and land-based community, which also sometimes appears as tension between ethnic nationalism and civic nationalism. Both are legitimizing systems, and we may like to think that legitimacy rather than coercion has the upper hand, at least by the end of the day. This, however, is not always the case. Chechnya is one case. The Holocaust is another.

KB: This dovetails with another question I'd like to ask, one that revolves around the weaponization of land. I'm interested in the way that land — or rather, the manipulation, demarcation, alteration, or appropriation of land — is used as a weapon in conflict, in the operations of power. Some great articles and books have been written recently on this very subject by authors like Stephen Graham and Eyal Weizman. Graham describes the bulldozer, for instance, and the sort of destruction it wrecks on land, as a weapon in the Israeli-Palestinian conflict, one that stands alongside guns and soldiers. In what other contexts has land been similarly instrumentalized?

RD: Well, it's interesting that you brought up the idea of the bulldozer as a weapon because it has occurred to me that *land* — understood not only as a terrain or territory but as a certain kind of property — is used, has been used, by the United States as a kind of weapon. Of course, we know that land was at issue in westward expansion, but displacement from the land was itself a weapon. I would say that a certain kind of displacement and dispossession still manifests as a weapon today, an economic and also a social weapon. This is where the idea of the bulldozer is interesting because

certain dispossessions, such as the demolition of housing projects, function in a similar manner, especially when new spaces aren't created for those displaced populations.

KB: That happened in New York in the 1980s. It's happening in New Orleans now.

RD: It happened in Baltimore in the 1990s, ongoing in Chicago. And I would also say that, given the current economic situation, there's a way in which property ownership…the kinds of mortgages that were sold to people without means, without a certain kind of social and political power, seem very analogous to me to the kinds of treaties that were negotiated with Native populations in the United States in the nineteenth century. These wind up being tools of dispossession in a less direct way, because what's happening is that these mortgages were sold to people who then couldn't sustain them, so their homes were foreclosed, they were dispossessed of their property, their land, their space. And now it's the same people who sold those properties to them who are coming in and buying the foreclosures and making millions once again.

UA: But was it intentional, in your view?

RD: You know, I don't think it was intentional in the most specific sense, but given that the mortgages were sold without a spirit of "Let's give homes to everyone"…

KB: It's moneymaking.

RD: It's a moneymaking scheme.

KB: It's a profit-making enterprise, and they targeted the elderly, they targeted the poor, and they targeted the people who didn't speak English.

RD:  The fact that it was about money in the beginning makes the cynic in me think that it worked out rather nicely for those who put these plans in place to begin with. So maybe an inadvertent kind of dispossession from land? But it strikes me that even if it's not intentionally a weapon, land has become, in a sense, a social and economic weapon here. I think parallels can be drawn to New Orleans, as you're suggesting, and in interesting ways. But given that we're talking about mortgages and capitalism, it may be that Jon has something to add.

JL:  Well, I hate to stand up for the mortgage brokers…[*laughter*] The last thing they want to do is have to occupy foreclosed homes that have lost 40 percent of their value. But I think where the analogy does hold between nineteenth-century dispossession and this kind of dispossession, which *is* dispossession, is a disconnect between the two parties as to the use of land, which has a moral overtone to it. So, with the present economic crisis…the idea with the mortgages was that we could funnel them through the securitization process, and we could spread risk, and in this way we could create wealth. However, the person buying the mortgage had absolutely no idea that this was what their land was meant for, even could be used for, or should be used for—which is the moral question.

Likewise, in the nineteenth century—it depends on which tribe you're looking at—the Native populations had an idea of the use of land, economically, culturally, and politically, that's nothing like the idea envisioned for it by westward

white expansion; where, in their vision, the Indians are not using the land the way the land should be used and can be used and, really, must be used—it has that kind of providential discourse to it that you mentioned earlier. Whereas Indians—again, some were engaged in agriculture and had a notion of land—but many of them were baffled by the idea that someone could own a piece of land.

UA:  So not as property but as…

JL:  Well, I think the issue, which feeds back into the earlier discussion about territorial integrity, is exclusion—that you could have an exclusive right to occupy and use the land.

UA:  There was no notion of borders? Really?

JL:  Well, there were borders. They were defined by how one might use the land and what one's entitlements were. For example, there's seasonal migration, so in certain seasons, certain tribes can fish in this stream…But the idea that individuals have exclusive property rights in particular tracts of land? Certainly not so much, if at all.

UA:  Right. So it's functional.

JL:  There's a Western history of this too, before the enclosure of land, in early modern Europe, where land had a bundle of uses, which might be distributed within a collectivity. You could plant crops, you could hunt, you could graze, and it was not exclusive. So, the enclosure movement entailed creating not only the notion of territorial integrity but also exclusivity.

RD:  Well, this brings us to the question of relationality. In the context of westward expansion and the displacement of Native populations, what you wind up having then—and maybe this is what you're suggesting—is something like not only an unequal standing among parties involved in the relations that are set forth or constructed within the space, but also multiple and disparate formulations of relationship to the land. When forced to coexist, these raise questions that emerge or manifest as conflict, given that the formulations of relationship put together in the space are disparate and incommensurate.

But it is important not to overidealize or look through a nostalgic lens to a moment prior to property or prior to capitalism because of course—and this is something that American studies and other disciplines have been thinking about a lot in recent years—there *were* borders. There were conflicts among Native populations. There were functional and traditional kinds of possessions of the land, so it's not as if one model trumped the other. This is probably why land became such a complicated space.

UA:  Was it sanctified? Was it perceived as earth, yet metaphysical to a certain extent?

RD:  On the part of Native populations? Yes, and that manifested in different ways given what particular culture one is talking about. But, yes, absolutely. That's interesting because it means that two different imaginings of the sanctity of land came into conflict—well, a hundred imaginings of the sanctity of land, but if you want to make a dichotomy of whites versus Native populations, religion played a role of course, very much so, in westward expansion, because the idea on the part of settlers and policy makers was that the possession of land and the dispossession of Native populations were divinely ordained.

UA:  And on the part of the Native populations, was land also perceived to be the real estate of God?

RD:  Well, the sanctity of land for most Native populations wasn't a matter of ownership or possession in the sense of *property*, and I think that was one of the major conflicts when it came to these different understandings of sanctity.

JL:  I also think there was a metaphysical relationship to the land for white settlers, which has to do with community and religion as well, but also selfhood. Your autonomy was — well, a bad pun — grounded in the ownership of land. That was the basis for your ability to act as a free agent and a moral agent. And also as a political agent. And I don't think…well, I'm curious — *self-determination* probably isn't an accident as a phrase, as opposed to *group determination*…I've always interested in why the word *self*…

UA:  Rather than, say, group or collective determination?

JL:  Yes.

KB:  When did that term come into usage? When did it enter political philosophy?

UA:  The one person who dissipated the principle in the global arena is Woodrow Wilson in the late 1910s. But even before him, Lenin and other socialists invented the term and its political use.

JL:  Right, self-determination of peoples…

UA:  Right, right. And Woodrow Wilson propagated it following the first World War to the extent that that it should be the guiding principle in dealing with the outcomes of the war and of course preventing something similar in the future.

JL:  We should take out a map…

UA:  Well, the main landscape was that of Europe. We had the Hapsburg Empire and the Ottoman Empire and of course the defeated German state. The question that was posed by Woodrow Wilson's Secretary of State, Robert Lansing, was: Who would be the *self* of *self-determination*? This sounds like a very noble principle, he said, but it was in fact a very dangerous one, because not being able to determine that *self* would be a prescription for the continuation of war. And perhaps not oddly, Hitler was abusing this same notion of self-determination when he annexed Austria and when he argued for the annexation of the Sudenten region in Czechoslovakia, which were populated by those who were either German or identified with German culture.

So the whole notion of self-determination was utilized for what one might call racial imperialism. Here again you have a novel notion, ideal and idea, that in real life can very easily be abused in the name of that collective, that very ambiguous self.

JL:  Do you think we could be heading towards a period where a kind of overlapping dual sovereignty is newly possible? You see this discussed particularly in the Israeli-Palestinian conflict — the idea of a one-state solution in which there are

different kinds of sovereignty that are more rooted in culture, ethnicity, and religion or peoplehood, but can inhabit the same space.

KB:  Would it be a federal model, which is something that Hannah Arendt…

JL:  Like New Jersey and Connecticut? [*laughter*]

UA:  I wish. Well, I don't know if I wish. On a personal level, I should say that I'm a Zionist, and as much as I agree that self-determination can be abused, I think self-determination is the right ideal. So, I do believe, for example, in the self-determination of the Jewish people. Self-determination should be understood along that ideal as both dual and mutual. Dual in the sense that I, the individual self, may determine my belonging to the collective self, which, in turn, may determine its preferred polity. You have to establish what is that collective identity in the first place. The other aspect that is always important is the mutuality of it, which is that it is the right of the self as well as the other.

Take, for example, the cases of Kosovo and Georgia in 2008. That was clearly, in my mind at least, other-determination rather than self-determination, because for the European Union, or at least for many countries in the European Union, the whole notion of Kosovo's independence was predicated on the idea that there is a Kosovar people. But there is no Kosovar people, at least from the perception of the people (or rather peoples) on the ground. They perceive themselves to be Albanians.

KB:  And there are Serbians who live in that same province too.

UA: Right. This is exactly the reason why for the European Union there was a need to, in a way, reimagine that community as a Kosovar people, as a civic community that will enable it to be inclusive, in the sense that it's both Albanian and Serb. But that's not the way the people on the ground perceive themselves. So there is obviously a clash between the self and the other. The same goes for Georgia.

In the case of Israel and Palestine, there is an interesting mismatch between the identities of the two communities. For most Jews their identity is in one way or another — and I don't use it as a provocative term — blood-based. The Jewish people imagine themselves by and large as an extended kinship. It's a kind of fictive super-family. For the Palestinian, I would argue, we're seeing a much more land-based identity. So for Israeli Jews, there is much more willingness to compromise on aspects of land, such as the international withdrawal from southern Lebanon, from Gaza, even the wall or the security fence between the West Bank and Israel. For the Israelis, the main issue is the existence of the people, so you can try to compromise some properties, some aspects of the land. But when land becomes the maker of your identity, rather than the marker of it, then compromising it is compromising who you are, not just an aspect of properties of your polity. And this kind of asymmetry, I think, is what lies at the root of that conflict.

KB: So you think Israelis don't perceive their identity as land-bound?

UA: It's not land-based.

KB: Not land-based. OK.

UA: The whole idea of Israel as an ethno-national state … its raison d'être was to guarantee the survival of the Jewish people. This is why the Zionists favored the Uganda Plan for a settlement in Africa at the beginning of the twentieth century, because the imperative was saving the Jewish people. This is why Zionists endorsed the Peel Commission Plan in 1937 that basically gave the Jewish people 25 percent of the land, of Mandatory Palestine. They agreed to it even though it was a small fraction of the land, because you need to save the people. Land is important, but it's not the imperative. The imperative is the people, and the people are, in a way, blood-based.

RD: Can I ask then, given what you've said about the idea that Jewish identity is blood-based, what accounts for both the symbolic and material importance of the settlement?

UA: One fact that we have to bear in mind is that for the last, more than four decades, since 1967, the land in Gaza and the West Bank was never annexed — all that period. And the reason for it, I think, quite clearly, is the fact that the imperative was and still remains the survival of the Jewish people, having a Jewish state. And annexing those territories means there is no longer a Jewish state, demographically and democratically speaking. But if we look at the settlers — and here again we might distinguish between the more extreme, usually religious element and the majority that went to those territories mainly because of economic incentives — you can get some discounts and perhaps higher standards of living …

RD: New apartments.

UA: Yes, economically speaking, there are lots of incentives.

RD: Yeah, sure, I get that.

UA: But for many settlers, there is indeed something that perhaps resembles the majority of the Palestinians' approach towards land. Here, for example, one may ask those settlers, would they rather — because of their perception of land as so sanctified, perhaps as the maker of their identity rather than only a marker of it — would they prefer to hold to the ground, stay where they are, but be part of a Palestinian state? Which is basically the choice of Israeli Arabs. They are part of Israel, which is now a Jewish state.

RD: So their land, in a really interesting way, is being used as a kind of … I don't want to say weapon … but it has a functional use within a larger claim to identity, which isn't land-based, which is blood or religion-based.

UA: There was at the beginning of the Zionist movement a faction called the Canaanite movement, and their argument was that we should shy away from Jewish tradition — and from that whole notion of a blood-based community throughout the millennium — and reimagine ourselves as a community that is in fact Canaan. In which, perhaps, more like the French Republican model, the core will be cultural, linguistic, the Hebrew language. Everybody who is on the land, who makes Hebrew his or her mother tongue, would be part of that community, and make up part of the existence of that polity. It never came to pass, because of Jewish objections and Arabs' objections. The two communities perceived themselves very early on as mutually exclusive. There was no willingness on both sides to ever truly imagine themselves being part of a unitary community, giving rise to one political structure. There were many attempts, all rejected, by both sides.

JL: What you're saying seems to explain why using land as a bargaining chip or using the settlements as a kind of bargaining chip would strike Palestinians as utterly perverse. That notion of bargaining could actually fuel the conflict because you're offending their sensibility.

UA: The formula that has been used for the last forty years has been land for peace. For most Israelis the meaning of that is that we are giving up land in the West Bank and Gaza, and in return, we receive peace. For the Palestinians, it's really the other way around. It's they who are giving land, about 80 percent of their land, which is the whole of Palestine, in exchange for peace of mind, free from the occupation. This kind of mismatch is really at the core of the conflict. The question that we must address in one way or another is to what degree a land-based people can compromise land. In the minds of many Palestinians, the Israeli presence in Palestine itself — not 1967 but 1948, even before that — is perceived to be a kind of colonialist invasion. Land there is not just aspects of the polity, it's at the core of their identity, and it makes compromise much more hard to get. Well, there are perhaps solutions but . . . [laughs]

RD: We might not find the solution today. [laughs]

KB: What is our dominant experience of land in the United States? It seems to

me that we understand land primarily as image, commodity, and property, but also as frontier, especially in the last decade, which has witnessed the rise of an imperial rhetoric on the part of the United States government.

RD: That's a big question, and I begin to answer it by saying that there are as many understandings or imaginings of land in America as there are Americans.

KB: Do you think there's something about land specifically that lends itself to that kind of flexibility?

RD: Yes. One of the questions you asked was what authors have done the most to shape our understanding of land, and I have several in mind, but one author in particular is W. J. T. Mitchell, who in the introduction to a collection of essays called *Landscape and Power* says something to the effect that landscape — and we're talking here about landscape and not land as such, but I think the terms in this case might be interchangeable — he says landscape is not a genre, it's a medium. I take that to be utterly and emphatically the case, meaning that land can be imagined infinitely. It can be anything to anyone. It can be used for multiple purposes. It can be one thing on one day and on the next something wholly other, depending on what the desired outcome might be. I think that's in part because in America — and I'm speaking generally here — land was initially imagined, by Europeans, as expanse, almost unfathomable, unimaginable expanse. Imagined or desired to be empty (but of course not truly empty).

If one looks at nineteenth-century accounts of encountering, say, the landscape of the Plains states, those accounts

say things like: It's almost inconceivable that this kind of flat expanse exists. I don't have the words for it, I don't know how to describe it — it is sublime in its essence. Because of that emptiness, or phantasmatic emptiness and expanse, I think land truly has become the thing that can be imbued with anything, and thus, has been used as a medium. That said, I do think there are a number of ways in which one can generalize about the status of land or how Americans imagine land. I think the frontier is absolutely in play here. The frontier, of course, in the geographic region now known as the United States no longer exists, but among many Americans, the idea of the frontier is still in play . . . This gets back to questions of self-determination . . . the myth of the frontier as a myth having to do with folks who work the land and struggle on the land and wrestle the land to the ground in order to determine themselves and become successful American citizens.

UA: It's very dynamic.

RD: It is.

UA: It's a kind of ongoing challenge that you have to meet in order to conquer not only the land but yourself. You are changing as your relations to the land develop, as you manage in a way to make it yours.

RD: Dynamism is exactly the word to describe this ongoing relationship to the land or the idea of the land. I would also say that land is sometimes geographic or national in the sense of something like homeland security, so land wound up figuring in — I don't want to say in a new way, but in a new way for those of us who are citizens of the twentieth and twenty-first centuries, with the introduction of the idea of homeland security. There was a way in which the idea of homeland security re-bordered a land that had been imagined as more permeable under the regime of globalization — that's yet another way that the land has been imagined or re-imagined.

I would also say there's a way in which land for many people, especially urban dwellers, or suburban dwellers, or even rural dwellers, rather than being a matter of property, which it was in the nineteenth century, is now in many cases equated with nature. Land is the thing you go to as a tourist or that you consume in a representation. There is a way in which land then comes to shade into landscape, which means it's mentioned as that thing, nature, which is other than one's normal existence. We might consider here things like ecotourism or even hiking, which is a form of consuming the land as a kind of commodity.

One more thing: Anne Whiston Spirn, who's a landscape architect and also a scholar of the history and theory of landscape, has said that it's interesting that we don't think of cities as land, because they in fact are. And they are because they are built on land but also because they have to negotiate land. They have to negotiate underground streams. They have to negotiate the natural on a constant basis. I think it's imperative that we remember that the urban is a land-space or a landscape. And that complicates what we said earlier about Americans being increasingly estranged from the land, because it is, in fact, the thing in which we exist constantly and persistently, we just don't realize it. Something about the way the land has been imagined as nature, the thing that

one goes to in order to consume, has made us forget that we are still living in and on a kind of land.

UA: Until we die and then we become part of the land. [*laughter*] Well, in some traditions, I guess.

RD: Depends on the kind of coffin. [*laughs*] If you're buried in a coffin you don't at all become part of the land.

UA: In Jewish tradition, that's how it works. You're put in the ground itself.

RD: That's interesting, given what we were saying about the status of the land in the Jewish imaginary of themselves as a collective, but I know we've moved on.

JL: Dynamism is probably the perfect word, but I'd like to pose another tradition, a counter-current, that has to do with land providing a sense of place and fixity and stability. I've just been teaching Henry David Thoreau and Wendell Berry, and Thoreau says very clearly: Everybody wants to go west and remake themselves, but you can do that right here. In order to be able to do that, though, you have to have a different relationship to . . . does he use the word *nature*? . . . which is an interesting question . . . but you do have to have a sense of place, which has to do with your natural surroundings.

RD: You know, he doesn't really use the word *nature*.

UA: Really?

JL: I don't think he does.

RD: Which is interesting.

UA: But Ralph Waldo Emerson did.

RD: Emerson, yes.

JL: Emerson, absolutely.

RD: *Nature*, capital *N*. [*laughter*] That's interesting, because I've written about Thoreau, and I've written around that idea, but never actually put my finger on the fact that he doesn't use that word *nature* in the explicit way that, say, Emerson does or we would, inferring a capital. Thoreau is a really interesting case. What you say about dynamism in Thoreau is so important, because even Thoreau's descriptions of the land and of traveling through the land and spending a week on the Concord and Merrimack Rivers are all about the multiple viewpoints from which one sees the landscape and the way in which the landscape itself is ever shifting. I'm thinking, of course, of the famous passage where he describes the sand shifting on the bank of the railroad tracks, but also the way in which he plays with language and posits multiple words for a single thing, like a river. That's all about the way in which the land as a medium is constantly shifting and transmuting before our eyes. Thoreau might be an exemplary figure for this conversation.

KB: Something came to mind as we were talking . . . a historical event, a protest by the citizens of El Alto, Bolivia, in January 2005, against the privatization of their water supply. This event seems exemplary of our moment in several ways. More than ever before, land, space, and natural resources are coming under the control of corporate entities, and this privatization of commonly held resources constitutes a kind of dispossession, an impingement on our autonomy. Clearly, it was experienced as such by the citizens of El Alto. Do you have any thoughts about that?

UA: I have only a book in mind, by José Saramago.

KB: José Saramago? He's one of my favorite authors. Which book?

RD: *The Cave*. That is a brilliant book.

UA: You see what I'm referring to? The whole notion of the tension between the land outside the mall and the mall itself. But I will be telling you … [*laughs*]

RD: We might not be able to actually talk about this because if you haven't read it … [*laughter*]

UA: It's almost extraterritorial, isn't it?

RD: Yes, it is, because what is imagined is a kind of space within a space that isn't necessarily a place. The mall is kind of non-place. I wonder if loss of place, and a kind of grieving in Bolivia and elsewhere about a loss of a sense of place, or a loss of place as a kind of refuge or a space of autonomy and self-determination, has something to do with the substitution of place with a kind of non-place, with a mall, with a fake urban pedestrian space.

UA: The capitalist nexus is very clear. It's a kind of anarcho-capitalism that takes the place of the state, because outside that mall, it's wilderness.

RD: That's very interesting. So that even though there's a substitution, these kinds of spaces are still experienced as a loss, because they're spectacular, because

they aren't places at all. Airports would, of course, be a typical non-place, but that's not exactly what I'm talking about here … the kind of reconstitution or faking of place, given the decimation of actual places and spaces, wilderness or otherwise.

JL: Like the Venetian Hotel, Las Vegas.

RD: Yes, exactly.

JL: Why go to Venice when I can go to Las Vegas? [*laughter*]

RD: Or the re-creation in suburban spaces of a kind of urban pedestrian walkway, so that malls now take the form of what one could describe as what America imagines to be the pedestrian shopping experience in a major European city.

UA: Which was frightening for me, I must admit, coming to the university only last year. Amazing, the mall culture here, it's like the hub of life.

JL: There's another lesson — and this goes back to space versus place, which we've been discussing in different registers — which has to do with the abstraction of capitalist exchange and how you can map it onto this kind of Newtonian grid within globalization. At the end of the day, though, in our work, it does have to touch down on specific, concrete places with actual people, doing actual concrete things in the world. You can see that in Bolivia, where it's hard to connect the dots between what's going on there and the kind of Wall Street finance that no one really understands. But there is an actual concrete connection, which creates a site for contestation and politics in things that are so diffused it's

hard to even wrap your mind around them, let alone do something about them.

RD: I think that reminds us of the importance of keeping in mind the microcosms of space, and it cautions us against generalizing and abstracting too much because, as someone like Rebecca Solnit would remind us, all spaces have real people doing actual material things in them, and every interaction between human and space is a significant interaction and those things are things that we ought not to abstract too far beyond.

KB: I'd like to direct the conversation towards ethics. I've been reading quite a bit of Judith Butler, whose recent work focuses on ethics, subjectivity, and modes of belonging. Key for Butler is the notion that relationality plays a role in the formation and reproduction of subjectivity: "We *are* our relations to others," Butler has said. This proposition has specific ethical and political ramifications, but it also has bearing on the way we use and live on land. Land is, after all, the site where human relations are produced, and for this reason, it's the site where we perform (or should perform) our ethical responsibility to others. What are your thoughts on the relationship between ethics and land?

RD: Well, I would say two things in response to this set of questions. The first would entail a tweaking of Butler's model of relationality. For me the land isn't just a site or space or container for relations. I see land as an agent in its own right, itself a kind of subjectivity, that forms relations with us and with which we form relations. Now, I'm not saying the land is alive as a human is alive, but of course it does act, so I would say that it's not a container or a space only, that it is one of the variables or subjects in this network of relationality.

The other thing I would say, having tweaked this model somewhat, is that the matter of environmental justice is very relevant here — environmental justice being the thing that asks us to think about the groups for whom the consequences of our actions are the most grave, and the disparate consequences among different populations in the United States, for example, of things like global warming and the disintegration and pollution of cities. I think the field of environmental justice is a space in which land and ethics come together in a really important way.

JL:  The word *belonging* is oftentimes juxtaposed with *becoming*…so this dynamism of the self becoming different and newly remaking itself, as a kind of end point of subjectivity, which I think you can associate with the liberal model of selfhood which Butler wants to pull the plug on, if you will. So, making *belonging* the endpoint of subjectivity already has a very different kind of ethical orientation. What you've just said, thinking about land or nature…that maybe as a person you can't act ethically if your orientation is either individual becoming or the belonging of different individuals within different kinds of communities. The circle for understanding subjectivity must be opened to include a sense of *the land*, however defined, as an agent.

UA:  My intuition was a bit different from that, although it's fascinating, regarding land as agent. Still, for me, it's much more a kind of container. Intuitively, I was speaking about family, the fact that homeland in the most mundane way…the fact that our responsibility to one another is not confined to that home, but to a large extent is delineated by the fact that you either stay or go — that your responsibility, which I think is something Butler does emphasize, manifests itself in your ability to feel at home, to *really* feel at home, to *truly* make that small or big piece of land your place.

Another book comes to mind, by Jean Améry. He's an Austrian-born Jewish author. He wrote, I think, quite a remarkable book about the Holocaust, *At the Mind's Limits*. In it, he also explored the question: How much homeland does one need? His argument was, from a perspective of a refugee, that one needs a lot of homeland in order to survive, in order to prosper…land is so much beyond land itself — it's the people. For him — it returns back to the notion we started with, that of security — land is security. This is what he emphasized, and this is what he stands to lose, because of the Holocaust. Even though we can return to the place, and the land is still there, but he cannot do that.

JL:  At a psychic level he cannot.…

UA:  Right. Because of time and because of the people that the homeland encompassed. So, that kind of security for him was forever lost. And he said that obviously, if you were an immigrant to another land, as he was, you can in time get used to new people and new traditions, a new way of thinking, perhaps you become more and more tuned to the different signals that surround you. But there is nothing like that homeland, that place from which you actually emerge, and being deprived of that sense of security, that land as a homeland, is a tremendous loss.

RD:  What you said about immigration and displacement and loss of home makes me think of an artist by the name of Tseng Kwong Chi. Do you know this work? He was born in Hong Kong in 1950 and came to Vancouver, British Columbia, with his family as a teenager, then wound up as a New York-based artist. He did a series of photographs of himself dressed in what looks like a Communist Party official suit, a "Mao suit," at various tourist sites around the country. He looks so out of place. The work is very much about the displacement he experienced, coming from one space to another, and finding himself in a very in-between status, not at home here, but no longer able to return and be home there. It's a compelling series of photographs — it's funny, but also tragic in its way, because the images are about estrangement from place and homelessness, and of course thus very much about the kind of homelessness that arises at a very large scale in a globalizing world. Now, my feeling is that the world has always been globalized, after a fashion, but let's just pretend we recently globalized. [*laughter*] So that's really interesting, to think about it in the way you're describing. This may or may not lead to us to the question of what art has to say.

KB:  Actually, I was hoping we could talk about that. I know that neither Jon nor Uriel are involved in art and art history to the degree of Rachael and I are, but Uriel posed a very interesting question to me over coffee a few weeks ago, which was…

UA:  I don't remember…

KB:  I've been thinking about it quite a bit. I asked one of the artists in this exhibition that same question: Can art have a philosophy? That's one of the questions I'd like to pose to the group. I'm also curious to know what sort of agency you think art can have in the ethical and political realm — not just visual art, but literature, film… Can you think of instances where art has had a demonstrable impact — psychic, material — on the world?

RD:  The role art can play is an interesting question.

KB:  It's another roundtable discussion.

RD:  The idealist and utopian in me wants it to have a role, and to have a viable one, but the cynic in me has not seen it have or play…

UA:  Really? Never?

RD:  I wouldn't say ever, but given the amount of art that aims to be political, that aims to make an intervention.… The politicalness and the impulse toward intervention of this art…Well, these things often happen in a particular space and for a particular audience. In that way, art can preach to the converted and not necessarily make a difference.

UA:  So it's an elite phenomenon?

RD:  I don't mean *elite* so much. I mean a phenomenon that may not fully extend and act as an agent in a truly public and political sphere. Now, that said, I think that certain kinds of art forms can, in fact, act in the public and political spheres. One example — I don't know if we would call this art with a capital A — is *An Inconvenient Truth*, which had a huge impact in terms of the conversation about global warming. I'm not saying that Al Gore's movie changed the face of politics. I'm also not calling it high art, but

it is a cultural form. It's a kind of representation.

So by way of saying this, what I'm suggesting — and I think that the work in the exhibition will manifest this or at least provide evidence for this — what I'm suggesting is that art in an expanded form or in a newly rethought form, by which I mean art as non-traditionally understood, can and has had real political and material consequences. It seems to me that the projects you've included in the exhibition, or many of them at least, aren't art in the sense it is usually understood. The lines between political activism and artistic production have blurred to the point of disappearing. In that sense, I think the idealist and the utopian in me can say, yes, there is a space for a certain kind of artistic agency and action in the public and political spheres. But one does have to be wary of what might be called the "seeing a political movie phenomenon," that is, when we go to a political movie, we watch it, and we feel as if we've done something, but we have in fact performed no material action. Looking at a work of political art isn't *doing* something.

KB:  True.

RD:  Maybe there's a way in which we can talk about the act of viewing as somehow different from the political act — the two aren't one and the same. Maybe there's a difference between awareness, which is generated by art, and actual change. Maybe these are two terms we can set in relation to one another.

KB:  I think so. For the Situationists, for instance, art and activism were inextricable. They thought of art as a way to provide viewers with tools to change or

revolutionize their own lives. In fact, they didn't think of viewers as viewers as all, but rather as potential collaborators. The Situationists completely reimagined their relationship to an art public, to an art-going audience.

RD:  Various iterations of what art historians call performance art might be understood in the same way — artists using their bodies as a medium in the public sphere in such a way that the audience becomes a participant…such that there is a kind of material effect, the implications of which are varied, but there is a literal, material effect, given that the audience is in many cases forced to participate and can't passively walk by or ignore. So that is also a site, as with the Situationists, for a kind of potential political act.

JL:  So you distinguish, then, between art that simply tries to crystallize or articulate the way we live, conditions as things are, versus art that is more explicitly trying to intervene politically. Or is that a distinction not really…I mean, what art is *not* political? Is there any kind of art that is *not* political?

KB:  Well, that's a very good point, and it's one that art historians like Rosalyn Deutsche have addressed. In various essays and round table discussions, Deutsche has argued that we need to expand our understanding of what constitutes a work of political art. According to Deutsche, even if an artist doesn't have explicitly political intentions, that doesn't necessarily mean his or her work lacks political agency or that it doesn't perform politically. So you're right, almost everything artists produce has a political currency.

UA: But that would make it almost mean-ingless, if everything is political.

KB: Well, that's the danger.

UA: So the *Mona Lisa* is political? [*laughter*]

KB: Well, Deutsche was answering a questionnaire distributed by the editors of *October* about artistic responses (or lack thereof) to the war in Iraq. I think Deutsche wanted to multiply the possibilities for incisive critiques of the war. Your own observation raises an important question, though: If all art is political, then where does that leave us? How do we distinguish between degrees of efficacy?

JL: I've been teaching Thoreau this semester. There's a passage in *Walden* in which he says: "When I look at the trees, I see leaves, but when my neighbors look at trees, they see lumber." When my students read that, it was incredibly emboldening: Yes, everyone sees lumber when they see trees, but we need to have environmental justice, we need to see trees as moral agents. That passage had an incredible political overtone to them. I didn't assign that passage from Thoreau for that reason — there's nothing Thoreau hated more than actual formal political partici-pation, he didn't vote, and he was proud of it — so there is a way in which certain cultural forms, centuries later, can then become mobilized as *overt* political tools.

RD: One thing you just asked, are there two kinds of art? Art that is overtly politi-cal and art that simply — although you didn't say simply — reflects the conditions in which we live. What's really inter-esting about that is that I think art that

simply — and now I'll say it — reflects the conditions in which we live can actually be some of the most incisive, instru-mental, political art. One of the things that art can contribute to the political sphere is the exposing of artifice by way of artifice. There's no better way to point to falsehoods, imaginaries, myths than re-artificing or remythifying them by way of art, so that one's attention is drawn to falsity by way of falsity itself. There's a way in which simply reflecting the condi-tions of our existence can be enormously political because it's the exposing of those conditions, which were perhaps hidden or lost to view or invisible, that I think art is especially adept at doing and that other forms, even literature, actual words, language can't.

KB: I agree, although I would phrase it slightly differently. Some of the most powerful, compelling, and incisive works of art are, in my mind, those that defamil-iarize the world in which we live, those that make all of the things we take for granted strange. The process of estrange-ment these works effect introduces dissonance or friction into our experience of everyday life. I think art-as-propaganda is potentially less effective, politically speaking, than art that operates in these more subtle ways.

UA: Yes, I think that's a good point. For me, at least personally, art should be subtle. When it becomes too political, I think it loses some of its beauty.

KB: And some of its dialectical energy.

RD: And it's too easily ignored if it's propa-gandistic. What propaganda, or art that wears its heart on its sleeve, runs the risk

of doing is giving us the familiar, right? We already have heard this, we already have seen this, therefore we can either believe it or not believe it. But what Kelly is saying is that art that makes things strange, that de-familiarizes, that de-naturalizes, doesn't allow us a familiar way in by way of which to accept or dismiss, and that means that no matter what we think, we have to think.

UA: Right. Exactly.

KB: Thank you, everyone. This was wonderful.

Catalogue

Jennifer Allora and Guillermo Calzadilla

Land Mark (Foot Prints)  2001–2
12 digital C-prints, each 46 × 60.5 cm (18⅛ × 23⅞ in.)
AP 1/3

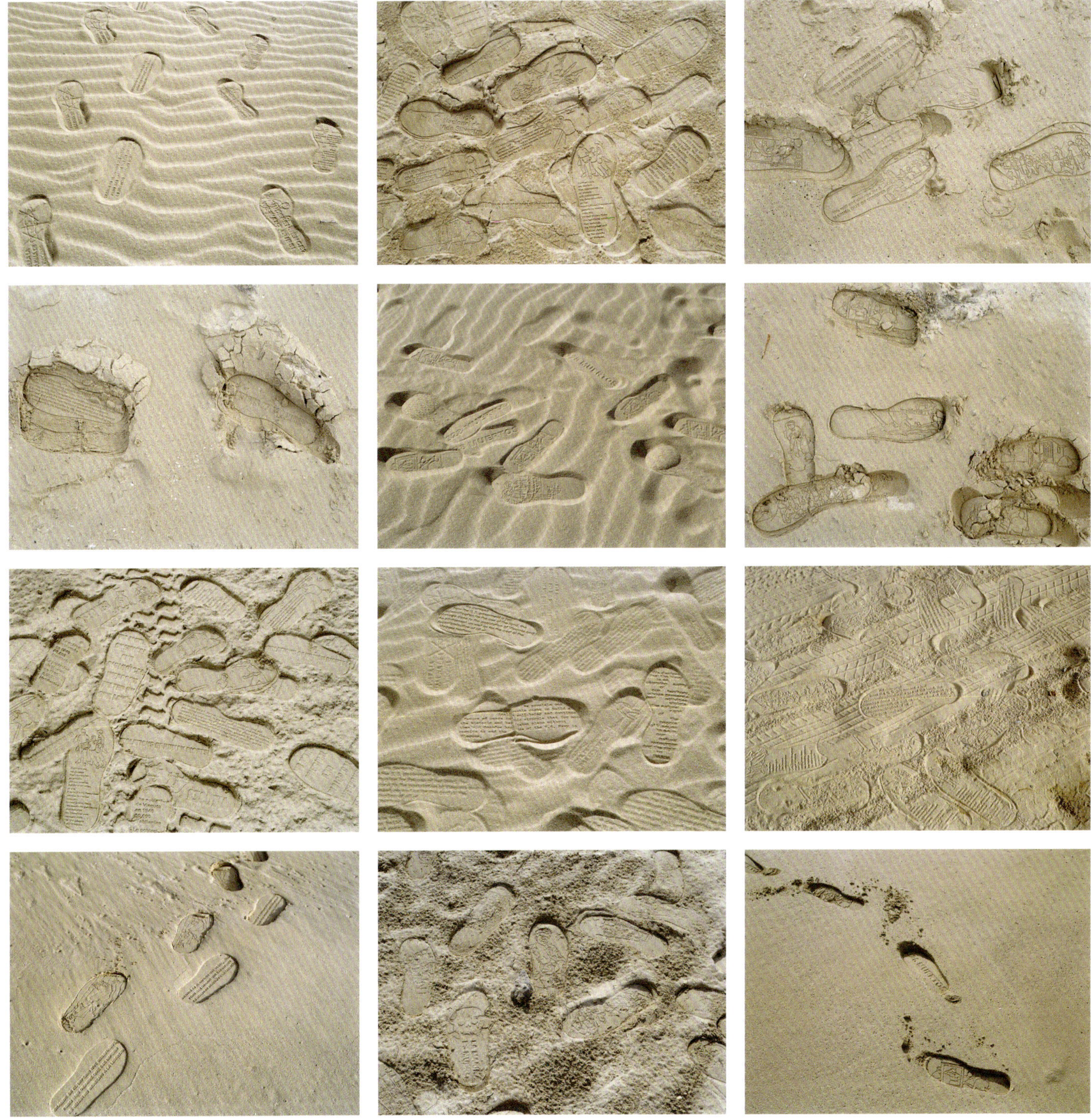

*Land Mark (Foot Prints)* (2001–2) is one of several works that Jennifer Allora and Guillermo Calzadilla have devoted to the subject of Vieques, Puerto Rico. The pieces in this series explore, represent, and ultimately challenge what the artists perceive as an intolerable social, political, and environmental situation.

After World War II, the United States Navy began using Vieques, an island roughly eight miles southeast of the Puerto Rican mainland, to store and test weapons, with devastating results for the local population and ecology. Many of the people whose way of life and means of subsistence were disrupted by the military occupation launched a civil disobedience campaign in the 1970s. Members of the Vieques Fishermen's Association were among the most vocal of these protesters. Established in 1976 in response to contamination caused by munitions testing, the group staged tactical acts of reclamation designed to upset military training exercises. The most dramatic of these occurred in 1978, when forty fishing boats dragging underwater traps effectively "tripped" oncoming ships by disabling their propellers. Tension mounted in 1999, when a rogue test bomb killed a civilian security guard named David Sanes. Family members of the deceased and other sympathizers trespassed onto restricted territory, using their bodies as human shields to prevent "one more bomb" from falling.[1] That same year, Allora and Calzadilla embarked on the first of many works intended to raise awareness about the plight of Vieques citizens suffering from eviction or pollution.

Under pressure from activists, among them Allora and Calzadilla, the U.S. Navy transferred expropriated portions of the island to the U.S. Fish and Wildlife Service — 3,100 acres on the east side in 2001 and 14,671 on the west side in 2003. In 2005, the U.S. Environmental Protection Agency officially added the area, now referred to as the Vieques National Wildlife Refuge, to its National Priorities List of Superfund sites.[2] Allora and Calzadilla have explored this post-occupation status in two videos that document young activists circumnavigating the island. In *Returning a Sound* (2004), a man identified as Homar rides a moped with a trumpet lodged in its muffler. In *Under Discussion* (2004–5), another activist named Diego pilots an overturned conference table across the open water. Both journeys take viewers on a scenic tour of the island. The drone of the two

motors is commemoratory of those who helped oust the military and blatantly confrontational at the same time. The uncertain fate of Vieques looms as each protagonist passes warning signs that read "NO TRASPASE, PERSONAL AUTORIZADO SOLAMENTE, PELIGRO EXPLOSIVOS — NO TRESPASSING, AUTHORIZED PERSONNEL ONLY, DANGER EXPLOSIVES." As of 2010, remediation is still underway, and it is unlikely that residents of Vieques will ever be justly compensated for the seizure and subsequent destruction of their property.

In these works, movement — whether on foot, by bike, or by boat — implies political mobilization, and *Land Mark (Foot Prints)*, the series of twelve photographs on view in this exhibition, was a step in this direction.[3] In 2001–2, Allora and Calzadilla staged a series of interventions with activist groups, trespassing onto a section of the bombing range wearing customized shoes. Imprinted on the soles were demands, grievances, and aspirations, many of them accompanied by pictures. The latter included portraits of individuals affected by the occupation, images from the Apollo 11 mission that landed the first man on the moon in 1969, and documentary depictions of previous and current civil disobedience campaigns, such as the one launched by the Fishermen's Association in 1978. When the activists encroached upon the beach, surveillance sensors registered the warmth of their bodies and temporarily halted weapons testing. In this way, Allora, Calzadilla, and their collaborators physically charged the property, transforming a so-called dead site — one considered inhospitable to human activity because it was too toxic, too damaged by weapons testing — into a productive art space and a locus for effective political action.

Allora and Calzadilla's collective action made rarely heard voices visible, creating a kind of land-based graffiti in the process. One might also understand their intervention as a literal enactment of a statement by Paul Klee, who once described drawing as the act of taking "an active line on a walk."[4] Indeed, *Land Mark* belongs to a tradition of works by artists such as Richard Long, which similarly collapse walking into drawing or writing. *Land Mark*, however, which documents the tactical movement of protestors on restricted land, represents a highly politicized version of Long's relatively anodyne strolls. In this respect, the work has more in common with Judi Werthein's

2005 project *Brinco*, in which the artist designed cross-trainers for border-crossing migrant workers from Tijuana while simultaneously selling limited-edition samples to boutique shoppers in San Diego.

Allora and Calzadilla often bring individuals together in collective effort. In *Chalk (Lima)* (2002), for instance, they provided oversized sticks of chalk to random passersby on the Paseo de Santa Rosa in Lima, Peru, who then used them to write on the asphalt. In *Untitled (Dance Floor)* (1997), Allora and Calzadilla created an unfixed charcoal drawing of teenage dancers on the floor of the Luigi Marrozzini Gallery in San Juan, Puerto Rico. The composition became muddied as visitors walked across it, creating an impression similar to the entropic, irreparably disordered sandbox evoked by Robert Smithson in a 1967 essay.[5] In *Land Mark*, one can read the accumulation of footprints in political terms, as an allegory of the forging of a single voice from many distinct ones. At the same time, the visual confusion created by the overlapping footprints registers the presence of conflicting perspectives among protestors and the fragile, often precarious nature of their negotiations.

The traces of Allora and Calzadilla's foray onto the bombing range were quickly consumed by the tides and winds. All that remains of their pedestrian transgression are twenty-four color photographs. While *Returning a Sound* and *Under Discussion* also recorded otherwise fleeting gestures, these videos privilege space, acknowledging the island's geographical limits. The photographs that comprise *Land Mark*, on the other hand, speak more to temporal constraints, to moments plucked from a series of other moments. This act of documentation is not incidental to *Land Mark (Foot Prints)*, as evidenced by the title, in which *mark* and *prints* have been deliberately separated from *land* and *foot*. Allora and Calzadilla's decision to disarticulate these two sets of words reinforces the impact of inscription and reproduction. Their two dozen mobile and reproducible photographs not only preserve the original gesture, but also guarantee its political and artistic afterlife.[6] MH

1 For a thorough account of the Vieques controversy, see Allora and Calzadilla, *Land Mark*.
2 U.S. Fish and Wildlife Service, *Vieques National Wildlife Refuge: Comprehensive Conservation Plan and Environmental Impact Statement* (Atlanta, Ga.: U.S. Fish and Wildlife Service, Southeast Region, 2007).
3 *Land Mark (Foot Prints)* is comprised of two sets of twelve photographs, which are shown and collected separately as independent works of art; the second set is included in *Nobody's Property*.
4 Paul Klee, *Pedagogical Sketchbook* (New York: F. A. Praeger, 1953), 16.
5 Robert Smithson, "The Monuments of Passaic," *Artforum* 6:4 (Dec. 1967): 48–51.
6 On this issue, see also Yates McKee, "Art and the Ends of Environmentalism." McKee describes the footprints themselves as embodiments of "virtuality, repeatability, and mobility" (ibid., 567).

Supplement:

Reading *Land Mark (Foot Prints)*
Kelly Baum

The men and women who infiltrated the United States Navy bombing range on Vieques in 2001–2 did so intending not only to interrupt weapons testing, but to signal their discontent with the occupation, both physically and symbolically. One can imagine the excitement and trepidation — not to mention the noise and activity — that accompanied their intervention (they were walking on a live bombing range, after all). None of this is retained in the photographic documentation, however; nor are the bodies and faces of the activists portrayed. In its afterlife, at least, an eerie silence as well as a discomforting absence attends *Land Mark (Foot Prints)*. This is part of what gives the work its charge, though: The photographs do not depict what we expect them to depict, and in so doing, they strain the category of documentation and give the poetic some breathing room.

But these photographs are not just silence and absence. Indeed, if anything, they contain a surfeit of expression, all of it embedded in the footprints themselves. As Margo Handwerker has discussed in the preceding essay, the activists who accompanied Allora and Calzadilla onto the bombing range wore customized soles on their shoes.[1] These soles and the words and images they contain spoke silently but assertively, giving voice to a host of positions, opinions, and grievances. Nonetheless, footprints often cross and obscure other footprints, compromising the marks' legibility and frustrating their communicative intent. It is possible to read this illegibility allegorically, of course: that is, as a measure of the sheer difficulty of speaking as a group, especially the difficulty of speaking coherently. Making oneself heard in the face of a power as intimidating at the Navy is no easy task; neither is coordinating the efforts of dozens of activists and synchronizing their often disparate agendas.

Beyond this, however, all those colliding footprints make for extremely (and surprisingly) luscious images. The footprints displace dry sand differently than wet sand, which in turn creates a variety of visual and tonal effects. Some of the footprints resemble drawings more so than depressions, and they tend to be quite subtle, even delicate. Others are more sculptural: these impressions — usually made in wet, heavy sand — read as caverns, with deep pockets of light and shadow. When the images and words overlap, moreover, they generate abstract patterns whose effect is in excess of the specific messages they contain.

It was with a little trepidation, therefore, that I decided to decipher as many of the footprints as possible, in part because such an effort had never before been made. The artists provided invaluable assistance — and not only with those footprints rendered wholly or partially illegible during the intervention.

For me, at least, clarity of image did not necessarily guarantee intelligibility of meaning, especially in the case of the images, and I had to seek the artists' help in decoding these as well. Clearly, Allora and Calzadilla's was a local action directed at a local audience, with all the senders and receivers working within more or less the same frame of reference. Their action had (and has) global consequences, and its aesthetic and political aims most certainly resonate with wider audiences. That said, translation from site-specific intervention to site-less exhibition is always fraught. My own text is an effort in support of just such a translation.[2]

**The images:** Some of the pictures are based on photographs of recent and past civil disobedience campaigns on Vieques. In one, we see military police dragging off a protestor, in another we see them clashing with a group of dissidents, and in a third, we see fishermen confronting Navy ships in 1978. Other soles depict temporary structures erected by dissenters as base camps within the bombing range, guards' booths, groups of fishermen, and even portraits of individuals. One footprint commemorates Carmelo Félix Matta, described by Allora and Calzadilla as "a homesteader who built his house on the buffer zone between the military issued resettlement tracks and the Navy-controlled land." As they recall, "his eviction was a highly politicized event, and it brought to the surface many underlying issues facing the island, especially those related to

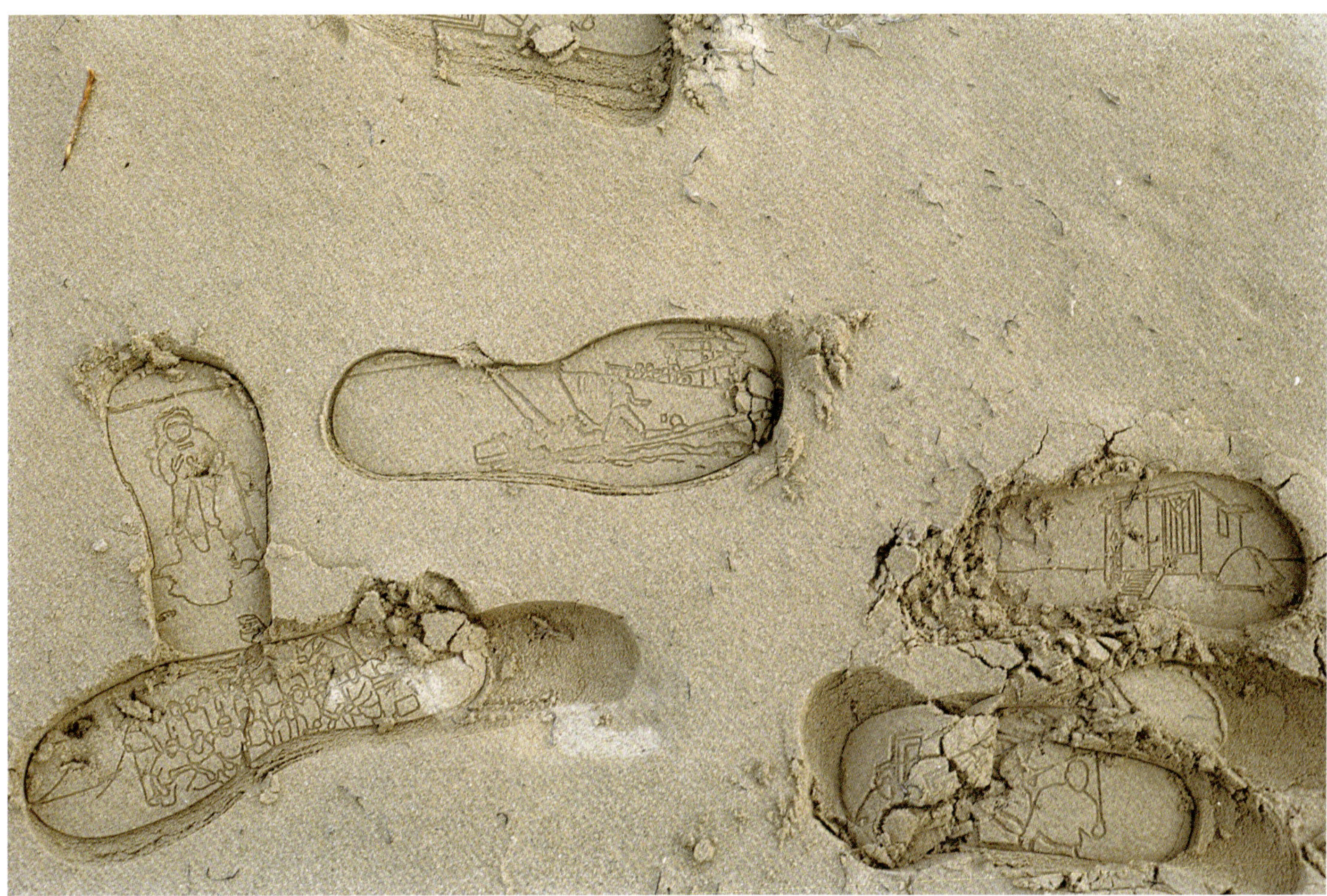

*Land Mark (Foot Prints)*, detail

land speculation and the island's future development."[3]

The soles also contain images that function symbolically: one represents a dove, another consists of a montage of flags and weapons (swords, planes, bombs, guns, and tanks), and a third is based on a well-known photograph from the 1969 Apollo 11 space mission.[4] Many images are joined with text. In one footprint, we see a map of the island. It is almost completely obscured by two large letter *X*'s: one indicates the Navy's ammunition storage facility on the west side of Vieques, the other the live firing range on the island's east side. The words next to the map read: "Fuera la marina de Vieques" (Navy Out of Vieques). A picture of a skull and crossbones is accompanied by the statement, "La Marina es muerte" (The Navy is Death). Together, these images and texts narrate the history of the island, including its occupation by the military and by individuals as well as the competing claims made on its land and resources.

**The words:** Many of the footprints contain only words, and they appear in either Spanish or English, suggesting the multiple audiences (both Puerto Rican and Anglo-American) for which they were intended. Sometimes the texts are short and to the point, both accusatory and declamatory—"Muerto" (Dead), "328 Muertos" (328 Dead), "Violations of Human Rights," "Warning: Civil Disobedience Will Continue"—while at other times they read like treatises, enumerating multiple demands and allegations.

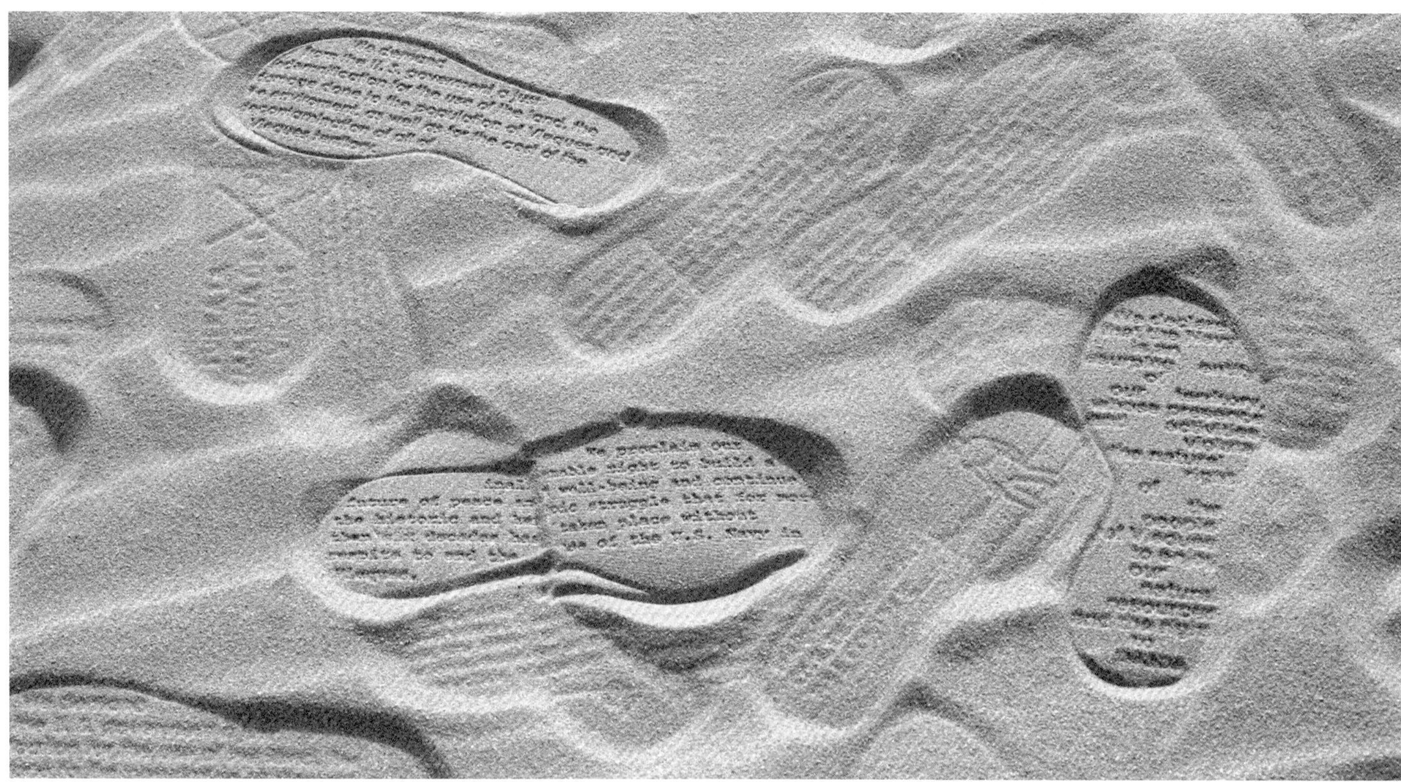

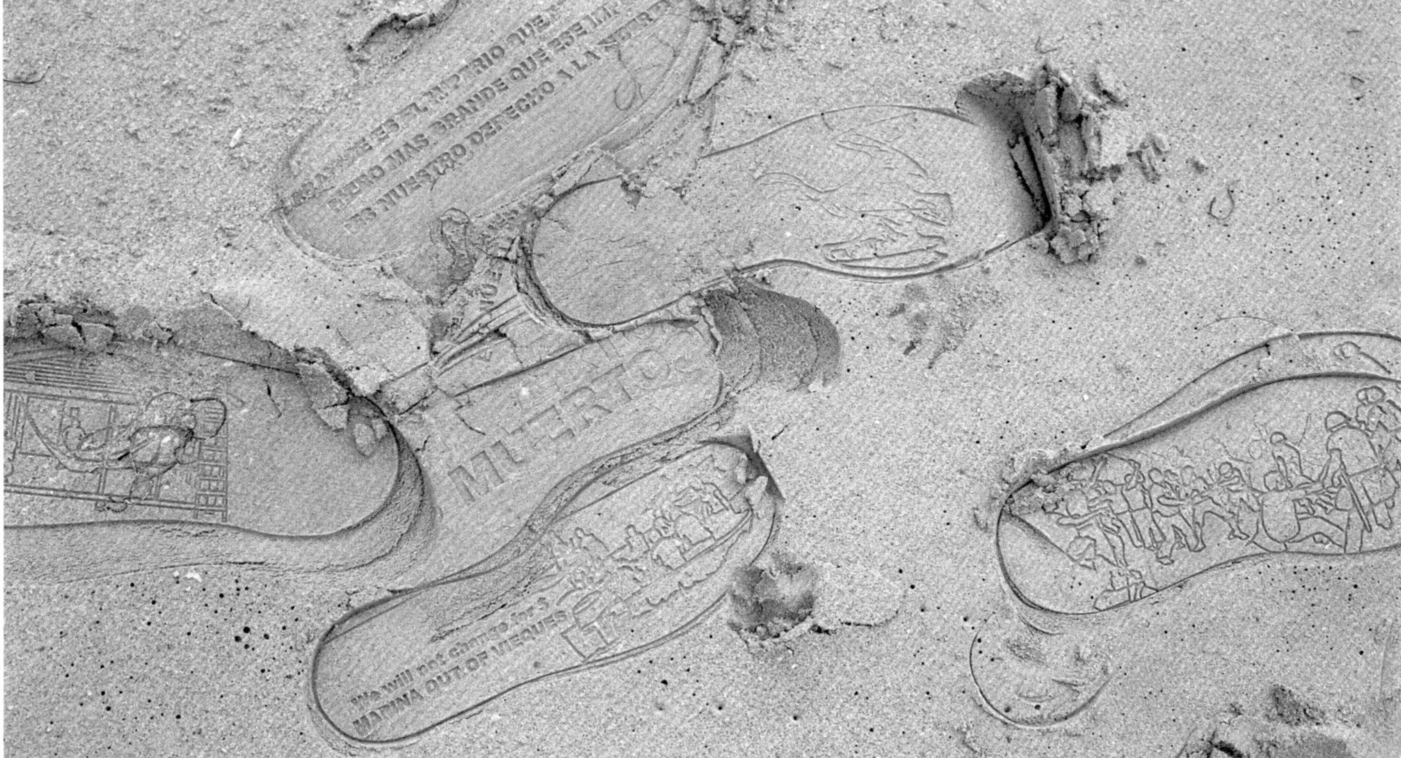

*Land Mark (Foot Prints)*, details

*No more chemical and biological weapons on our land.*

*We will not change for $. Marina [Navy] out of Vieques.*

*Grande es el imperio que desafiamos, pero mas grande es el derecho a la libertad (Great is the empire we challenge, but greater is our right to liberty).[5]*

*La población de Vieques en 1940, 30,000 habitantes…la población de Vieques en 1998, 8,000 habitantes (The population of Vieques in 1940, 30,000 people…the population of Vieques in 1998, 8,000 people).[6]*

Several of the longer texts that appear in the footprints are excerpted from the "Declaration of Ultimatum of the People of Vieques to the United States Navy," a 1999 document that called for the Navy's complete withdrawal from the island.[7]

*We the people of Vieques, with the unanimous support of all of Puerto Rico's community sectors and with the support of the Puerto Rican government, demand that the United States military forces in Vieques, Puerto Rico cease permanently all war practices, exercises, and other activities; the immediate departure of all its personnel, equipment, and artifacts from the island municipality; and the return of all presently occupied territories by any branch or department of the U.S. Armed Forces to the municipality of Vieques.*

*We proclaim our inalienable right to build a future of peace and well-being and continue the historic and heroic struggle that for more than six decades has taken place without respite to end the abuse of the U.S. Navy in Vieques.*

*We accuse the U.S. Navy of thwarting, for more than half a century, the healthy development of our economy, forcing our people to emigrate in search of work and well-being, with the resulting family disintegration.*

*We demand from the U.S. government a just indemnification for the use of the land, the damage done to the population of Vieques and to the environment, as well as for the cost of the decontamination of all Vieques territory.*

*Furthermore, we declare that repression or arrests will not weaken the determination of the Puerto Rican people to rescue from the United States Navy the territorial patrimony that belongs by historical and natural right to the people of Vieques.*

1  The soles consist of silicone castings made from a Plexiglas template that was cut on a laser. Jennifer Allora and Guillermo Calzadilla, e-mail message to author, March 24, 2010.
2  Many of the texts on the shoe soles are printed in capital letters, underscoring the declamatory nature of the statements. I have placed the texts in sentence case here and have added punctuation where necessary for greater ease of reading.
3  Allora and Calzadilla, e-mail message to author, January 1, 2009. My thanks to the artists for their help in deciphering the footprints.
4  The photograph in question was taken by Neil Armstrong, and it shows Buzz Aldrin in the foreground, along with several overlapping footprints. Why would a Viequense activist choose an episode from the lunar landing in 1969 for his or her custom-designed soles? What relationship is he or she establishing between Aldrin and Armstrong's footprints—footprints associated with the Cold War, the space race, and the ideology of scientific progress—and those deposited on Vieques? What analogy is being drawn here, what political and symbolic synonymy established? Is it between two iterations of American imperialism (galactic and hemispheric) or is it between two instances of (re)clamation (American and Viequense)? Put another way, is this particular footprint an exercise in critique or self-critique? Was it intended, perhaps, to problematize the very notion of property as well as the act of territorialization itself? Might it also signal a long view of Vieques history, a history comprised of hundreds of years of migrations and occupations, with the result of calling into question the authenticity of any single claim of ownership?
5  This particular activist is quoting Pedro Albizu Campos. Between 1930 and his death in 1965, Campos served as the leader and president of the Puerto Rican Nationalist Party. A skilled orator, polylinguist, and canny politician, he played a key role in the Puerto Rican independence movement, for which he was imprisoned by the United States on numerous occasions. Unfortunately, I was unable to determine the precise source or date of this quote in time for publication. Many thanks to Jane E. Boyd for calling my attention to the quotation.
6  The severe population decline in Vieques was due in large part to the Navy's occupation of two-thirds of the island's land mass and the loss of economic activity this posed to its residents. Allora and Calzadilla, e-mail message to author, January 1, 2009.
7  In some cases, the wording on the shoe soles differs slightly from the original text, which is available online in both Spanish and English. See Robert Rabin, e-mail to Military Environmental Forum (MEF) newsgroup of the Center for Public Environmental Oversight (CPEO), August 2, 1999, http://www.cpeo.org/lists/military/1999/msg00236.html.

Francis Alÿs

The Green Line: Sometimes Doing Something Poetic Can Become Political
and Sometimes Doing Something Political Can Become Poetic  2007
Video installation with various components, dimensions variable

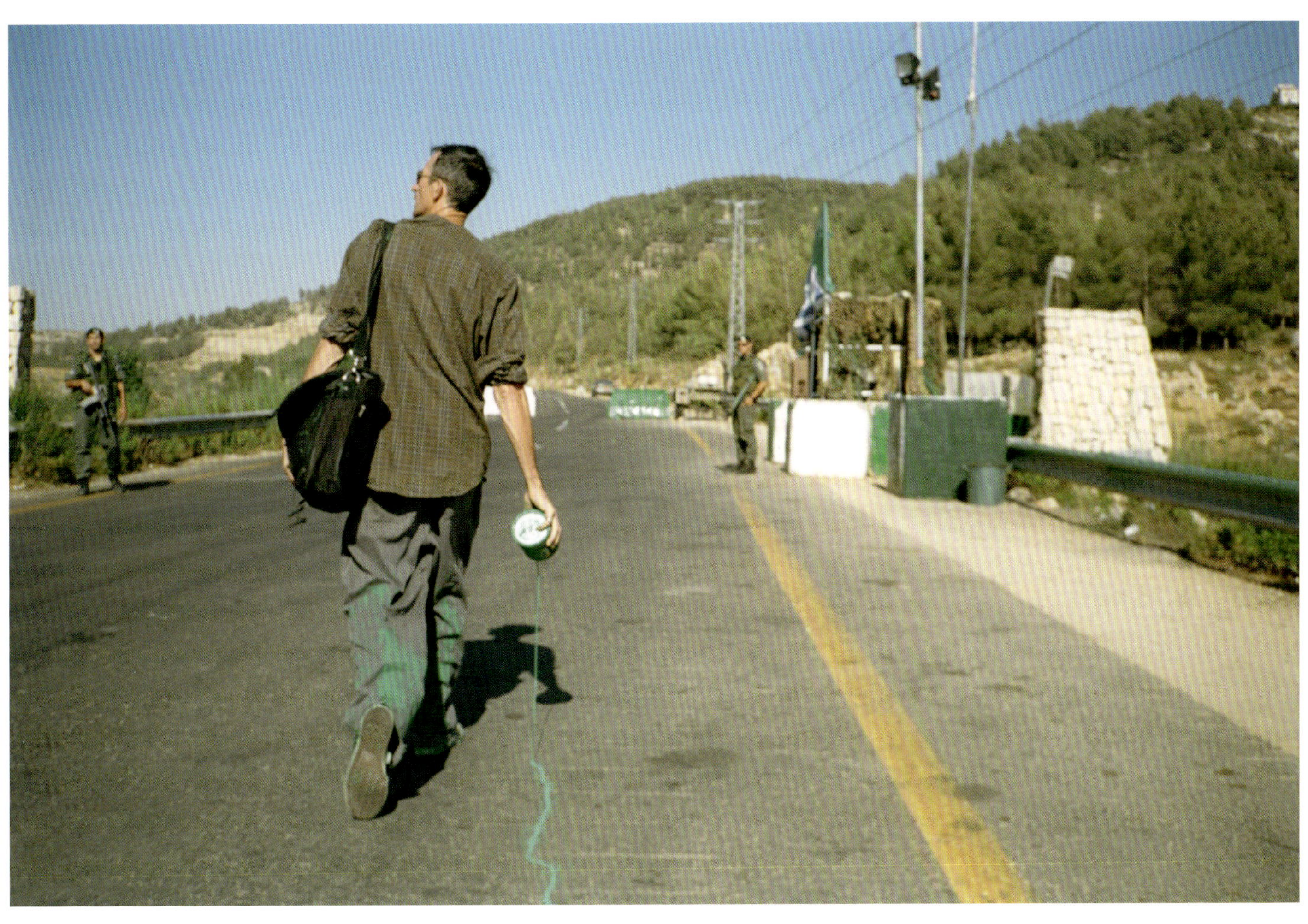

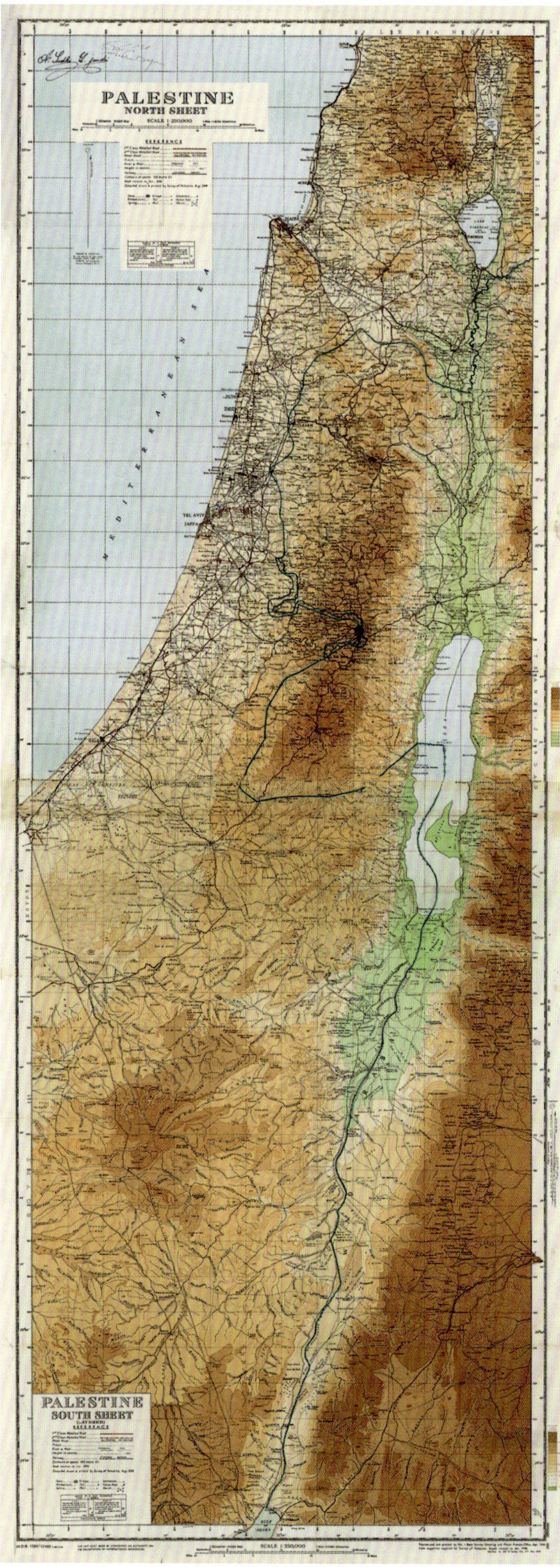

PALESTINE
NORTH SHEET
PALESTINE
SOUTH SHEET

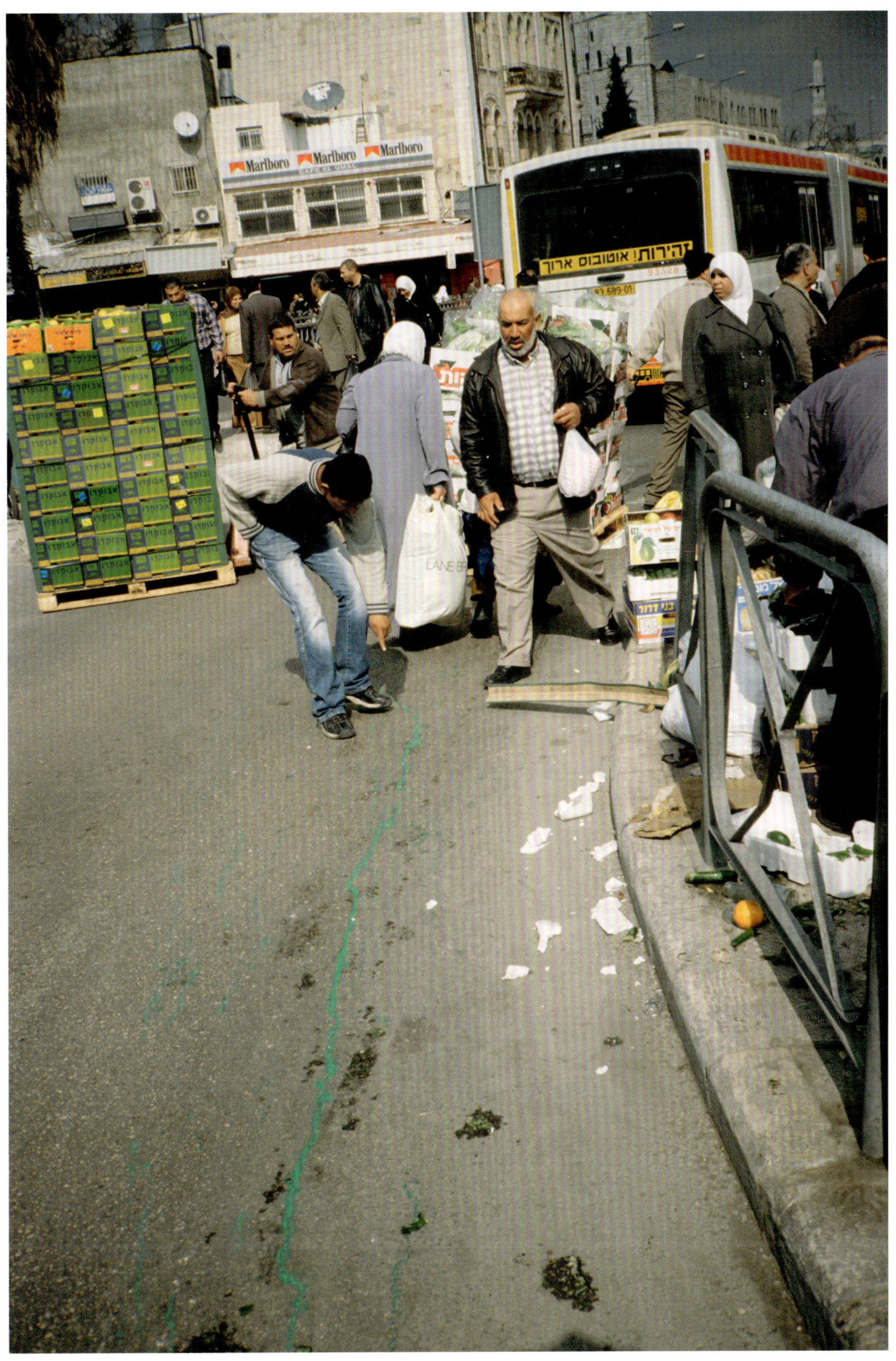

Francis Alÿs first punctured a can of paint and allowed the contents to leak onto a city street in 1995, while drifting through a working-class neighborhood in São Paulo, Brazil.[1] Almost ten years later, as he prepared to perform a similar action in Jerusalem, the Belgian-born artist retrospectively cast the dripping of blue paint in São Paulo as a "poetic gesture, a *beau-geste*."[2] By introducing the subject of aesthetics, Alÿs implicitly complicated the question of the political that he so earnestly wished to foreground as the central issue for his subsequent work, *The Green Line* (2007), also known as *Sometimes Doing Something Poetic Can Become Political and Sometimes Doing Something Political Can Become Poetic*. Although it seems as if *The Leak* prioritizes the poetic over the political, the latter is, in fact, the backdrop against which the poetic is played out. How could it be otherwise in a city where the megastructures of western modernization stand only feet away from the hastily assembled favelas of the urban poor?[3]

In Alÿs's intervention in Jerusalem, carried out in June 2004, the artist traced the boundaries of the Green Line, a 1948 armistice line that once separated the eastern and western parts of the city but that has since been trumped, first by Israel's 1967 occupation of East Jerusalem and then again by the West Bank Barrier, begun in 2002. Many of the artist's statements about *The Green Line* focus on the potential for an artistic action to court both the political and the poetic. In his concern with the meaning and effect of actions, Alÿs may have sensed a crisis of art's efficacy in the face of political violence.[4] In the 1960s and 1970s, artistic interventions (performances, installations, happenings, and other practices that foregrounded real-time experiences as they occurred in real space) were key weapons in the fight against media apparatuses that numbed and alienated individuals. Over time, however, these modes of artistic production have become absorbed into the institutions of bourgeois culture. There, they act as markers of individuality in an era in which identity is constructed against and through media events. These events pose self-consciously as aestheticized forms of supposed real life (as in the recent, rapid proliferation of reality television).[5] In this context, the fact that viewers encounter formerly radical interventions in the form of photographic and video documentation is striking, as it thoroughly contradicts the stated claims of many of the medium's practitioners.[6]

For his part, Alÿs appears to embrace the dissolution of "presentness" by media and art alike, as seen in the video documentation of *The Green Line*. When the latter is displayed in museums and galleries, visitors are invited to select a soundtrack using a touch-screen monitor. Each soundtrack is excerpted from a longer conversation between Alÿs and a group of Palestinian, Israeli, and British interlocutors, each of whom watched an early version of the video and then provided feedback. Once accessed by the viewer, their comments and critiques serve as a discursive layer that complicates the seemingly straightforward visual evidence.[7]

As a result, Alÿs's video not only presents the dripping of the paint as it unfolds before our eyes in real time (a fiction belied by the extensive editing); it also stages the mediatized realm—the realm of reception via video—into which the action necessarily enters. The voice-overs shift between personal experience and critical assessment, based on the speaker's perceived relationship to Jerusalem. Some express their own opinions of the Green Line, dealing only cursorily with Alÿs's intervention. Others take a detached, analytical approach, examining the status of his action more than their own connection to the politics, history, and experience that the Line both represents and catalyzes. The artist's narrativizing of an ostensibly simple and modest act through the voices of people external to its execution operates on numerous registers. On the one hand, it seems to critique or perhaps even to correct the original artistic action by reconnecting it with the history, political landscape, and people it sought to engage, but at too great a distance to have much effect. On the other hand, Alÿs's decision to make available to the viewer the doubts and responses of other individuals questions that action's political efficacy. In other words, the voice-over negates much of the lyrical quality of the artist's stroll through the city and its environs, returning us repeatedly to the fraught geopolitical context in which the walk occurred. It also makes us constantly aware, through the observations of a few key interlocutors, that the artist's tracing of the Green Line, for all its incendiary potential, actually raised few eyebrows.[8]

If the lyrical mode and its accompanying evocation of individuality often emerge from an artwork's formal terms, even if only as a repressed echo, then Alÿs's axiom—"sometimes doing something poetic can become political and sometimes doing something political can become poetic" — constitutes a valid questioning of the potential for any artistic action to fully square with history.[9] However, we should not forget that the artist's maxim also addresses the possibility of a political gesture becoming poetic. *The Green Line* thus demonstrates how the historical and the social can be translated into the aesthetic pleasure of the here and now, the personal and the individual. Perhaps, Alÿs seems to suggest, the lyrical release occasioned by an encounter with the poetic can prompt precisely the sort of self-reflexivity, the freedom from ingrained ways of thinking, that intractable political and ethical dilemmas require.

In video and photographic documentation, presentness and immediacy always cede to absence and aestheticization. Instead of decrying this result as a loss, Alÿs proposes that we recuperate it as a site of possibility. Indeed, it was just such a site — a site not only of criticality, but of spectatorial distance — that he carved out for viewers when he altered the original video and added excerpts from his interviews. Positioned thus, at several removes from the action, viewers are allowed to actively process the images before them, instead of simply absorbing more fragments from their daily confrontation with the digitized wash of information emanating from televisual screens. AB

1  I purposely use the term *drifting* to evoke the historical context of Situationist *dérives*, which critics have often cited as precedents for Alÿs's wanderings. See, for example, Cuauhtémoc Medina, "Fable Power," in Medina et al., *Francis Alÿs*, 74–78.
2  Alÿs, *Sometimes Doing Something Poetic*, n.p.
3  For a detailed historical discussion of the favelas and their relation to urban poverty in Brazil — still relevant after more than thirty years — see Elizabeth and Anthony Leeds, "Brazil in the 1960's: Favelas and Polity, the Continuity of the Structure of Social Control," *LADAC Occasional Papers* 2:5 (Austin: Institute of Latin American Studies, University of Texas, 1972).
4  When Rosalind Krauss examined the proliferation of video in the late 1960s, her influential account focused on the medium's engagement with the terms of narcissism.

According to Krauss, this engagement was signaled by early video's tendency to stage feedback loops that would constantly bring the subject of the work up against his or her own image and/or actions. For Krauss, the most successful videos staged their narcissistic documentation self-consciously. I would place Alÿs's *The Green Line* in this line of critical video. By overlaying audio that is clearly temporally removed from the action we see on the screen, the artist interrupts the work's otherwise documentary nature. Krauss, "Video: The Aesthetics of Narcissism," *October* 1 (Spring 1976): 50–64. See also Anne M. Wagner, "Performance, Video and the Rhetoric of Presence," *October* 91 (Winter 2000): 59–80.
5  Even before the existence of the culture industry, people did not have "authentic" or "natural" identities (or an accurate sense of

individuality) that have since been lamentably lost. Rather, in recent years, our senses of identity and individuality have evolved closely in relation to media apparatuses.
6  Much of the work on display in the present exhibition is symptomatic of this contradiction.
7  Alÿs tends not to privilege the original performance and intervention over and above the resulting documentation. As he says, "it's really two moments. Two different, consecutive lives of a single piece: the events and the transmission or translation of the events. One very local life, and another one that operates as a product for export." See Alÿs and Medina, *When Faith Moves Mountains*, 66. Although Alÿs is speaking here about his 2002 work *When Faith Moves Mountains*, the same seems to hold true for *The Green Line*.
8  For example, one interviewee delighted in the fact that Alÿs acted

almost as a terrorist in slipping back and forth across the Green Line's borders, trying to look as innocuous as possible. Alÿs, *Sometimes Doing Something Poetic*, n.p.
9  My invocation of the lyrical is indebted to T. J. Clark's claim that the crisis for the modernist artwork was the attempt to eradicate the lyrical aspects of art because they appeared absurd in our time (in particular, the illusion "of a singular voice or viewpoint, uninterrupted, absolute, laying claim to a world of its own"). See Clark, "In Defense of Abstract Expressionism," in *Farewell to An Idea: Episodes from a History of Modernism* (New Haven: Yale University Press, 1999), 401.

Yael Bartana

**Kings of the Hill  2003**
Video, color with sound,
7:30 minutes

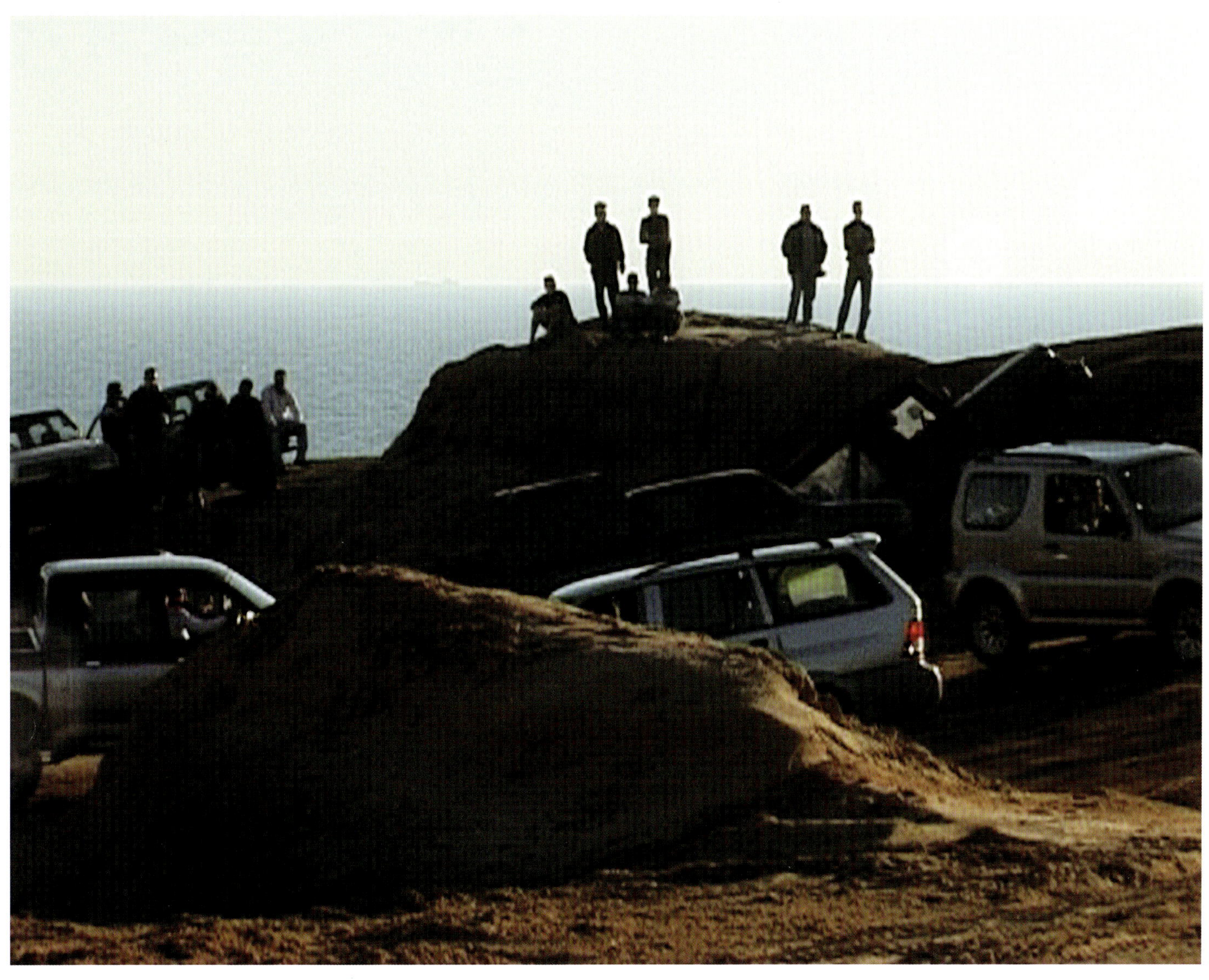

Still from *Kings of the Hill*

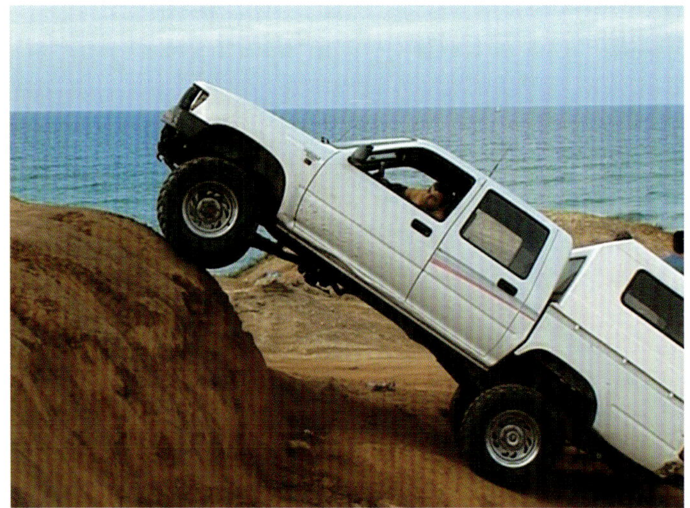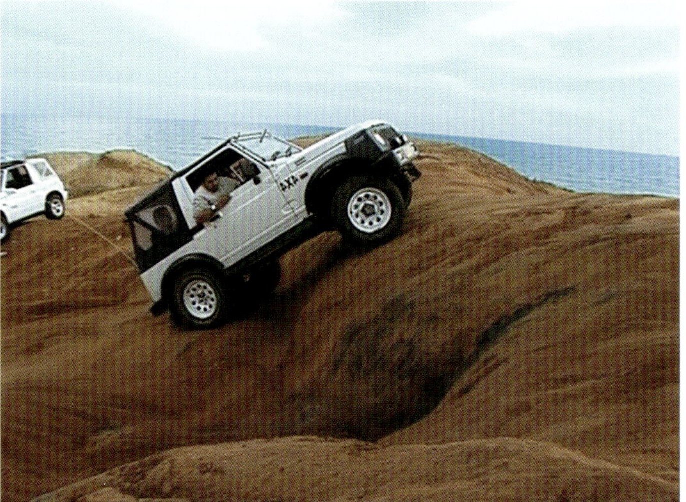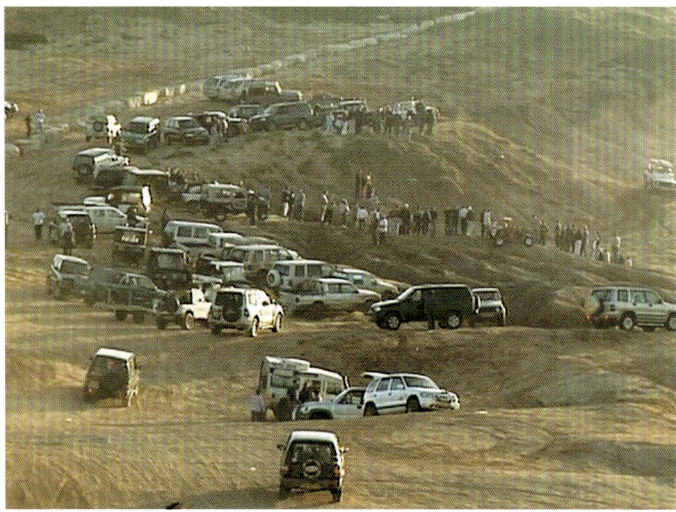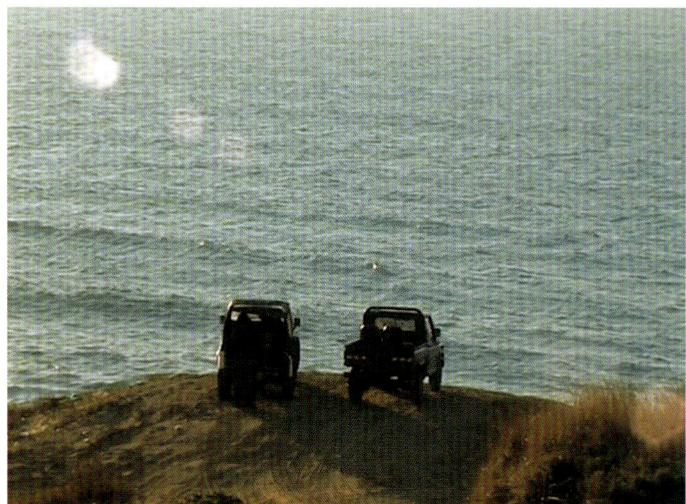

Stills from *Kings of the Hill*

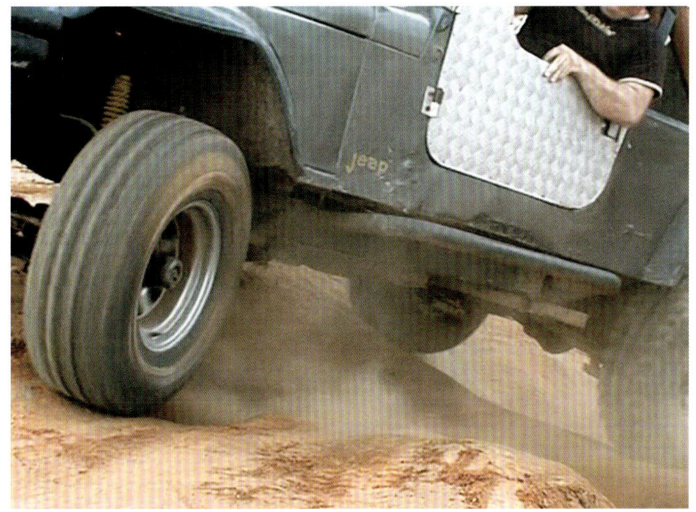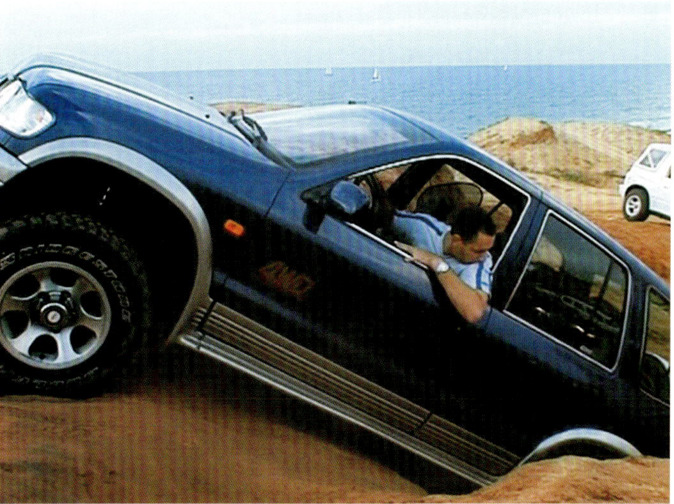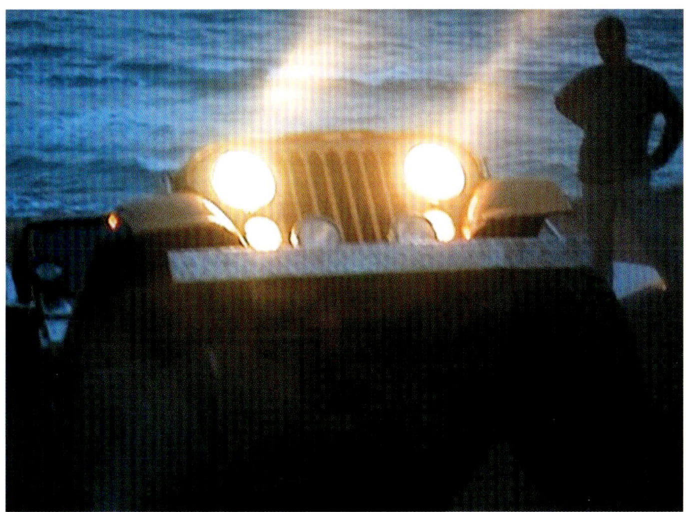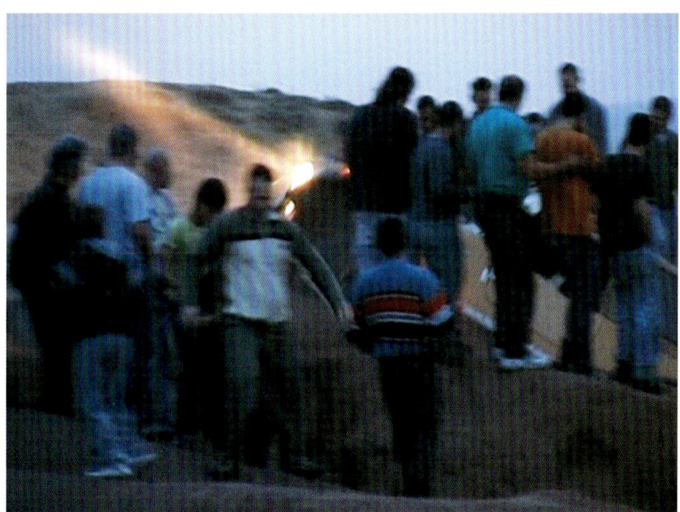

Stills from *Kings of the Hill*

Yael Bartana's *Kings of the Hill* (2003) portrays a landscape besieged. Video footage documents pickup trucks, jeeps, and sport-utility vehicles charging and clambering over the ragged slope of a beachside dune. On the outskirts of a coastal development, drivers—male and middle-class—push their machines to extreme all-wheel-drive feats and failures. Factory-model four-by-fours rally, Sisyphus-like, against boulder-like formations and up near-vertical grades. In a slow-moving free-for-all, wheels spin, dust spews, and tire-treads gouge.

Bereft of commentary, Bartana's video plays as a near-abstract sequence of images, a seven-and-a-half-minute montage. Neither narrated nor subtitled, it reads as raw footage, visual evidence of a place and witness to a scene. Yet *Kings of the Hill* is not without editorializing. Bartana's camerawork is tightly edited to depict part of a single late-afternoon gathering. More-over, her video has a title, which functions like a caption, labeling the images with a slight variation on the better-known phrase "King of the Hill." Also called King of the Mountain or King of the Castle, this is a children's game in which individual players attempt to gain and then maintain a single piece of land, the lone position at the top of an elevation. King of the Hill is an example of zero-sum competition, as well as a metaphor for rule by force and hierarchical control. Similarly, Bartana's video evokes the pleasures and pitfalls of aggression, the violence and destruction of testosterone-fueled conquest. Considered within the context of the artist's practice, *Kings of the Hill* also reads as a specific comment on Israel's paramilitary society and its destructive conflict with Palestine.

Bartana creates photographs, films, videos, sound works, and installations that probe the construction of identity, primarily in her native Israel. As she says, "I am focusing on Israel in order to ask: what is this place where I grew up?"[1] Now a resident of Amsterdam and Tel Aviv, Bartana is uniquely suited to approach her subject both etically and emically—anthropologists' parlance for observing with the distance of an outsider and the access of an insider. Considering the relationship of individual to place, in particular a cultural or national landscape, Bartana focuses on ritual behavior as a shaper of identity.

Over the past decade, Bartana's videos have addressed subjects ranging from Israel's state-mandated military service

(*Profile*, 2000) to Purim (*Ad De'lo Yoda* and *When Adar Enters*, both 2003) and Yom Hazikaron—Israel's Memorial Day and minute of silence, which commemorate the fallen of the Arab-Israeli conflict (*Trembling Time*, 2001). Through these short vignettes on customary life in Israel, Bartana offers alternative narratives to those promoted by state or military media, often imbuing moments intended to celebrate victory and heroism with ambiguity and uncertainty. Her works, some of which mime visual and verbal propaganda (*Summer Camp* and *Mary Koszmary*, both 2007), also question the didacticism voiced by sovereign power. In so doing, they achieve a criticality akin to that described by Chantal Mouffe in a recent essay on art and activism.[2]

Bartana's videos often mix seriousness with playfulness, revealing the ideological import of sport and festival, forming a caricature of power, or otherwise obliquely addressing political issues. *Wild Seeds* (2005), for example, depicts a hillside wres-tling game—"Evacuation of Gilad's Colony"—over two adjacent projections. One video presents a group of teenage pacifists forming a human knot, while two other teens, representing government authorities, try to forcibly extricate their friends. A second video shows their screams and exasperated outcries, audible from the first video, as English subtitles isolated on a black background. As the viewer's attention shifts between the images and words, attributing different narratives to each, *Wild Seeds* slips between a general image of roughhousing and a metaphor for forced evacuation—specifically Israel's 2005 disengagement from the Gaza Strip.

Similarly, the dune bashing in *Kings of the Hill* can be under-stood as an allegory of Israel's settlement and sovereignty of the territories designated as "occupied" by the United Nations. Following the Six-Day War of 1967, Israel gained control of the West Bank, East Jerusalem, the Gaza Strip, and the Golan Heights, quickly establishing settlements in historically Arab regions, including areas planned for the foundation of an inde-pendent Palestinian state. Although Israel ceded some internal jurisdiction of the West Bank and the Gaza Strip to the Palestine Liberation Organization in 1993 and officially evacuated settle-ments in Gaza in 2005, the territories remain contested turf.[3] Freely traversing a putatively off-limits terrain, the protagonists in Bartana's video echo this conflict, facing off against one another and competing for routes on the limited space of the sand dunes with movements that read as both invasion and Zionist self-realization. Israel, as embodied by the men seen here, is truly King of the Hill.[4]

*Kings of the Hill* also simulates the spectacle of war and its folly, showing environmental damage at the hands of technology. Bartana often focuses on moments in which machines are forced into absurd, if not foolish, positions by their drivers' stubborn attempts to achieve domination over the territory. In a few slow-motion sequences — Bartana's heaviest editing touches — the aggression, often amusing, appears increasingly violent. In one particular twilight scene, a jeep (the civilian descendant of military engineering) assaults a steep incline, its engine revving from the struggle and its headlights beaming like searchlights across the land and into the sky, scattering a crowd of excited onlookers.

For all its depictions of competition and individual effort, *Kings of the Hill* ultimately captures an image of community.[5] As an increasing number of vehicles challenge the summit, a swelling crowd of pedestrians lines its ridges. The amateur contest is also a spectator sport. Bartana pictures the gathering as an afternoon-*cum*-night of collective leisure, a high-octane, off-road, twenty-first-century version of George Seurat's famous painting *A Sunday on La Grande Jatte — 1884* (1884–6). Some of the vehicles carry entire families (or at least their male members), while scenic views of the adjacent Tel Aviv coastline feature sailboats and condominiums. A soundtrack otherwise comprised

of motors and horns includes waves and breezes. The video's dominant narrative progression is the picturesque setting sun. One late-afternoon shot shows a woman and a girl — perhaps the only females depicted — relaxed on a central outcropping, picnicking, almost indifferent to the action around them.

In *Kings of the Hill*, Bartana strategically deploys both metaphor and metonymy. Metaphor is apparent in the video's many allegorical readings, in the poetic, provocative resonances the artist allows to emerge. On its own, though, metaphor tends to gloss the specifics of the two objects it compares, in this case, the ritual on the dunes and the politics of Israel's occupation. As a favored rhetorical tool of the same propagandist politics Bartana seeks to question, metaphor runs the risk of generating aesthetic pleasure instead of critical thought.[6] The artist mitigates this risk through recourse to metonymy, specifically by maintaining a contiguous relationship to her subject through the ostensible objectivity of the camera's gaze. Created during two months of observation, *Kings of the Hill* is a kind of minor ethnographic study, a document of a macho ritual performed and spectated in a society permeated by military convention. The hill Bartana depicts is unsettled Israeli land, while its aggressors are Israeli citizens, the same individuals who shape national policies on Palestine (even if they do not personally enact them). Even Bartana's title can be understood metonymically. Her off-road kings are the cultural, if not biological descendants of King David, the slayer of Goliath who founded Jerusalem on the remains of his enemy's fort and established a united Jewish state. **KM**

1  Yael Bartana, artist's statement for Prague Biennale 4, 2009, http://www.praguebiennale.org/artists/illusion/bartana.php.
2  Mouffe argues that critical art "foments dissensus" and contributes to "questioning the dominant hegemony." See Chantal Mouffe, "Artistic Activism and Agonistic Spaces," *Art & Research: A Journal of Ideas, Contexts and Methods* 1:2 (Summer 2007), http://www.artandresearch.org.uk/v1n2/mouffe.html.
3  Following United Nations Security Council Resolutions 242 (1967), 446 (1979), 465 (1980), and 478 (1980), as well as declarations by the High Contracting Parties to the Fourth Geneva Convention and the International Committee on the Red Cross, the areas seized by Israel in the Six-Day War are considered "occupied" by international law. For full texts of the resolutions, see the UN Security Council website at http://www.un.org/Docs/sc/unsc_resolutions.html.
4  This can be interpreted literally, as the Israeli assault on Ammunition Hill in Jerusalem was one of the fiercest battles of the Six-Day War. This assault precipitated the capture of East Jerusalem and the Temple Mount, the eastern of the two hills upon which the Old City is built and a holy site significant to both Judaism and Islam. Moreover, the 1947 United Nations Partition Plan for Palestine called for the formation of a Jewish state to encompass 56% of the Palestinian state outlined in the 1922 British Mandate of Palestine — a majority stake that has only been increased following the 1949 Armistice Agreements and the Six-Day War. See Howard M. Sachar, *A History of Israel: From the Rise of Zionism to Our Time*, 3d ed. (New York: Alfred A. Knopf, 2007) and Mark Tessler, *A History of the Israeli-Palestinan Conflict*, 2d ed. (Bloomington: Indiana University Press, 2009).
5  See Rachel Taylor, "Yael Bartana, *Kings of the Hill*, 2003," Tate Collection Online Text, http://www.tate.org.uk/servlet/ViewWork?cgroupid=999999961&workid=81205&searchid=21124&tabview=text.
6  See Charles Gaines, "Reconsidering Metaphor/Metonymy: Art and the Suppression of Thought," *Art Lies*, no. 64 (Winter 2009): 48–57.

Andrea Geyer

**Spiral Lands / Chapter 1**  2007
Four panels from an installation comprised of nineteen fiber-based photographs
and text; brochure with footnotes; three panels, each 70 × 170 cm (27 ½ × 68 in.),
fourth panel 70 × 230 cm (27 ½ × 90 in.)

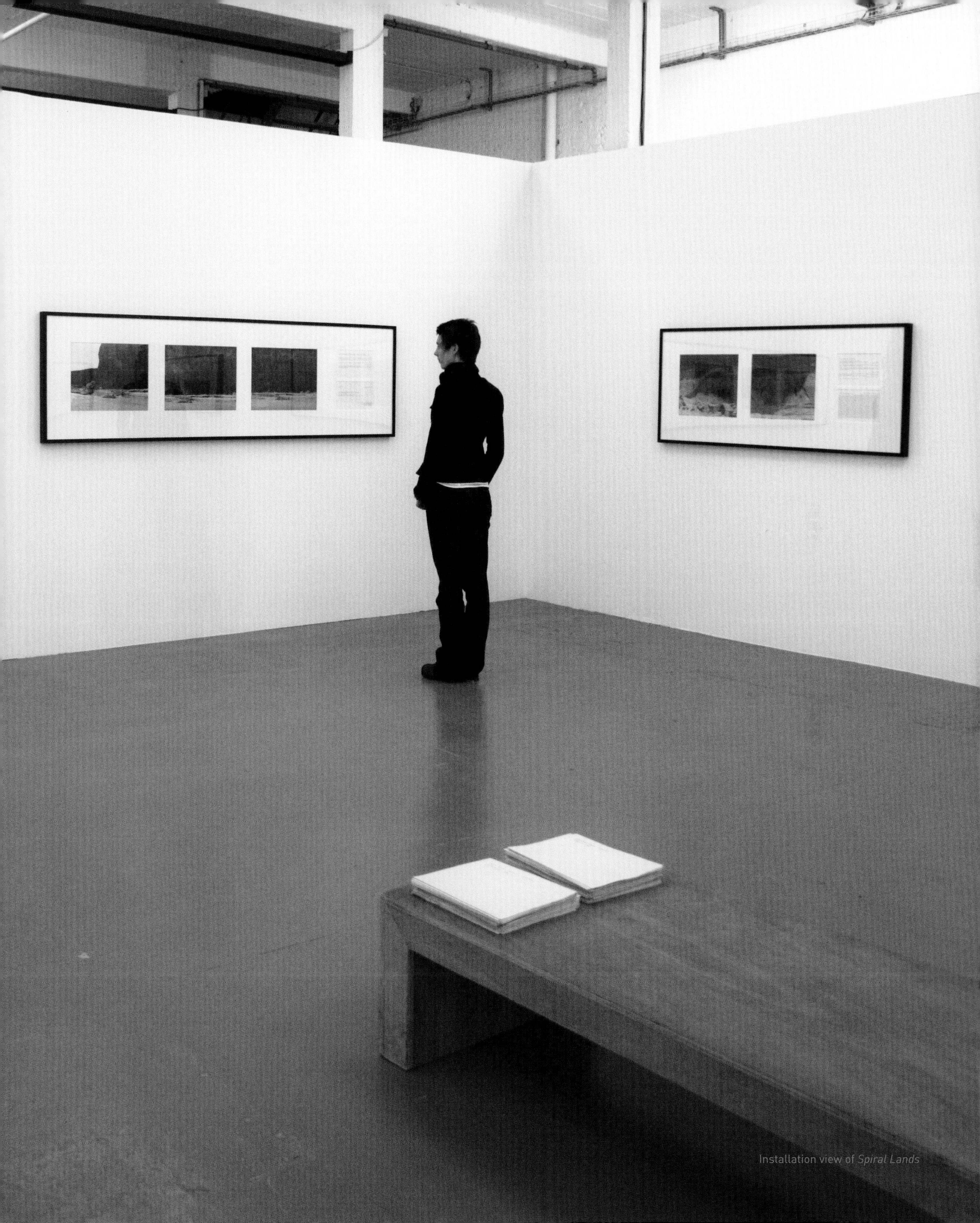

Installation view of Spiral Lands

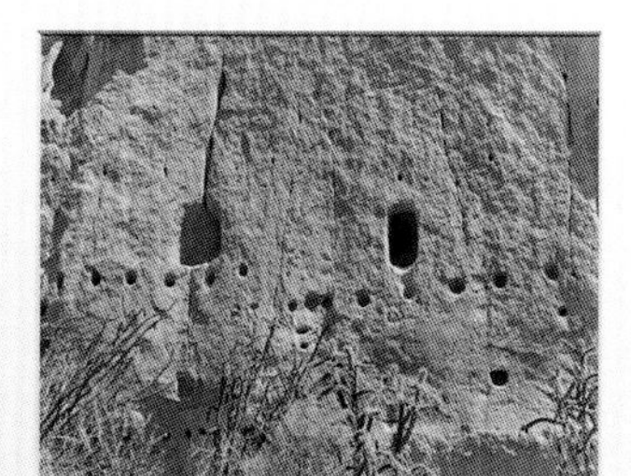
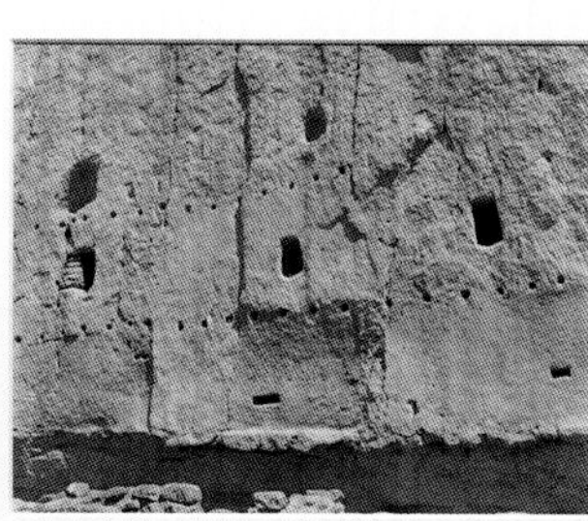
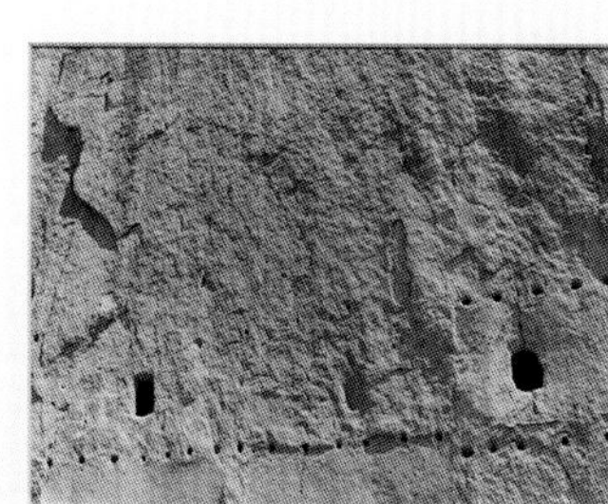

Overcoming the Wilderness[22]

...

With Protestantism rising[23] in the so-called New World, the British added to their statues of what constituted the right to hold title over land, that such rights could only be respected and granted to those individuals who not only showed desire but ability to "develop" the land, exercising "dominium" over nature, subduing the "wilderness" to convert it into "domesticated" land. [24]

1754 — 1763   The French and Indian Wars.[25]

1763   *Proclamation of King George III.[26]... And whereas it is just and reasonable, and essential to our Interest, and the Security of our Colonies, that the several Nations or Tribes of Indians with whom We are connected, and who live under our Protection, should not be molested or disturbed in the Possession of such Parts of Our Dominions and Territories as, not having been ceded to or purchased by Us, are reserved to them, or any of them, as their Hunting Grounds — We do therefore, with the Advice of our Privy Council, declare it to be our Royal Will and Pleasure, that no Governor or Commander in Chief in any of our Colonies of Quebec, East Florida, or West Florida, do presume, upon any Pretence whatever, to grant Warrants of Survey, or pass any Patents for Lands beyond the Bounds of their respective Governments, as described in their Commissions: as also that no Governor or Commander in Chief in any of our other Colonies or Plantations in America do presume for the present, and until our further Pleasure be known, to grant Warrants of Survey, or pass Patents for any Lands beyond the Heads or Sources of any of the Rivers which fall into the Atlantic Ocean from the West and North West, or upon any Lands whatever, which, not having been ceded to or purchased by Us as aforesaid, are reserved to the said Indians, or any of them ...*

1775   The War of Independence.[27]

1776   The Declaration of Independence. ... *We hold these Truths to be self-evident, that all Men are created equal, that they are endowed by their Creator with certain unalienable Rights, that among these are Life, Liberty, and the pursuit of Happiness ...*

---

1783   The Treaty of Paris[28] *Article 1: His Britannic Majesty acknowledges the said United States, viz., New Hampshire, Massachusetts Bay, Rhode Island and Providence Plantations, Connecticut, New York, New Jersey, Pennsylvania, Delaware, Maryland, Virginia, North Carolina, South Carolina and Georgia, to be free sovereign and independent states, that he treats with them as such, and for himself, his heirs, and successors, relinquishes all claims to the government, propriety, and territorial rights of the same and every part thereof ...*

1787   The Constitution of the United States of America. *We the People of the United States, in Order to form a more perfect Union, establish Justice, insure domestic Tranquility, provide for the common Defence, promote the general Welfare, and secure the Blessings of Liberty to ourselves and our Posterity, do ordain and establish this Constitution for the United States of America ...*

1787   North West Ordinance.[29] *Article 3: The utmost good faith shall always be observed towards the Indians; their lands and property shall never be taken from them without their consent; and, in their property, rights, and liberty, they shall never be invaded or disturbed, unless in just and lawful wars authorized by Congress; but laws founded in justice and humanity, shall from time to time be made for preventing wrongs being done to them, and for preserving peace and friendship with them.*

1803   Louisiana Purchase Treaty. *Article 6: The United States promise to execute such treaties and articles as may have been agreed between Spain and the tribes and nations of Indians until by mutual consent of the United States and the said tribes or nations other suitable articles shall have been agreed upon.*

1848   The Treaty of Guadalupe Hidalgo.[30]*... Considering that a great part of the territories, which, by the present treaty, are to be comprehended for the future within the limits of the United States, is now occupied by savage tribes, who will hereafter be under the exclusive control of the Government of the United States, and whose incursions within the territory of Mexico would be prejudicial in the extreme, it is solemnly agreed that all such incursions shall be forcibly restrained by the Government of the United States whensoever this may be necessary; and that when they cannot be prevented, they shall be punished by the said Government ...*

...

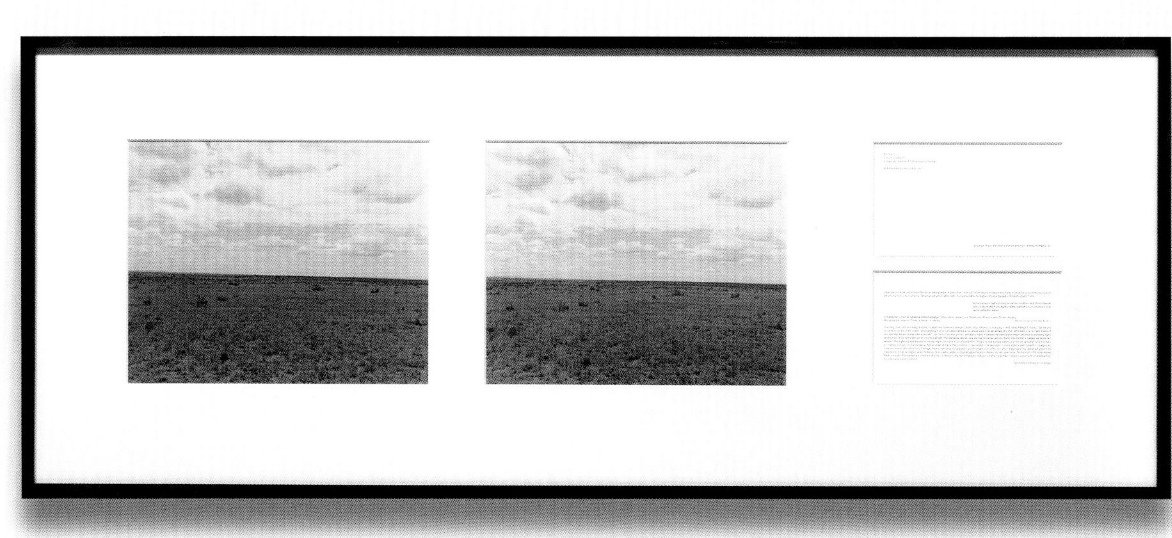

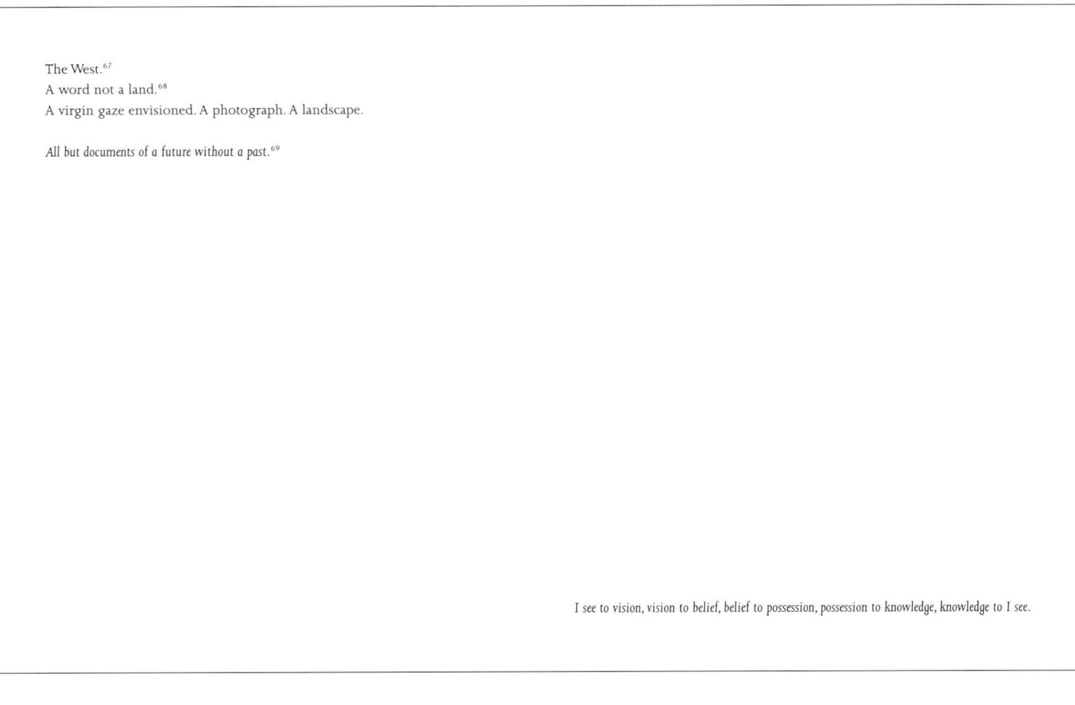

The West.[67]
A word not a land.[68]
A virgin gaze envisioned. A photograph. A landscape.

*All but documents of a future without a past.*[69]

*I see to vision, vision to belief, belief to possession, possession to knowledge, knowledge to I see.*

I learn about a book called *Wonder Places* by the photographer William Henry Jackson[70] whose name I recognize from being scratched in stone at Mancos Canyon. The introduction to the book reads: *The red man will pass into oblivion before many years have flown, but the glory of the scenes they dwelt in will never be eclipsed.*[71] 1894.

*The West had long privileged scopic enterprises and visual modalities, and by the mid-nineteenth century an observational visualist hegemony became a persistent focus of modernism in social, scientific, and aesthetic endeavors.*[72]

*A wholesale shift in vision. An observational, perspectival paradigm.*[73] Mass culture. Surveillance. Observation. All was at stake. All was changing. Photography. A conquest of land, of people, of meaning.                    Dictating silence, dictating absence.

Vanishing, I am told. Becoming invisible, in rapid and mysterious manner. Chiefly with reference to conjuring. I think about Edward S. Curtis,[74] the famous documentarian, the noble worker, photographing to secure *a permanent ethnological and pictorial record of the fast vanishing race, which shall preserve it for the student hundreds of years after it has been lost from the surface of the earth.*[75] For Curtis a life time project. *After nearly a century of systematic deprivation of space, resources and culture by missionaries, soldiers and government officials, Native Americans were now also confronted with humanitarian reformers, social and physical scientists, and artists that lent their authority to assimilate and dissolve their identities.*[76] Curtis photographed people as statues, staged, costumed icons of themselves.[77] Why is no one smiling? A project worth one and a half million dollars. An expression of care via documentation. And an image of a gaze. Once pictured — non-subject, wild and other — Curtis' subjects were doomed to disappear by common consent. After all, it was J. P. Morgan himself who financed the project. 40,000 images of 80 tribes. 722 plates of photogravures. Handmade paper from Holland of rich tone and highest grade. Binding in three-quarter Levant, an irregular grained morocco leather. 500 sets. Made to last. The Portfolio of *The North American Indian*, a wonder of bookmaking. A document of what J. P. Morgan's business investments were actively destroying. What remains is a monopoly in imagemaking, the only vision meant to prevail.

A picturesque, preemptive nostalgia.

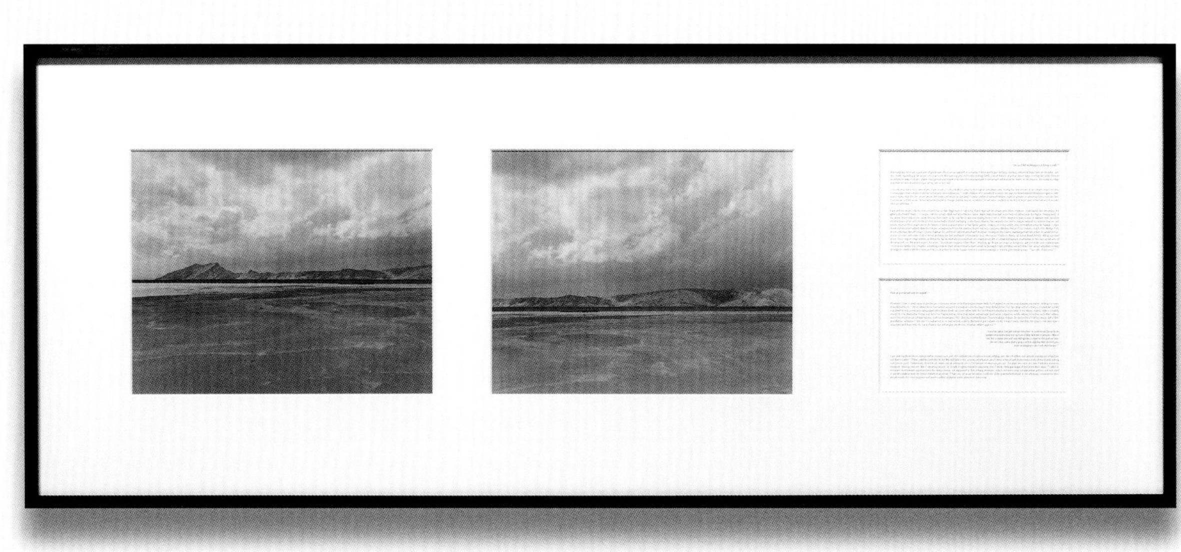

This land does not belong to us. It belongs to itself.[111]

Following the dirt road, I pass a set of gatehouses. There are unmanned. It is Sunday. I drive slowly past the large smoking chimneys. Then there are the lakes, one, two, three, expanding as far as one's eyes can reach. Shimmering grey and white, moving slowly if at all. Sounds of pumps. Heavy tarps covering the banks. There is no bird to be seen. Coal slurry lakes. Fine ground coal mixed with water for easy transport. I turn around and look at the desert. In the distance, the mountain ridge guards storm clouds announcing a spring rain soon to fall.

I am told that the Four Corners Power Plant is one of two coal-fired plants in this region. Both plants rate among the fifty dirtiest in the United States. The Four Corners plant leads a nationwide list in nitrogen-oxide emissions.[112] It also releases 851 pounds of mercury per year. An Environmental Protection Agency (EPA) report shows that the two power plants and their coal mines in San Juan County combined released thirteen million pounds of chemical toxins into the Four Corners' air in 2000 alone. Those toxins are inhaled by Navajo, Jicarilla Apache, Southern Ute and other residents in the Four Corners area of New Mexico, Colorado, Arizona, and Utah.[113]

I am told that people call this area a second Cancer Alley. High rates of cancer are found especially in teenage girls, about seventeen times higher than the average for girls in the United States.[114] I am also told that people think that John Wayne's cancer death might have had to do with his presence in this region, filming most of his career. Direct links to the cancer have not been made to the coal but to uranium mining. From 1944 to 1986, about four million tons of uranium were mined in 10,000 mines, all located on the 27,000-square-miles of land belonging to the Navajo Nation. The uranium was used to supply material for nuclear weapons and nuclear reactors. Most important in the history of these uranium mines is that Navajo people, working or living nearby, were never informed of the hazards to their health that the mines posed. Many died of the consequences. When the uranium boom was over, companies like Kerr-McGee Corp, Conoco, Gulf, Mobil, Phillips, TVA, Pioneer Nuclear, United Nuclear, Climax Uranium Co., and Foote Mineral abandoned the mines, leaving the fine yellow uranium powder, like pollen, to nature's forces, to soil, to water, and worst of all to the air, polluting the lives and lands of thousands. In a 1986 memo, Charles A. Reaux, an Indian Health Service official stationed in the Navajo region, responded to an EPA study that showed the extreme levels of contamination. He recommended against involvement in the clean-up because of the projected cost. The health service, he wrote, "should only monitor tribal efforts." Not long ago Reaux, no longer at the agency, said that if the same contaminants "were in the middle of Los Angeles, something would be done about it because there would be thousands of people living around them." But Navajo shepherds moving through the desert with their herds and the locals in their far-flung hogans were not numerous enough to warrant government action. "That's life," Reaux said.[115]

Gains are privatized and losses are socialized.[113]

December 2006. A small camp of people just 10 minutes south of the Farmington Power Plant. A car parked across the road stopping contractors drilling for water. Doda Desert Rock.[114] No to Desert Rock! This land is occupied. A common voice not heard. Sithe Global Power, LLC, has proposed to construct a hybrid dry cooled coal-fired electric power-generating plant called Desert Rock, as a joint effort with the Diné Power Authority, an enterprise of the Navajo Nation. Sithe is privately owned by The Blackstone Group and Reservoir Capital Group, New York-based international investment companies worth billions of dollars each. The lobbyist named for Desert Rock is Frank Maisano, with the Washington, D.C., firm Bracewell & Giuliani. That is Rudolph Giuliani the former New York City mayor and a 2008 presidential candidate.[115] The site of construction is on land held in trust by the Federal government for the Navajo Nation; therefore, the project will enter into a long-term land lease with the Navajo Nation that will require the Bureau of Indian Affairs' approval.[116]

Since I have been a child, here and there were places we moved around. During the hot<br>
summers we've moved around with our herds of sheep. Back then it was a time when we<br>
only lived in shaded arbors and tents. And right here is where we truly made our home.<br>
But now I hear a power plant is going to be built right here where the herd grazes.<br>
It sets an imbalance in me. I really don't like this.[117]

I am told that Desert Rock is projected to produce each year 10.5 million tons of carbon dioxide, adding onto the 29 million tons already coming out of San Juan and Four Corners.[118] These numbers, provided by the EPA and Sithe's own account, would place Desert Rock as the second-highest emitter of carbon dioxide among new power plants. Furthermore, Desert Rock could emit an estimated 114 to 555 pounds of mercury per year. The plant does not meet new California emissions standards, creating concerns that if adjoining Arizona or Nevada toughen emissions standards, they'll revoke their patronage of the Desert Rock plant.[119] Called an economic development opportunity for the Navajo Nation, and supported by their tribal government, Sithe is not foreclosing its employment politics, and even tried to get $85 million from the Navajo Nation as tax credit.[120] They also show no intention to sell any of the generated electricity to the adjoining communities. Most people nearby live without power and need to collect drinkable water, often from miles away.

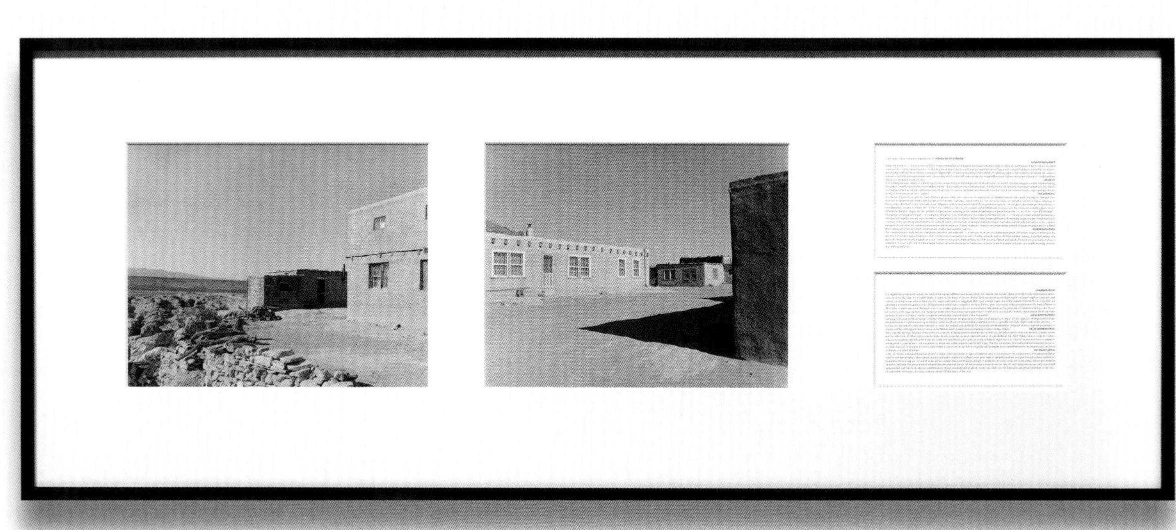

I have been told an American Indian Theory of **JUSTICE AS INDIGENISM**[137]

**ACKNOWLEDGMENT**

Indian claims stories — rich sources of oral history that contextualize and humanize the Indian experience while revealing the inadequacies of the record as it has been constructed — can be a powerful source of liberation for all Americans. To enable national demythification, Congress should pass legislation to establish and fund an independent truth and reconciliation commission charged with (1) investigating Indian claims afresh; (2) allowing Indian voices to enrich and debunk the sanitized national record with their oral histories; and (3) persuading the U.S. to formally acknowledge the wrongs inflicted upon Indians over the period since 1776 and enable the telling of a new national creation-story.

**APOLOGY**

After persuading many citizens to acknowledge harm to Indian tribes and individuals, the U.S. should relieve the burden of its national guilt-complex while advancing the process toward forgiveness by recommending that the U.S. government issue a formal apology, on behalf of the U.S. and all its citizens past and present, as symbolic recognition of the role of public and private actors in past acts of genocide, land theft, and ethnocide. National church and corporate boards might apologize for acts in which these institutions were complicit.

**PEACEMAKING**

If a theory of justice is to span the chasm between peoples, ideas, and objectives, its enunciation and implementation will require negotiation. Although their resilience is unquestionable after a half millennium of extreme challenges, Indian tribes are now too numerically and militarily inferior to impose solutions by force; on the other hand, reason, principle, moral obligations, and the aspirational values of a constitutional republic, erected upon prior sovereigns with whom it is interdependent, conspire to restrain the U.S. While the conflict has been waged primarily on battlefields and in courtrooms, the origins are rooted largely in cultural differences difficult to exaggerate: the "problem of learning how meaning in one system of expression is expressed in another" is one of the "most difficult tasks"... Recognition of mutual sovereignty — a companion obligation to the establishment of a multicultural ethic of respect — will require a cross-cultural hermeneutics, which in turn mandates the clearing of barriers to communication and the sharing of stories, fears, hopes, and dreams. By restoring a large measure of legal personality to Indian tribes, identifying shared interests obscured by history and emotion, tempering tendencies toward extremism, and tutoring both parties in the common humanity of each other, U.S.-Indian negotiations can usher in a new era of peace and justice. Fittingly, the ancient Indian method of dispute resolution known as Tribal Peacemaking can guide the journey toward greater mutual understanding and trust.

**COMMEMORATION**

The commemoration of the history of genocide, land theft, and ethnocide — is necessary to ensure that future generations will neither forget nor perpetuate the injustice toward the original inhabitants of the U.S. Erection of monuments at sites of Indian genocide and on the National Mall, naming of public buildings and parks after Indians of historical significance, and creation of a wing in the National Museum of the American Indian with specific focus on the gross human injustices suffered by Indian people will serve these transformative and deterrent purposes. Posthumous pardons should be granted to Indians executed for resisting genocide and land expropriation.

**COMPENSATION**

It is impossible to objectively quantify the value of the injuries inflicted upon Indian people over history, and morally odious to try. Moreover, compensation cannot reach, let alone discharge, the wrongful deaths of ancestors, the denial of the use of tribal lands and resources, and legal assaults on Indian religions, languages, and cultures. These harms can never be repaired with money, and Justice as Indigenism (JAI) theory would regard any wealth transfer from the U.S. as a symbolic act undertaken in further recognition of moral responsibility, rather than a settlement of claims for loss, grief, and trauma. Although endowment of a fund sufficient to allow tribes to repurchase some lands and to serve as a social support net for the poorest Indian individuals, and in particular off-reservation Indians who do not presently enjoy the legal, medical, and educational entitlements their tribal counterparts receive, would not be incompatible with the application of JAI theory to the question of justice for Indians, money is simply an unimportant, and potentially even a dispensable.

**LAND RESTORATION**

A necessary precondition for the exercise of power of self-government, the generation of wealth, the propagation of culture and the expression of religious belief is the secure possession of a physical space upon which to center these forms of human endeavor and from which it is possible to exclude others hostile to this activities…[1] In sum, the recovery of a land mass sufficient to create the material preconditions for economic self-determination, religious freedom, and self-governance is crucial, and thus JAI proposes land restoration to the furthest limits possible short of imposing injustice on non-Indians."

**LEGAL REFORMATION**

Taken together, the legal doctrines of discovery and conquest, as incorporated in domestic law, as well as a judicially unenforceable trust doctrine, plenary power, and the subversion of Indian rights reserved under treaties, constitute an interconnected matrix of legal disability that refers Indian rights to property, culture, religion, development, and self-government, no matter how broadly any given generation of non-Indians might choose to construct and protect them, to perpetual reinterpretation, appropriation, and suppression by future non-Indian majorities and hostile judges. That this system must be transformed if the impediments are to be swept away and those rights secured to their bearers is a proposition that follows logically, but has largely gone unstated heretofore by theoreticians concerned with justice on behalf of Indians.

**RECONCILIATION**

If the U.S. restores a meaningful measure of land to Indian tribes and amends its legal and political order to ensure respect for and protection of fundamental Indian rights to self-determination, a new regime of peace and justice worthy of emulation and export must be rewarded with the most precious gift Indians can bestow: forgiveness. By forgiving the U.S. and all its people in a solemn ceremony broadcast globally to symbolize the dawn of the new relationship, Indians will finally be allowed to heal, and all Americans will be released from the chains of history and freed to forge a better tomorrow. The U.S. and Indian tribes are not only intertwined geographically and historically, they are interdependent. Indian autonomy and prosperity on the one hand, and U.S. legitimacy and global leadership on the other, are inseverable, with each a necessary condition for the full realization of the other.

The work of German-born, New York-based artist Andrea Geyer is inspired by a longstanding commitment to social justice. Originally trained as a photojournalist, Geyer brings to light repressed narratives and explores the conditions of democracy, citizenship, and subjectivity in both the past and the present. Such is the case with *Spiral Lands/Chapter 1*, the first of three projects about the ongoing conflict between the United States government and indigenous Americans.

Geyer began *Spiral Lands* in 2003, after a cross-country drive brought her and fellow artist Sharon Hayes to the Navajo Nation, which covers portions of Arizona, Utah, and New Mexico. The project gained momentum as she pondered the increasing prominence of manifest destiny in American political rhetoric after the terrorist attacks of September 11, 2001. In addition to the research she conducts in New York, Geyer has traveled to the Southwest many times, usually to the Navajo Nation, although she has also visited nearby pueblos (Zuni, Acoma, San Ildefonso, Hopi, and Laguna). Her trips "followed stories" learned about from others or read about in books.[1] Geyer conceives of herself as a visitor rather than a researcher, and the people she spoke to were encountered by chance, whether on the street, in museums and restaurants, or on tours through tribal parks. That said, there is a strong investigative thrust to *Spiral Lands*. Geyer might not identify as an archivist, but the retrieval of history through research and interviews is an integral part of her artistic process.

*Spiral Lands/Chapter 1* consists of nineteen panels that pair text with black-and-white photographs. The images represent land-sites associated with Native Americans, and they mimic (albeit imperfectly) the conventions of nineteenth-century landscape photography, which was itself harnessed to the doctrine of manifest destiny. A few of the pictures offer indisputably dramatic views, but most eschew the sublime for the pedestrian. Conspicuously absent are Native Americans: this omission has important political ramifications, a point to which I will return at the end of this essay. The photographs appear in twos or threes, each group depicting the same land-site from slightly different perspectives. The multiplication of points of view suggests stereoscopic photography, but it also signals the rejection of a single, authoritative subject position. The passages of text with which the photographs are juxtaposed accomplish a similar

feat, multiplying and dispersing the authorial voice. These texts include excerpts from eighteenth-century British proclamations and colonial mandates; laws and treaties between the United States and Native Americans; editorials from nineteenth-century newspapers; writings by Native American and Anglo-American scholars; documents from the American Indian Movement, an activist organization founded in 1968; corporate reports; and diaristic entries written by the artist but attributed to another's voice. Nearly all these accounts focus on land as it factors into either the government's imperial ambitions or the struggle for compensation, reclamation, and self-determination on the part of the indigenous peoples of the Southwest.[2] As framed by Geyer, moreover, land resides not just at the intersection of competing claims of ownership, but also at the center of conflicting definitions of home, place, property, and identity.[3]

When *Spiral Lands* is on display in galleries and museums, the land-sites represented therein remain unidentified. This is a deliberate choice on Geyer's part. While unfamiliar to most Anglo-Americans, these land-sites are immediately recognizable to local indigenous peoples.[4] Geyer prefers to prolong rather than resolve this contradiction, since it signals so effectively the politics of history and knowledge. At the risk of deflating precisely the tension Geyer wishes to retain, however, it is useful to decode the land-sites depicted in the four panels featured in *Nobody's Property*. One shows the remains of the Long House cliff dwelling, once home to the Ancestral Pueblo people who resided in the area between 1150 and 1550 C.E. The ruins are located in what is now New Mexico's Bandelier National Monument on the Pajarito Plateau in the northern Rio Grande Valley, south of Los Alamos and northwest of Santa Fe. In the second, mustangs graze near the highway on the eastern edge of the Navajo Nation, in an area called the "Checkerboard" because of the many peoples who claim ownership of it. A coal slurry lake, part of the Four Corners Power Plant located in the Navajo Nation west of Farmington, New Mexico, appears in the foreground of the third panel. This lake serves as a potent symbol of the systemic acts of environmental injustice committed by corporations and the United States government.[5] Represented in the last panel is the Acoma Pueblo near Albuquerque, New Mexico, a community settled centuries ago.[6]

Geyer operates within the documentary tradition, but her relationship to it is extremely precarious, even taxed. Faith in the ameliorative possibility of documentary photography was strong in the past (for instance, in the 1930s, when the Farm Security Administration hired photographers to capture the hardships of the Great Depression), but this belief fell into decline by the 1960s and 1970s. According to critics, the problem was not merely documentary photography's spurious claims to objectivity, but also its latent paternalism, its indulgence in a kind of pornography of suffering. In the end, some wondered if documentary photography simply disenfranchised its subjects a second time.[7] Related, but different, anxieties led Gilles Deleuze to commend Michel Foucault in 1972 for demonstrating the "indignity of speaking for others."[8]

Artists in the 1960s and beyond were certainly no less skeptical about speaking on another's behalf, but instead of rejecting the documentary tradition, they revised it. For them, Deleuze's words were less an injunction than a challenge. How might one speak about others without displacing and violating them? How might one marshal documentary photography in the service of social justice without confirming the very inequities one hopes to disable? Martha Rosler attempted just that in her 1974–75 project, *The Bowery in Two Inadequate Descriptive Systems*; Steve McQueen has done much the same in two recent videos on mining operations in the Congo and South Africa; and Geyer accomplishes a similar feat in *Spiral Lands*.[9] Like Rosler and McQueen, moreover, Geyer does so by deliberately withholding not only information, but the "other" itself, or at least its physical countenance. Native Americans are merely implied in these pictures, never shown, and no faces or bodies are made available to the viewer's gaze, a desire traditional ethnographic photographs were all too willing to satisfy. That said, what our seeing eye is denied, our reading eye is granted: the voices of many generations of indigenous peoples who address the viewer directly, in their own words. It is through her strategic orchestration of absence and presence, visibility and invisibility, therefore, that Geyer adapts and advances the tradition of documentary photography.[10] KB

**1** Andrea Geyer, e-mail message to author, February 2, 2009.

**2** 138 footnotes accompany *Spiral Lands/Chapter 1*. These provide sources for the texts in the panels and include additional insights, ruminations, and information.

**3** Most indigenous peoples believe that land is irreducible to property, that it cannot be bought or sold. This belief is tested, though, by claims to self-determination, which today revolve around land rights. On this issue and the Western Shoshone, see Rebecca Solnit, *Savage Dreams: A Journey into the Landscape Wars of the American West* (Berkeley and Los Angeles: University of California Press, 1994), 28–30, 159–69, 186–90.

**4** Geyer, e-mail message to author, February 2, 2009.

**5** Corporations have long located many of their most toxic plants (coal) and mines (uranium, gold) near or on Native American land, and the United States has done the same with its most dangerous bombing ranges and waste facilities (nuclear). In many cases, these entities do so with the approval of tribal governments, for whom such leases represent rare opportunities for economic development. In this way, poverty and dispossession begets more poverty and dispossession. See Solnit, *Savage Dreams*, 56–57, 77–86, 137, and Solnit, *Storming the Gates of Paradise: Landscapes for Politics* (Berkeley and Los Angeles: University of California Press, 2007), 38, 115–34. On these issues and the resulting tensions among corporations, environmental activists, indigenous residents, and tribal governments, specifically as they pertain to the Navajo Nation, see Katy Bolger, "Fallout," *Brooklyn Rail*, Dec. 2009–Jan. 2010, http://www.brooklynrail.org/2009/12/express/fallout.

**6** Simon J. Ortiz of Acoma Pueblo heritage is collaborating with Geyer on *Spiral Lands/Chapter 3*. All the panels from *Spiral Lands/Chapter 1* are reproduced in Geyer, *Spiral Lands/Chapter 1*, intro. Janet Catherine Berlo (London: Koenig Books, 2008). Berlo sheds light on the landmarks in panels no. 4 and no. 19 and identifies the mountain in panel no. 1 as *Dibéntsaa* (Hesperus Mountain in Colorado), which features prominently in the Navajo creation story. On the spiral and its relationship to Native American cosmology and calendars, see ibid., v–vi, and Geyer's panel no. 7.

**7** Some Native American communities have similar objections to photography. See, for instance, the large number of "Photography Forbidden" signs that appear on indigenous lands and at indigenous landmarks (as in Geyer's panel no. 15). See also Geyer, *Spiral Lands*, 93, 133 n. 102.

**8** "Intellectuals and Power: A Conversation between Gilles Deleuze and Michel Foucault," in Foucault, *Language, Counter-Memory, Practice: Selected Essays and Interviews*, ed. Donald F. Bouchard (Ithaca, N.Y.: Cornell University Press, 1977), 209. Deleuze's comment arises in the context of a larger discussion about the strikes and protests in May 1968, the role of the intellectual, and Foucault's own activism, especially with regard to prisoner's rights. Instead of lobbying in the conventional sense of the word, Foucault strove to create opportunities for prisoners to express their claims in their own voices.

**9** I am thinking specifically of McQueen's *Western Deep* (2002) and *Gravesend* (2007). See Demos, "Art of Darkness" and "Moving Images of Globalization." It is fruitful to consider Geyer's work in relationship to Judith Butler's discussion of the ethics of representation. For Butler, the ethical efficacy of representation lies in its failure to capture its subject's suffering, and in its determination to demonstrate that failure. See Butler, *Precarious Life*, 144.

**10** It is clear from the texts and footnotes that accompany the images of the Checkerboard that Geyer is in dialogue with nineteenth-century documentary photography, especially the landscapes of William Henry Jackson and the Native American portraits of Edward S. Curtis. See Geyer, *Spiral Lands*, 63.

Joana Hadjithomas and Khalil Joreige

Wonder Beirut (History of a Pyromaniac Photographer)  1998–2006
Six Lambda prints mounted on aluminum,
each 70.5 × 105 cm (27 ¾ × 41 ½ in.)

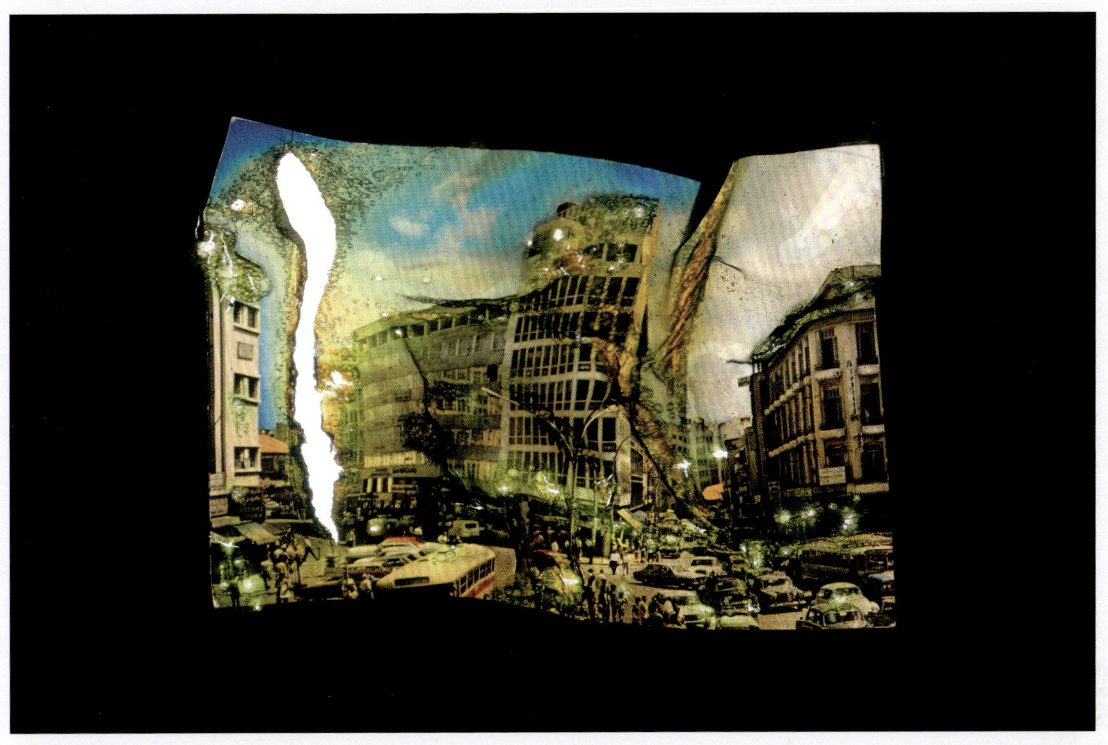

#6 (Rivoli Square)

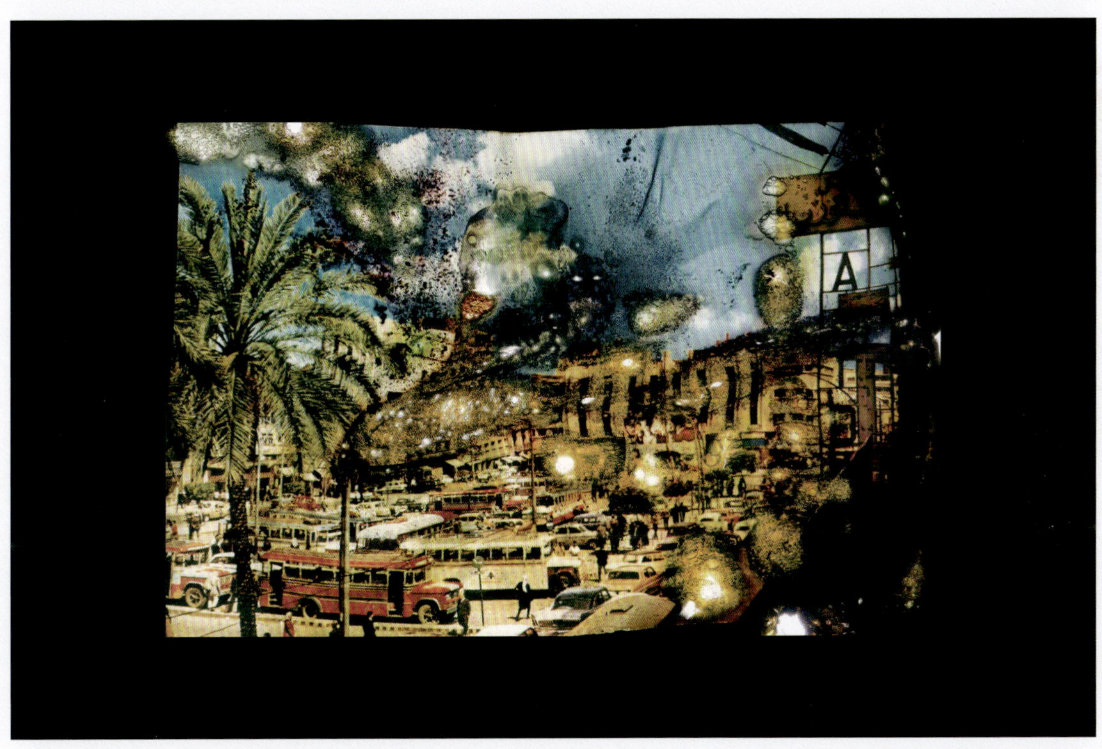



#15 (Rivoli Square)

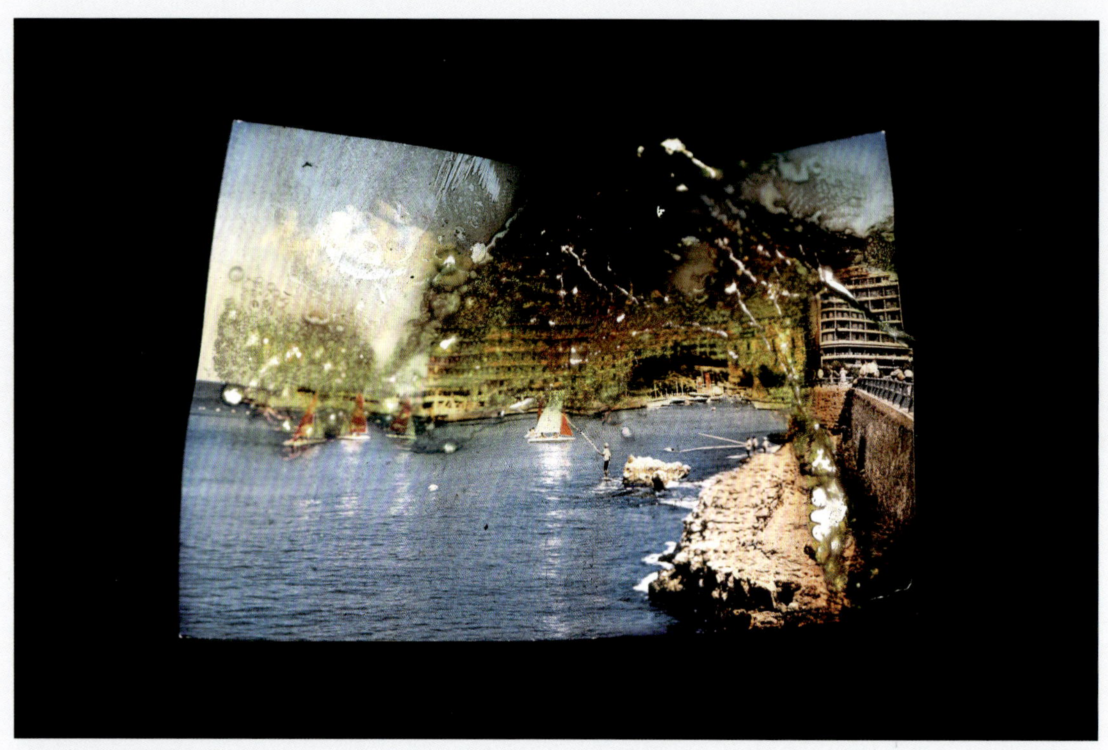

#10 (The Sea Shore)

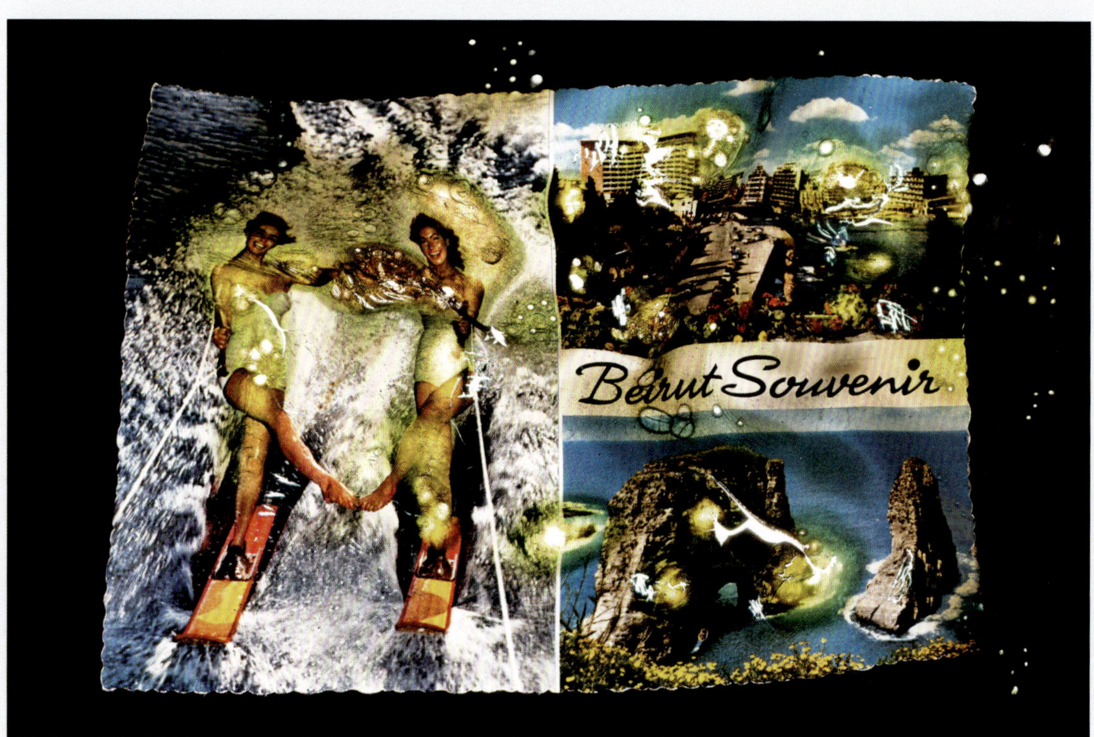


#13

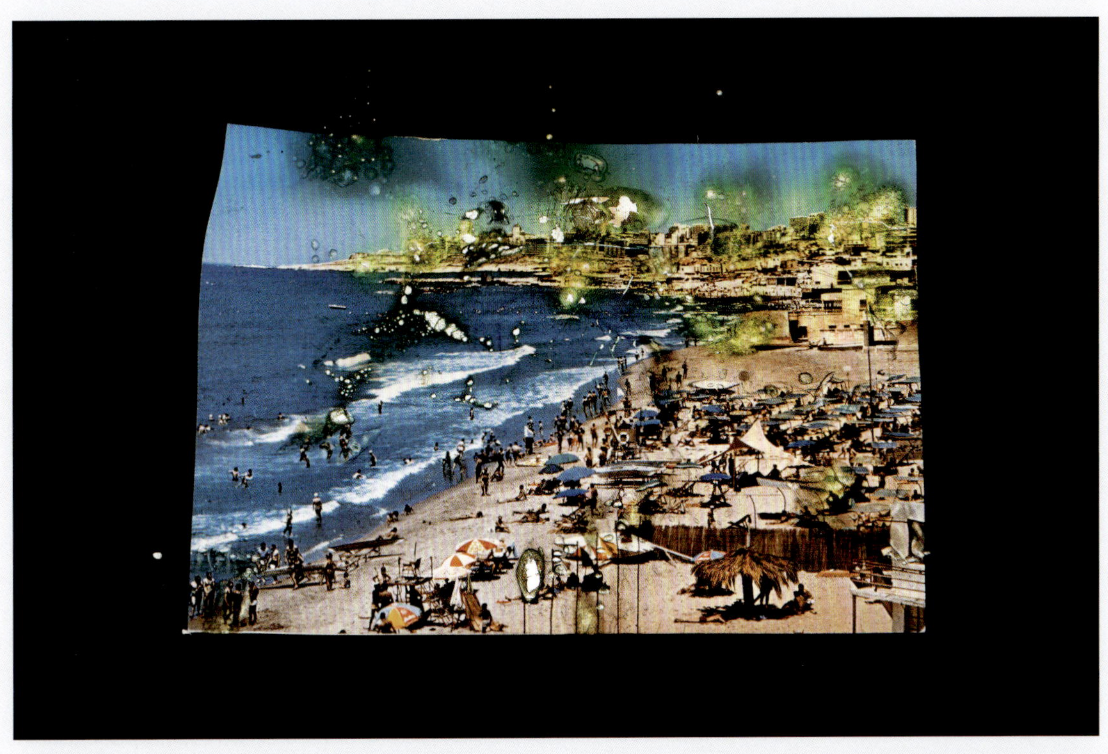

#21 (Beaches in Beirut)

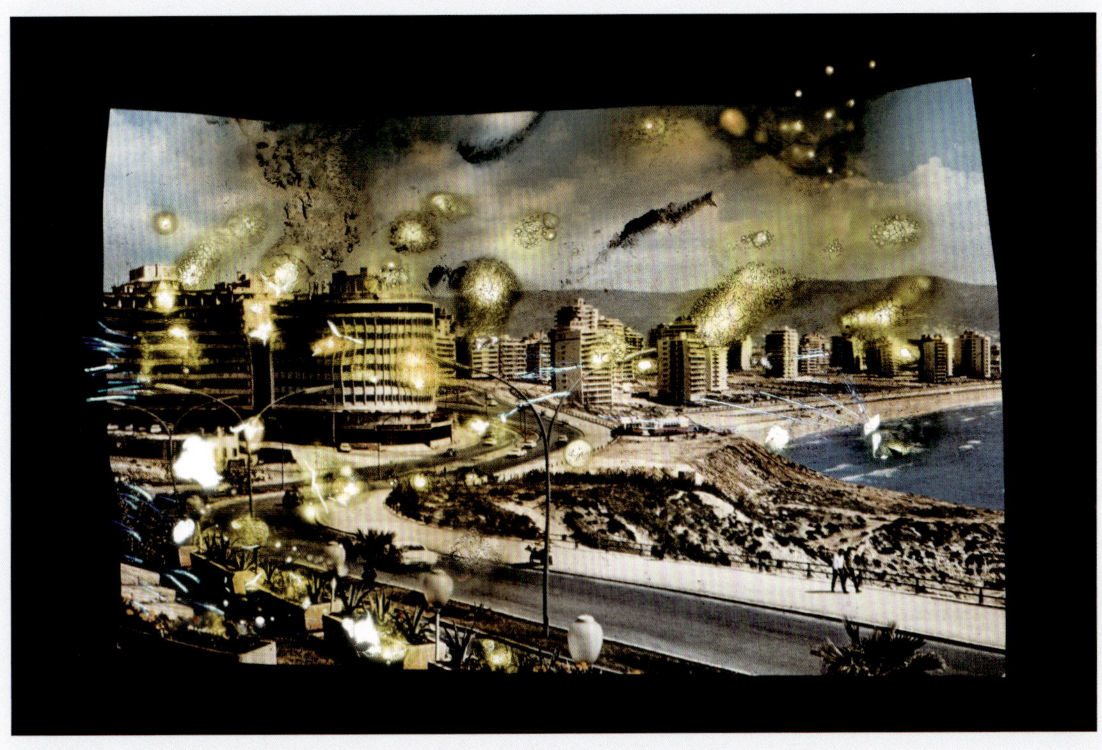

#22

Between 1998 and 2006, the Lebanese filmmaker-artists Joana Hadjithomas and Khalil Joreige created several iterations of the *Wonder Beirut* project: *The Story of the Pyromaniac Photographer*, then *War Postcards*, and finally *Latent Images*. The first consists of digital Lambda prints mounted on aluminum, the second, postcard booklets, and the third, an assemblage of film rolls. All purport to archive the work of Lebanese photographer Abdallah Farah.

As the story goes, Farah was only sixteen years old in 1968 when the Lebanese Tourism Agency commissioned a series of postcards and a calendar from his father's studio. Several photographers were assigned to the project, including Farah, who was so successful at capturing precisely the image the city wished to project—a cosmopolitan Mediterranean Riviera— that his postcards are still sold in stores today. However, when the Lebanese civil war broke out in 1975, Farah began to burn his negatives in secret. Night after night, he synchronized his pyro-cartography with "the destruction of buildings, which were progressively disappearing in front of his eyes, ravished by bombardment and street battles."[1] These nocturnal activities only came to light in the late 1990s, when Hadjithomas and Joreige discovered Farah's damaged negatives and decided to print them.

In the prints produced by Hadjithomas and Joreige, Farah's postcards appear as incandescent still lifes. Each image, framed by a thick black border that sets off its bright, saturated colors, evokes a magnified contact sheet placed on a light-box or a miniaturized projection on a cinema screen.[2] In this way, Hadjithomas and Joreige transform Abdallah's original postcards from clichéd tourist souvenirs into dreamscapes, pseudo-ravaged by iridescent bubbles of melted color and glowing ruptures. The luminescent effects are heightened by backlighting shining through the open ruptures.

But while it is true that the postcards on which Hadjithomas and Joreige's prints are based are still available today, Farah himself is a fictional character. As with *The Atlas Group* (1989–2004), a project by fellow Lebanese artist Walid Ra'ad, *Wonder Beirut* can be described as an instance of what Carrie Lambert-Beatty calls the parafictional mode.[3] In such works, real facts are woven into fictional narratives, their interface shrewdly managed by the parafictioneer. It might thus be appropriate to consider parafiction as an open investigation into the nature of plausibility.[4]

Precisely how is plausibility produced in *Wonder Beirut*? The notion of *trucage*, French for trick, seems particularly relevant given Hadjithomas and Joreige's entwined interests in cinema and photography. The term is commonly used to denote either the production of a special effect, or the creation of an impression of narrative causality through the skillful editing and sequencing of images. *Trucage* generates the illusion that no gaps, whether narrative or structural, exist. These gaps in fact remain, and as Paul Virilio explained, "viewers do not manufacture mental images on the basis of what they are immediately given to see, but on the basis of their memories, by themselves filling in the blanks and their minds with images created retrospectively."[5] As with parafiction, *trucage* implies a degree of deception, but it also rests on the assumption that things left unsaid, unwritten, or unseen can be just as powerful as those made explicit.[6] Christian Metz has written that "in film, the temporal gaps between one image and the next create natural interstices (or spaces) that allow audience members to develop interpretations that transcend what was initially circumscribed by the filmmaker."[7]

In *Wonder Beirut*, these interstices can be found across a range of supposedly archival evidence. The project's cognitive setup, for instance, operates through the cross-referencing of visual images with the parafictional texts provided by Hadjithomas and Joreige. Contradictions between the visual evidence and the "official" story create a fertile tension allowing for interpretation—or creative misinterpretation—on the part of viewers. In the case of *Wonder Beirut*, the assemblage of still photographs becomes the starting point for stories to play out uniquely in each viewer's imagination, mimicking the porous narrative structure that exists naturally in film.[8] Joreige uses the phrase "latent images" (as in images projected into the imagination of the viewer) to describe the operation at work in *Wonder Beirut*. These "concepts of latent, residual images, of disappearances, of phantomatic appearances, of documents made fictitious, or of fictions turned into document" make up the terrain explored and the material utilized by *Wonder Beirut*, a project that intertwines the cinematic and the parafictional.[9]

If *Wonder Beirut* partakes of the parafictional, it might be because the city itself exists today in an ambivalent state between fact and fiction. Forgetting, misremembering, and reimagining are inevitable aspects of life in a postwar city such as Beirut, where developers and government officials are systematically restoring many of the buildings lost or damaged during the civil war.[10] These efforts to "reauthenticate" Beirut dovetail with the country's larger efforts to rebuild its national identity, public image, and tourist industry. As Elizabeth Outka has argued, such commercialized versions of nostalgic nationalism and authenticity create a sense of timelessness that seems to hold out the promise of healing and stability.[11]

Ironically, the architectural whiteout staged in Beirut effectively removes the possibility of nostalgic desire, described by Susan Stewart as "an act of memory" in which "the past is constructed from a set of presently existing pieces.[12] Even as the war destroyed parts of pre-war Beirut, so too does the reconstruction of this new Beirut constitute an act of destruction in itself, one in which war memories are being erased by the city's now disconcertingly surreal physical resemblance to an earlier past. One can only imagine the sense of dissonance upon seeing postcards of old Beirut sold in bookshops as romantic souvenirs, at the same time that present-day Beirut is being transformed into a shiny new version of that past. When nothing appears to be missing or changed, mourning is no longer necessary, or even possible.

As the violent history of Beirut is transformed into a vision of beautiful amnesia, Hadjithomas and Joreige attempt to reclaim this lost territory through tourist postcards, the very images that work to produce this artificial history.[13] With this paradox in mind, we can now view *Wonder Beirut* as an intervention that seeks to restore a history of trauma and ruptures to a city in the process of being forcibly separated from its past. In this respect, memory and nostalgia are the artists' means as well as their subjects. Hadjithomas and Joreige counter nostalgia—a romantic sensibility manipulated by market and institutional forces—with critical attempts to resuscitate history before it is completely erased. ML

1  Joana Hadjithomas and Khalil Joreige, description of *Wonder Beirut*, on the artists' website at http://www.hadjithomasjoreige.com.
2  "On Translation," transcript of panel chaired by Stephen Wright, with speakers Tony Chakar, Joana Hadjithomas, Khalil Joreige and Rabih Mroué, in *Public Time: A Symposium*, ed. Suzanne Cotter (Oxford: Modern Art Oxford, 2006), 29.
3  Lambert-Beatty, "Make Believe," 54.
4  Ibid., 72.
5  Paul Virilio, *The Vision Machine* (London: British Film Institute; Bloomington: Indiana University Press, 1994), 3.
6  "*Trucage* exists only when there is deceit. We may agree to use this term when the spectator ascribes to the diegesis the totality of the visual elements furnished him." Christian Metz, "*Trucage* and the Film," *Critical Inquiry* 3:4 (Summer 1997): 667.
7  Ibid., 671.
8  Although *Wonder Beirut* is comprised of single photographs, they are conceptualized and presented in ways that intentionally evoke a cinematic sensibility. Indeed, the project can be seen as an effort to replicate or engineer the experience of cinema from still images. In the booklets that comprise *War Postcards*, for example, a temporal narrative is generated through the sequencing of still images that unfold accordion-style, not unlike a cinematic storyboard.
9  "On Translation," 29.
10  Saree Makdisi, "Beirut/*Beirut*," in *Tamáss: Contemporary Arab Representations*, ed. Catherine David (Rotterdam; Witte de With; Barcelona: Fundació Antoni Tàpies, 2002), 31. According to Makdisi, present-day Beirut is not just a shiny new version of past Beirut, but a much "improved" version that only gestures towards authenticity (ibid., 30).
11  Elizabeth Outka, *Consuming Traditions: Modernity, Modernism, and the Commodified Authentic* (Oxford: Oxford University Press, 2009), 8–9.
12  Susan Stewart, *On Longing: Narratives of the Miniature, the Gigantic, the Souvenir, the Collection* (Baltimore: John Hopkins University Press, 1984), 145.
13  Jalal Toufic, *Undeserving Lebanon* (n.p., Forthcoming Books, 2007), 95 n. 12, http://www.jalaltoufic.com/downloads.htm. Toufic's theories on catastrophe have gained currency among several prominent artists and filmmakers, including Hadjithomas, Joreige, and Ra'ad. According to Toufic, when a surpassing disaster takes place, the loss of culture goes beyond the superficial destruction of buildings and objects. What is actually lost, however, may only be perceptible upon its subsequent "resurrection"—through art, for instance. See also Toufic's recent book, *Withdrawal of Tradition Past a Surpassing Disaster* (n.p., Forthcoming Books, 2009), also available on his website.

Emre Hüner

**Juggernaut** 2009
Video, color with sound,
21:10 minutes

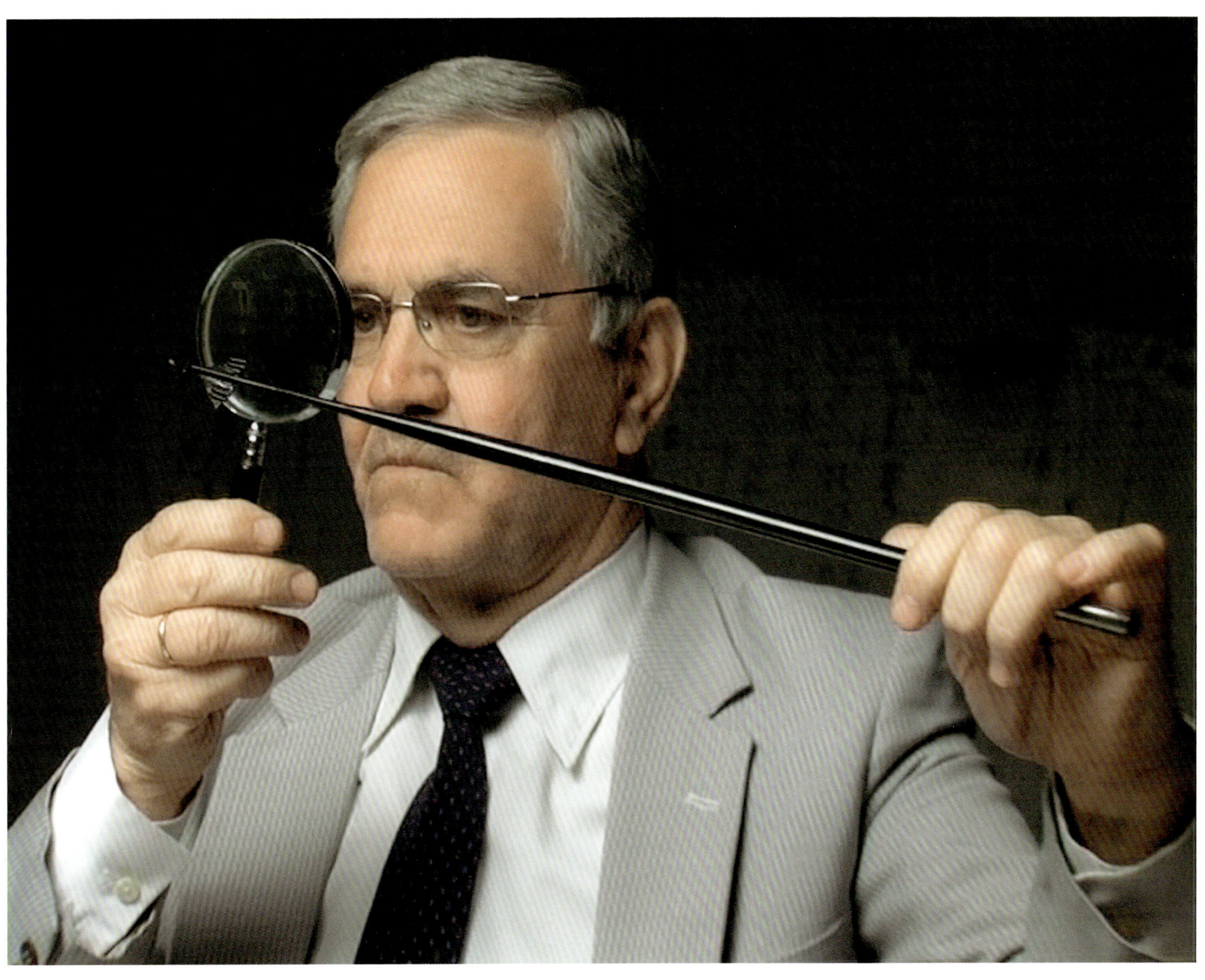

Still from *Juggernaut*

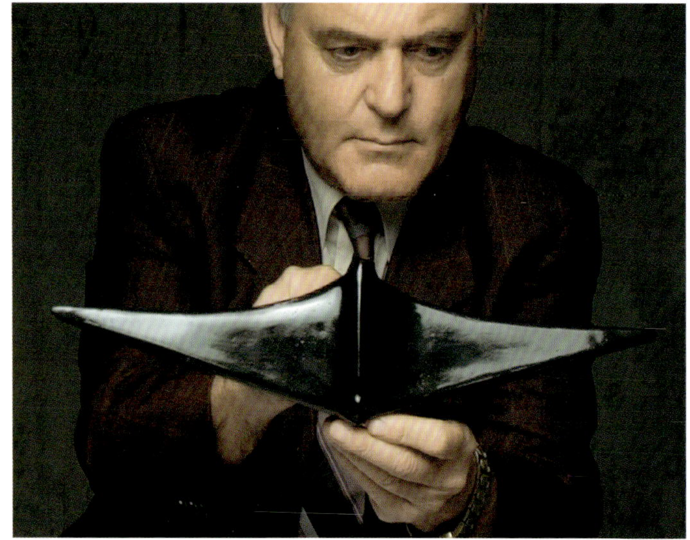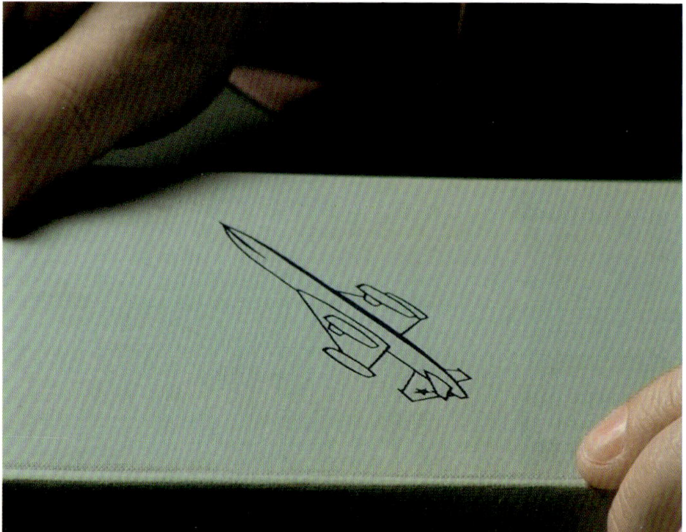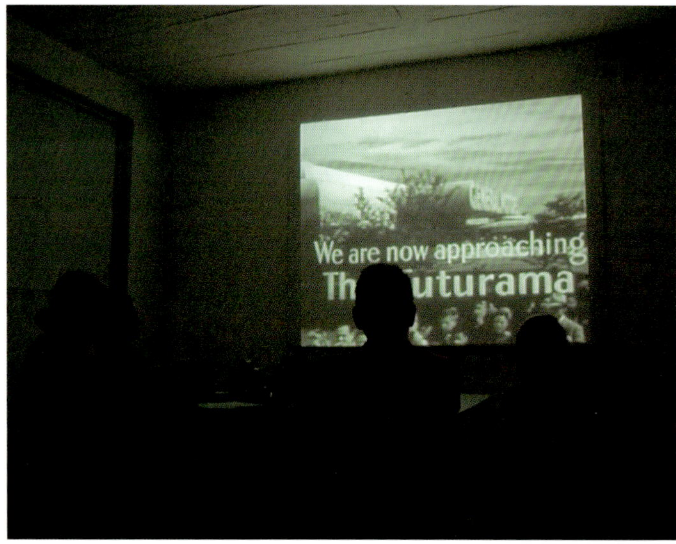

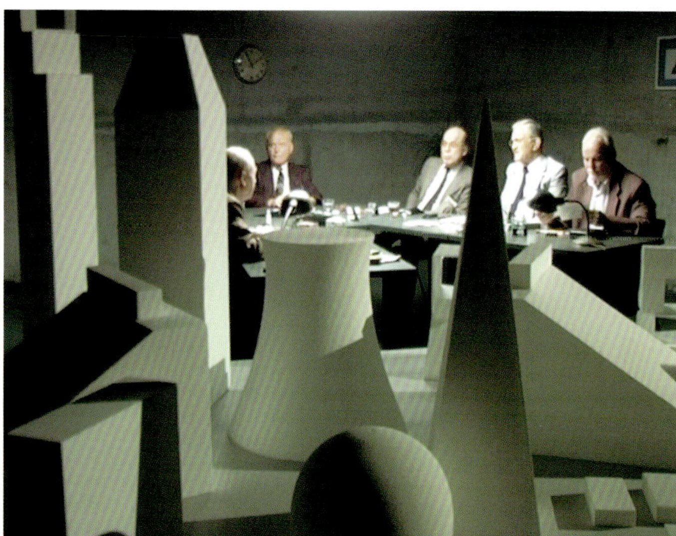

Stills from *Juggernaut*

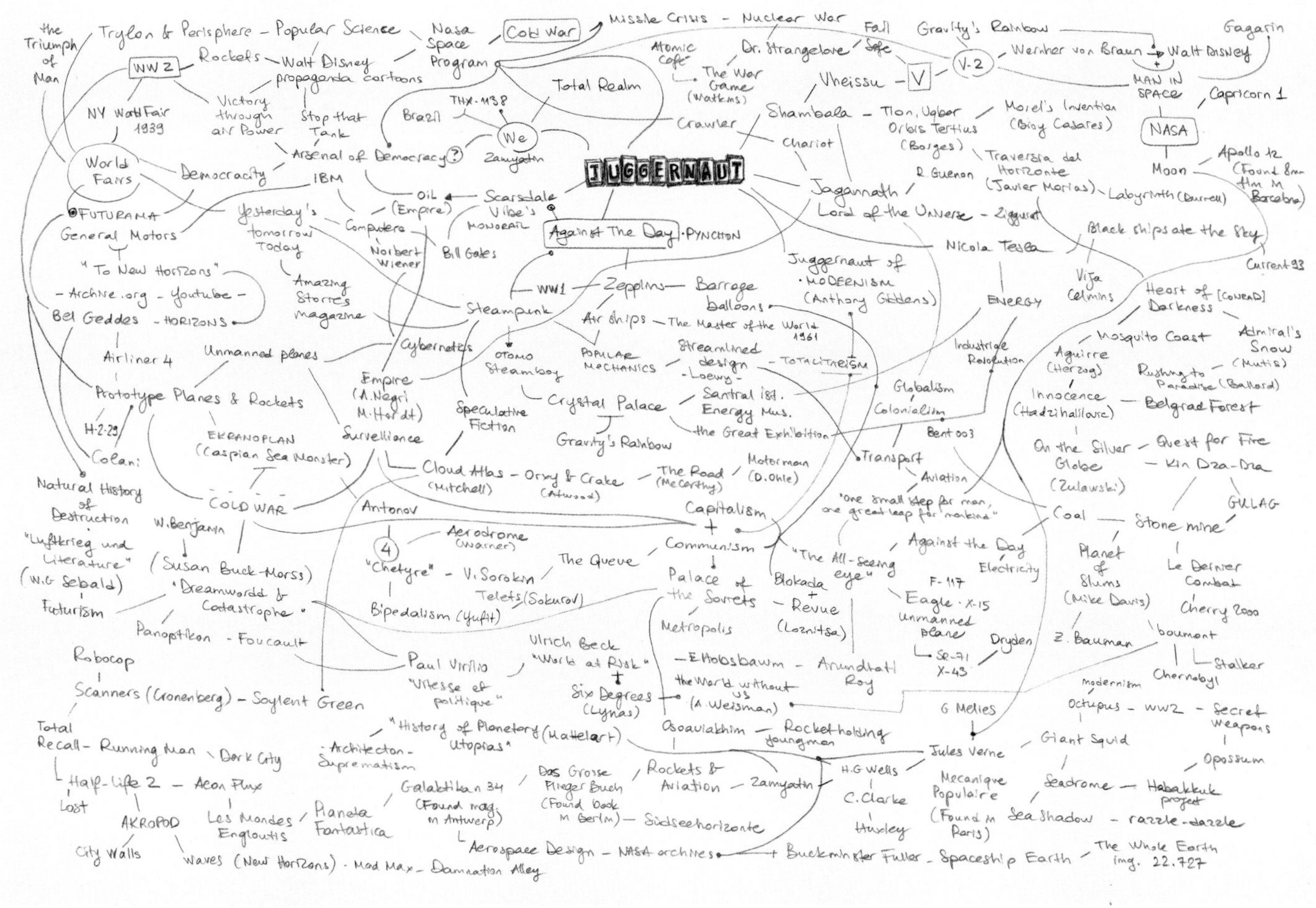

*Juggernaut Mindmap*, 2009. Pencil on paper, 50 × 34 cm (19 ¾ × 13 ½ in.) Courtesy of the artist and Rodeo Gallery, Istanbul

Emre Hüner's *Juggernaut* begins idyllically, if not optimistically. The video opens with a live-action sequence, based on archival images of Russian aviation clubs of the 1930s, in which young men encamped amongst forested ruins handle model rockets, search with binoculars, and wait, presumably for some airborne event. Their gear is immaculate and their mood hopeful.

Their anticipation, however, remains unanswered as the video cuts to another series of live-action sequences and then to a montage of archival footage. Scenes of late-middle-aged men examining handheld models of wing shapes jump to a mid-century cartoon of a space capsule and then to early footage shot from actual NASA space capsules. Hüner's video includes full-screen presentations of each clip as well as views of the men seated around a V-shaped table, watching the clips as projected filmstrips. The image of one such film reel, finished but still spinning, signals the conclusion of *Juggernaut*'s introductory passage. At this point, the soundtrack changes from jazzy to menacing, and the video's dreamlike progression takes on a nightmarish trajectory.

*Juggernaut* proceeds ominously, contrasting visions of aeronautical aspiration and invention with images of technology's violent application and destructive results. Simultaneously, Hüner mixes documentary and dramatic forms, suspending the narrative between fact and fiction. The video's next sequence is emblematic. Here, seven gentlemen — including those seen previously — converse excitedly (if not smugly) in the windowless viewing room. Hüner's camera pans across an adjacent table covered with architectural models, including the spire-like Trylon and ball-shaped Perisphere from the 1939–40 World's Fair in New York City. The view then cuts to animated and documentary footage of both structures, as seen in *To New Horizons* (1940), a filmic tour of General Motors' Futurama fair pavilion. "Come, let's travel into the future. What will we see?" intones the portentous voiceover. Hüner's video responds with hyperbolic portrayals of assembly-line world war from two Disney propaganda cartoons, *Stop that Tank!* (1942) and *Victory Through Air Power* (1943) — a parade of militarization that captivates at least one of the viewers. The spectacular montage asserts that the promises of flight, mass production, and mechanized life — if not the motivating ideals of modernity itself — have coalesced into a juggernaut.

Derived from the Sanskrit for "Lord of the Universe," the term *juggernaut* refers to an uncontrollable, destructive force and connotes inexorable violence, stampeding momentum, and collateral damage.[1] Sociologist Anthony Giddens recently employed the term to characterize the perpetual, profound, and erratic change of contemporary society.[2] Equally foreboding, Thomas Pynchon's 2006 novel *Against the Day* invokes the juggernaut as a personification of capitalist drive.[3] Hüner's *Juggernaut* similarly utilizes its name to convey ruinous social development. In deference to Giddens, the video presents the advances of modern, industrial civilization as double-edged; they are as likely to fulfill utopian ambition as to provoke global cataclysm. Hüner also counts Pynchon as an influence, and *Juggernaut*, like the novelist's writing, spins an allusive and cryptic but critical fiction. The video as a whole poses a series of questions: What is the driving force of this juggernaut of modernity? Who is directing it? And to what horizons is it taking us?

Rather than delivering decisive answers, the video depicts the acts of dreaming and investigating — ventures which, following Giddens, are themselves suspect. Hüner's gentlemen are likely culprits in modernity's crimes, but they are also potentially its forensic investigators. Diverse in appearance and accoutrements, they suggest various origins and occupations — bureaucrat, entrepreneur, scientist — while sharing an analytical investment in twentieth-century visions of the near future. These representations, and the video itself, however, take on an increasingly troubling tone. The young men in the forest reappear, with gliders instead of rockets; the video then shifts back to the bunker, where the gentlemen doodle, smoke, and ruminate listlessly. Finally, near the end of *Juggernaut*, a live-action sequence captures a ragtag group of men and women lingering despondently in an abandoned quarry.

Together, these three episodic narratives could be interpreted chronologically — as an evolution towards apocalypse, for instance — or they could be read synchronically, as a series of simultaneous yet different worlds. Hüner's archetypical characterizations and frequent crosscutting foster a sense of temporal ambiguity. Jumping between historical pictures, documents of the future-past, and contemporary images, the video disrupts the viewer's attempt to place its narratives precisely within the timeline of the twentieth century, or indeed in any linear story line. One cannot determine whether the gentlemen, isolated in their chamber of representations, are reflecting on past events, witnessing events as they unfold, or fantasizing about the shape of things to come. Despite the pretense of scientific rationality—one of *Juggernaut*'s ostensible subjects—the video subsumes the sequential thinking of cause and effect to a more rhizomic, if not chaotic logic of association and conglomeration.[4]

*Juggernaut* can likewise be understood as a sort of cabinet of curiosity, a structure Hüner has explored previously. In his 2005 animation *Panoptikon*, for instance, the artist assembled an inventory of worldly objects, including nautical gadgets and anatomical parts, all drawn by hand. He then animated this *Encyclopédie*-like archive, creating a fantastical world of biological and technological conflict that evokes the Ottoman miniatures of his Turkish heritage. *Juggernaut*'s own *wunderkammer* is distinctly videographic, and it exclusively displays artifacts of modernity. Besides representations of experimental aircraft (the Russian Ekranoplan, the American XB-70 Valkyrie, a flying wing plane), the video's protagonists consider dazzle camouflage from World War I, the East German propagandist textbook *Weltall Erde Mensch* (Universe, Earth, Man), and even octopuses. In a cartoon, the sea creature appears as a globe-smothering monster, a personification of imperialism, while in a live-action scene, it is reduced to a biological specimen, the dead carcass of modernity picked over by one of Hüner's analysts.

The persistent looking, watching, and probing in *Juggernaut* imitate the concept of "reflexive modernization" espoused by Giddens and fellow sociologist Ulrich Beck.[5] In this phase in the development of modern society, institutions recognize and confront the failure of their systems of rationality. Beck's *Risk Society*, in particular, considers the global hazards spawned by our imperfect mastery of technology, which is only compounded by our attempts to compensate for them.[6] Hüner's video reiterates the fallibility of progress: Dirigibles appear as both urban transport and city bombers, and the skyward-looking promise of the depicted futures is contrasted with views of a neglected earth. By the same token, martial invention, through resourceful adaptation, can lead to humane achievement, as in the case of the V-2 rocket, developed in Nazi Germany but later adapted to the Saturn V superbooster.

Likewise, the relationship of Hüner's gentlemen (and *Juggernaut*'s viewers) to their objects of study is not quite cynical. Their conclusions and judgments might invariably instigate negative effects, but they might also engender positive futures and reformative solutions. As a result, *Juggernaut*'s final comment, appropriated from *To New Horizons*, has a realist as well as ironic tone: "And so we see…A world with a future in which all of us are tremendously interested. Because that is where we are going to spend the rest of our lives. In a future which can be whatever we propose to make it." KM

1  The Hindi *Jagganāth* is a name for the Hindu deity Krishna, an avatar of Vishnu, the sustainer of the universe. The negative connotations of the English version *juggernaut* originate in the misapprehensions of European colonials, who observed the idol of Jagganath parading in an immense cart during the annual Rath Yatra festival in Puri, India. Ever since Westerners witnessed chariot wheels crushing celebrants—whether accidentally or willfully—*juggernaut* has denoted an immense object on an unwavering path of destruction.

2  The experience of living in late modernity, according to Giddens, feels like riding a runaway, unsteerable juggernaut—charging towards uncertain futures, imperiled by the risks of technology, the blind spots of specialized knowledge, and the unpredictability of countermeasures. See Anthony Giddens, *Modernity and Self-Identity* (Cambridge: Polity Press, 1991), 27–32, and *The Consequences of Modernity* (Stanford, Calif.: Stanford University Press, 1990), 151–54.
3  In a sardonic comment on the inequities of state-sponsored

plutocracy, Pynchon christens the diabolical mining magnate Scarsdale Vibe's personal train "The Juggernaut." Moreover, Lew Basnight, a "Psychical Detective" on the trail of "anarchistic scum," realizes that he's been playing the wrong side, but concedes that a switch to anarchy "might be too late, already past the point where anybody stood a chance against the juggernaut that had rolled down on the country and flat stolen it." Thomas Pynchon, *Against the Day* (New York: Penguin Press, 2006), 31, 43, 47, 181.

4  See Hüner's "mindmap" for the video, reproduced in this catalogue.
5  See Giddens, *Modernity and Self-Identity* and *Consequences of Modernity*; Ulrich Beck, *Risk Society: Towards a New Modernity*, trans. Mark Ritter (London: Sage Publications, 1992); and Beck, Giddens, and Scott Lash, *Reflexive Modernization* (Stanford, Calif.: Stanford University Press, 1994).
6  Beck et al., *Reflexive Modernization*, vii.

Matthew Day Jackson

**August 6th, 1945** 2010
Burnt wood and lead,
2.44 × 3.14 m (8 × 10 ft.)

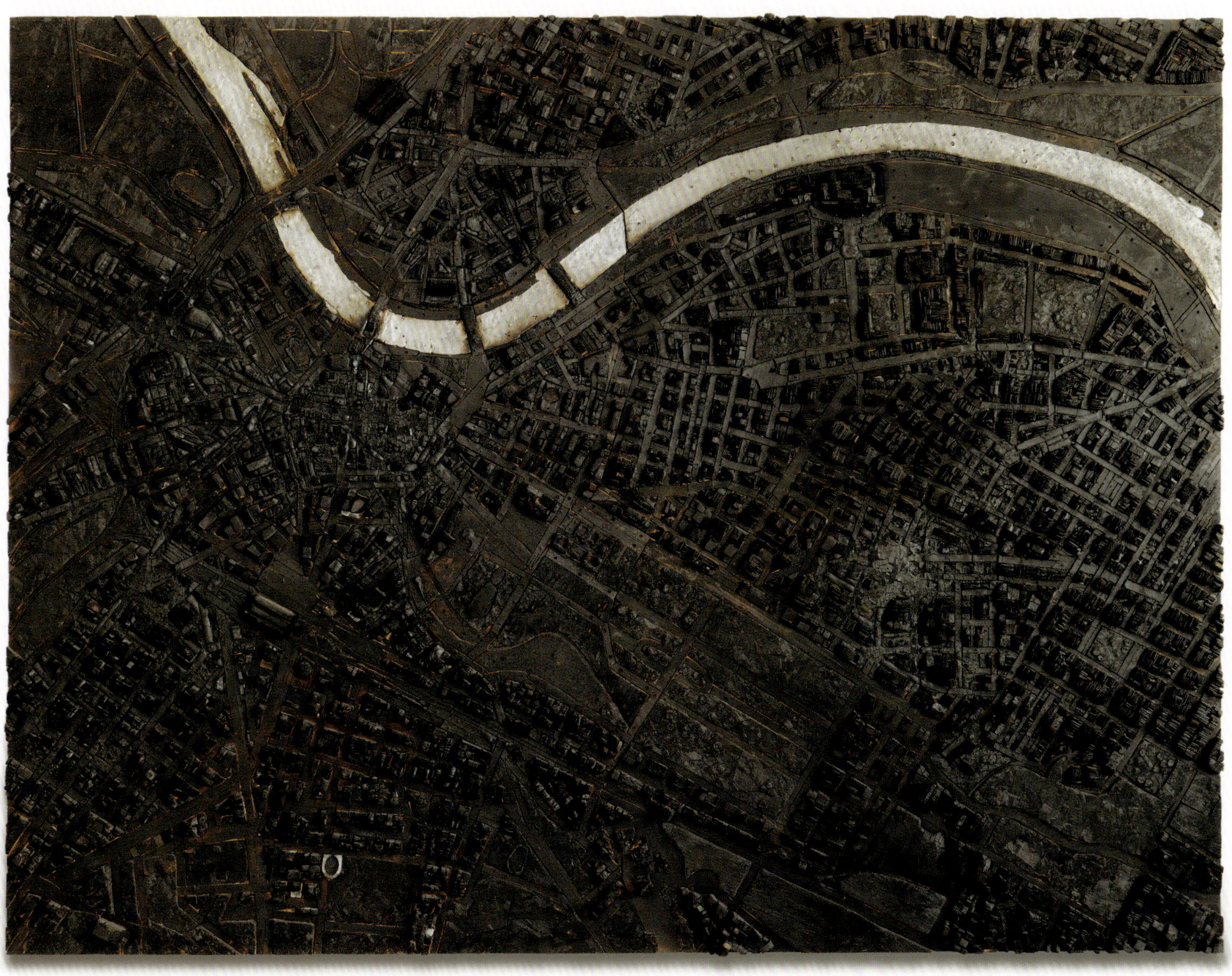

It is common to say that Matthew Day Jackson's work ranges widely over numerous subjects, that it is interdisciplinary in spirit, and that it reflects the artist's polymathic sensibility. All this is true, but it is equally true that a single (and singular) topic animates a great deal of Jackson's work. Bill Arning alluded to it when he described the artist's sculptures, videos, installations, and performances as investigations into the "positive and negative applications of science and technology."[1] Jackson's meta-subject, in other words, is contradiction, specifically the contradictions that animate human progress and that human progress generates in turn. Theodor W. Adorno and Max Horkheimer explored similar terrain in their 1944 text *Dialectic of Enlightenment*, but Walter Benjamin summarized it best when he wrote in 1940; "There is no document of civilization that is not simultaneously a document of barbarism."[2]

*August 6th, 1945* (2010) belongs to a series of works begun in 2008 when Jackson was an artist-in-residence at the MIT List Visual Arts Center in Cambridge, Massachusetts. The works share titles, media, and points of view. Each is comprised of melted lead and pieces of scorched wood, arranged to suggest the burnt remnants of a flattened city as seen from above. The aerial perspective is a fascinating object lesson in the visuality of power and knowledge, and Jackson uses it to considerable effect. Here, the viewer has no choice but to identify with a synoptic, possessive point of view, one that seeks to secure its referent and subject it to the full arsenal of human science. Aerial perspective — associated with entities as diverse as astronauts, cartographers, airplanes, and surveillance satellites — abhors the particular and admits to no complexity; abstraction, systematization, and generalization are its idiom.[3]

If the point of view established in *August 6th, 1945* belongs to any one person, though, it is to Paul Tibbets, the bomber pilot who captained the Enola Gay to Hiroshima, Japan, in the first week of August, 1945. As we might expect, one of the assemblages — but only one — represents Hiroshima. The others depict Washington, D.C., and Dresden, Germany (*Nobody's Property* features the latter). The work's title, therefore, generates as much confusion as it does comprehension. It places us squarely in the final months of World War II, but it leaves many questions unanswered. After all, only Hiroshima suffered

on August 6, 1945 (Nagasaki was targeted three days later, on August 9). The bombing of Dresden, a joint effort by the British and American air forces, took place February 13–15, 1945.[4] Because World War II was fought almost exclusively on foreign soil, moreover, American cities were mostly spared the destruction suffered by their Japanese, British, and European counterparts. Jackson nonetheless includes Washington, D.C., in his gallery, just as he dates the Dresden firestorm to a moment seven months later. Why the "mistake"? In all likelihood, August 6, 1945 is the artist's ur-date: the day some of the twentieth century's most important scientific and technological advances were wasted on weapons.[5]

This helps explain the title, but what of the choice of cities, and why the United States capital specifically? Jackson's decision implicates the American government in the havoc it wreaked upon other countries, but his is not merely an accusation. If anything, the artist wants to say that destruction disregards borders, that devastation is measured by more than just rubble, that violence has consequences for victims and perpetrators alike. Japanese anguish, he implies, is America's too: when it detonated "Little Boy," the United States won the war (a war some say it was already winning), but lost its moral compass. Even more importantly, the attack on Japan triggered a series of events — the arms race, weapons testing, uranium mining — that exposed the American population and landscape to both the reality and specter of nuclear catastrophe.[6]

The *August 6th, 1945* series is haunting and powerful. Even though it reflects Jackson's longstanding interests in land and landscape, as well as the relationship between nature and human beings, it differs considerably from his previous work. In pieces such as *Lean-to* (2007), for instance, a kind of shelter-*cum*-sculpture, and *The Lower 48* (2006), a series of forty-eight photographs representing anthropomorphic rock formations in each of the contiguous states, our affinity with land is brought to the fore.[7] Here, Jackson equates land with home: land as home to humanity in general (its collective birthright, its breadbasket) and land as home to Jackson in particular (the artist often utilizes material from his family's homestead).[8] That said, the artist troubles our identification with land as much as he facilitates it. Even in these earlier works, identification often resembles occupation and narcissistic projection, rather than mythopoetic communion.[9] The sites where such attachments are staged, moreover, always bear traces of social conflict and territorial disputes. Take *Undead Landscapes* (2007), consisting of thirty-three photographs, each representing the location of a battle or injustice whose significance Jackson describes in the accompanying captions. Before snapping the photographs, the artist added a wood sculpture of his own raised fist to the scenes. Associated with social justice movements of the 1960s and 1970s, the raised fist connotes both solidarity and contestation.

There is a long way to travel, though, between *Lean-to* and *August 6th, 1945*. While the former more or less avows our felicitous identification with nature, the latter irrevocably scrambles it. Instead of recognition, Jackson orchestrates alienation, and instead of reciprocity, he engineers domination. Of course, the contradictory, sometimes antagonistic, sometimes salutary relationship between nature and human beings is a function of Jackson's larger concern: the dialectic of progress and regression. The artist's approach to this dialectic is itself dialectical. *August 6th, 1945* certainly prioritizes violence and destruction, but other works made during and after his residency at MIT privilege hope and redemption. This is the case with a piece that serves as the unofficial pendant to *August 6th, 1945*: *Little Boy and Fat Man* (2009), a fifteen-minute video shot in the Wright Brothers' wind tunnel in Cambridge. Here, models of the nuclear bombs that destroyed Hiroshima and Nagasaki appear suspended in both time and space. They fall, but never land, much as Zeno's arrow only approaches, but never reaches, its target.[10] KB

1  Bill Arning, ed., *Matthew Day Jackson: The Immeasurable Distance* (Cambridge, Mass.: MIT List Visual Arts Center; Houston, Tex.: Contemporary Arts Museum Houston, 2010), 13. The dialectic between creation and destruction was especially palpable in Jackson's 2007 exhibition, *Paradise Now!*, organized by Annette DiMeo Carlozzi at the Blanton Museum of Art at the University of Texas at Austin. A brochure about this exhibition is forthcoming.
2  Walter Benjamin, "Theses on the Philosophy of History," in *Illuminations*, 256; Max Horkheimer and Theodor W. Adorno, *Dialectic of Enlightenment*, trans. John Cumming (New York: Continuum, 1994). As Adorno and Horkheimer write in the introduction to *Dialectic of Enlightenment*, we "set ourselves nothing less than the discovery of why mankind, instead of entering into a truly human condition, is sinking into a new kind of barbarism" (ibid., xi). The answer, we learn, is due not only to the rise of the culture industry and the spread of Fascism and anti-Semitism. Rather, if human beings regress with every act of progress, it is because of contradictions immanent to progress itself. These contradictions are precisely what Adorno and Horkheimer mean by the phrase "dialectic of Enlightenment." According to them, Enlightenment thinking sows the seeds of its own destruction. Devoted wholly to generalization, systematization, and abstraction, it admits to no deviation or particularity, substituting myth for truth. Directed towards the instrumentalization of nature and man, it promises freedom but delivers domination. This kind of mechanical, unreflexive thinking, which perverts the founding principles of the Enlightenment, found its ally in both totalitarianism and industrial capitalism. Under the conditions of Enlightenment, where "madness" derives from the same source as "rationality," rationality becomes a form of madness (205).

3  It is no accident that the aerial point of view plays such a central role in Jackson's *August 6th, 1945* series. Much of his research at MIT focused on the development of nuclear technology and the 1969 Apollo 11 space mission, both of which utilize, facilitate, and suggest just such a perspective.
4  For information about the Dresden bombing and the city's general reluctance to confront the tragedy of this event as well as its role in World War II, see George Packer, "Embers," *New Yorker*, Feb. 1, 2010.
5  Speaking of the parallels between the paranoiac anti-Semite and the positivist thinker, Adorno and Horkheimer write that the paranoiac's "discernment is used up in the circle drawn by the fixed idea, just as human ingenuity is liquidated in the area determined for it by technical civilization." *Dialectic of Enlightenment*, 195.
6  This burden was not (nor is it) shared equally among America's peoples and regions. Along with soldiers, ranchers, and Native Americans, the West has suffered the brunt of nuclear testing and uranium mining.
7  For *The Lower 48*, Jackson traveled across the country for several months, locating and documenting geological formations with distinctly human characteristics.
8  Pillars from Jackson's Nebraska homestead appear in *Cannon (Based on first wheeled vehicle to cross the continental divide, 1872)* (2006) as well as in *Lean-to* (2007), which also includes a wall Jackson salvaged from a house in Austin, Texas.
9  Jackson speaks to this point in a 2007 interview with Ingrid Spencer, "The Voice of the Artist," *Articulate: The Blanton Museum of Art Magazine* (Winter 2007): 11.
10  Tom Morton would seem to have this work in mind when he mentions Zeno's paradox in "Flat Maps: Six Notes on Matthew Day Jackson's *The Immeasurable Distance*," in Arning, *Immeasurable Distance*, 45.

Lucy Raven

China Town  2009
Photographic animation,
color with sound, 51:30 minutes

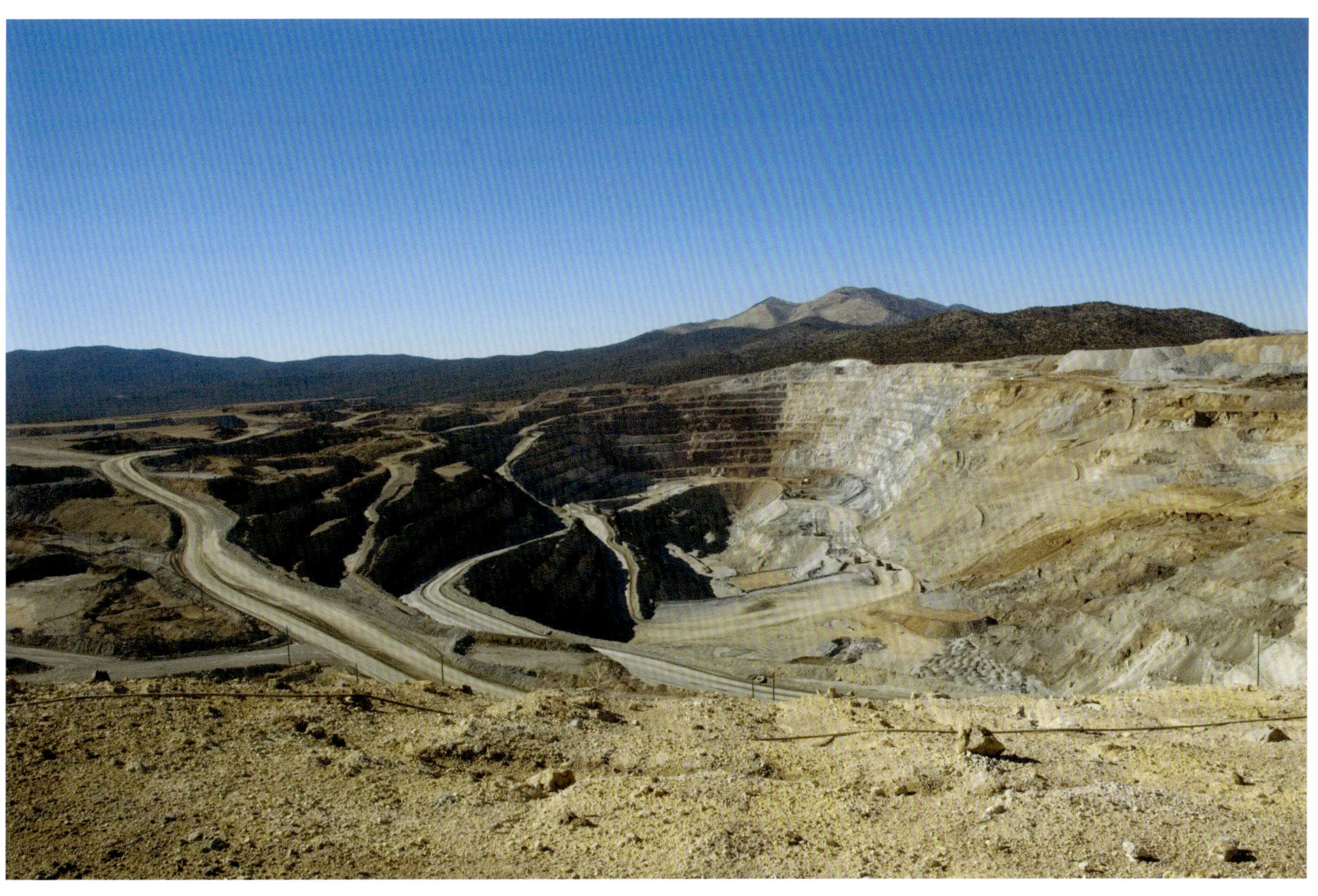

Still from China Town

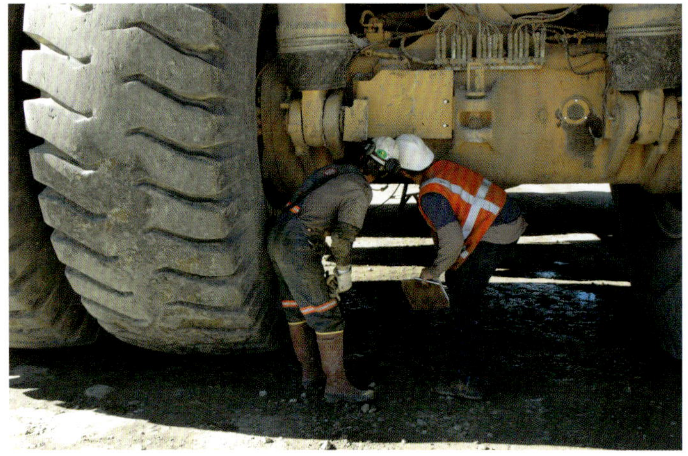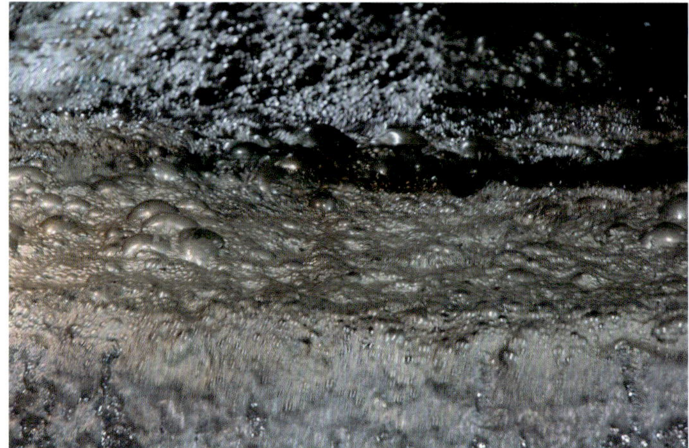

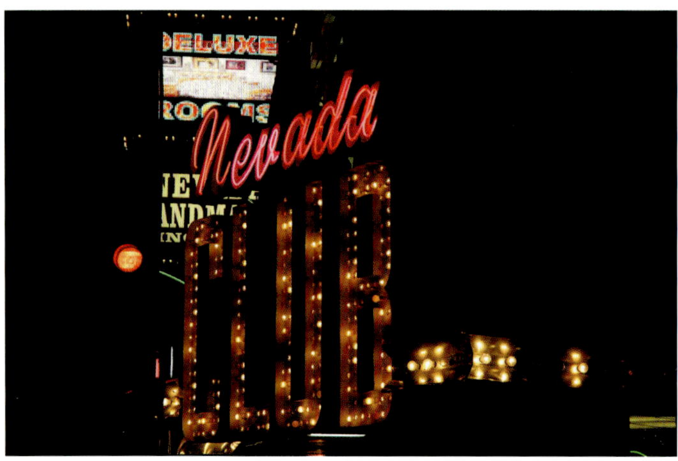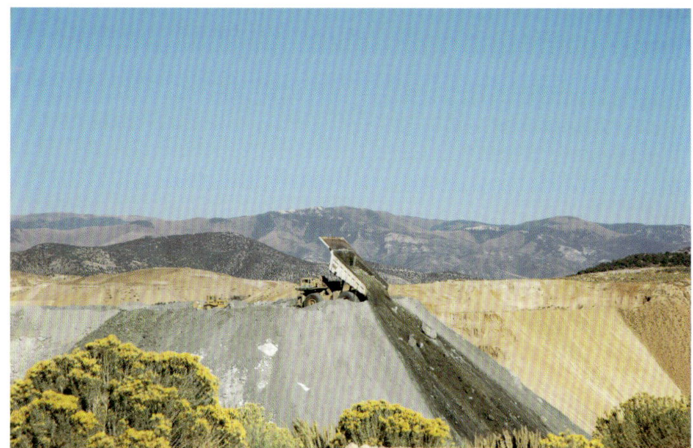

Stills from *China Town*

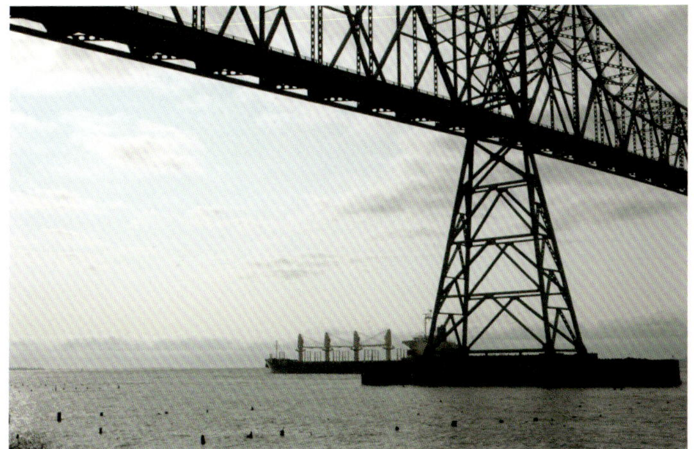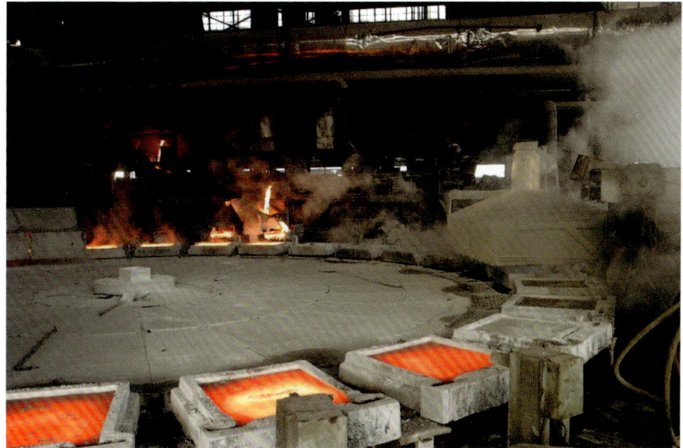

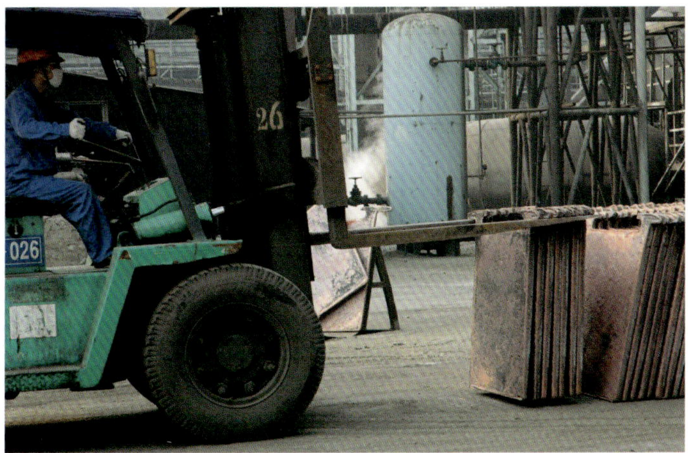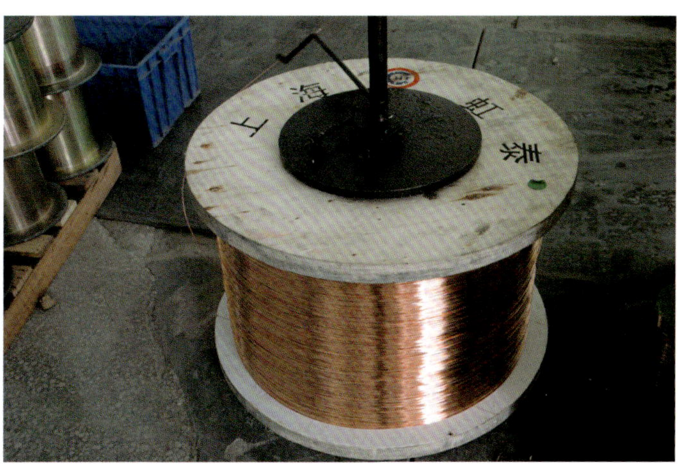

Stills from *China Town*

In the last ten minutes of Lucy Raven's *China Town* (2009), the artist's camera attends a video presentation at the information center of the Three Gorges Dam, in Sandouping, Hubei, China. Through Raven's lens, we observe a round theatre encircled by a single panoramic screen and occupied by standing, craning visitors. A 360-degree video projection spins the tale of the Three Gorges, from the formation of the Himalaya forty million years ago to the valley's status as home to the world's largest public works project and electricity-generating plant. Footage of demolition and dump trucks cuts to cockpit views of flights over the Yangtze River, while a heroic soundtrack exalts the Three Gorges as the "blossom of the Changjiang civilization."

The sequence above mirrors the approach of *China Town* itself. Like the video in Sandouping, Raven's animation appropriates the guise of filmic nonfiction, offers a wide view of history, and depicts land as an economic resource. In contrast to the seamless spectacle and authoritative voice of the nationalist-tourist video, however, Raven's exposé is speculative. *China Town* is discontinuous at both the narrative and formal levels. The story it recounts would seem to be straightforward — the global processing of copper ore into a ductile transmitter of electricity — but Raven allows it to hop sideways and skip forward. The camera, too, stutters and stammers, visibly jostling and jerking from frame to frame. A tale about connectivity, Raven's account is decisively disjointed, dodging streamlined and idealized views to assess the particulars of two systems: the consumption of land and its representation.

*China Town* opens with views of Ruth, Nevada (population 512) at dawn and the "silence" of buzzing power lines. It ends fifty minutes later with scenes of a room-sized, three-dimensional model of electrified Beijing. In between, the animation tracks an alchemical course of raw material transformed into energy and the consequent expenditures and waste. We see detonations and lab tests, digging, crushing, and trucking; we hear conversations, hydraulic pumps, and reverse drive signals. We follow the ore on conveyor belt, truck, and train from Nevada to a ship at the Port of Vancouver in Washington State. At just over halfway through the film, we arrive in China, where more cranes, boats, and trucks lead to the smelters of the Jinlong Copper Company, Limited. Here cathodes are refined and wire spun, presumably for use in the immense generators at the Three Gorges Dam.

Along the way, the narrative jumps to the ostensible next step in the manufacturing process, while the trip detours to the slot machines of Hotel Nevada, a living room in Ruth, and an earthmover mechanic. Raven's camera frames a peripheral view: neighborhoods, third shifts, historic photographs, and models of the future. When the copper is in transit, the camera turns to the adjacent landscape. Likewise, perspective changes regularly, meandering to a distant panorama, a passenger-seat point of view, or the close look of a microscope. In this accumulation of particle-like images and sounds, there is neither narration nor subtitles to orient the viewer, just the consistent, human-scaled but impersonal lens — a tour without a guide.

*China Town* can be alternatively described as a travelogue, a documentary, or an industrial film, but it stretches the definition of each, in particular the overarching idea of film itself. *China Town* is composed entirely of still shots, over 7000 digital photographs taken by the artist with a single-lens reflex (SLR) camera over the course of almost three years during multiple trips to Nevada, Washington, and China. Each trip yielded a batch of raw images, which were then edited together to create animated sequences with individual cadences. The result is something akin to a rapid-fire slide presentation or a decelerated filmstrip; events and places are sifted instead of streamed. Sound, also collected on site, is paired with the appropriate image, but the real-time continuity is only an illusion, and a fragile one at that. The subtle inconsistencies between what we hear and see further the ambiguity of the largely ambient soundtrack, which inherently manifests an indeterminate relationship to its source. These discrepancies between sound and sight signal a gap in experience. In this respect, *China Town* builds upon a genealogy of filmmaking, including the works of Chris Marker and Alexander Kluge, which utilize montage to produce and disrupt narrative simultaneously. Kluge's theory of montage, in particular, provides an instructive model. By composing a film from a variety of visual and sound elements, and emphasizing the editing cuts between them, Kluge arouses the spectator to activate his or her imagination in the construction of the film's meaning.[1]

As a collection of impressions, *China Town* also continues the spirit of Robert Smithson's itinerant essays, in particular "The Crystal Land" (1966), "A Tour of the Monuments of Passaic, New Jersey" (1967), and "The Spiral Jetty" (1972). Both Raven and Smithson scout out trails marked by the geologic and the industrial, and both explore the contradictory logic of the spiral. For Smithson, the spiral suggests accretion and entropy; likewise, Raven's video traces a movement outward that doubles back on itself.[2] The open-pit mine in Ruth even forms a conic helix. As an electric rope shovel digs "toward China," displaced American land in the beds of haul trucks literally spirals outward on its way across the globe, only to return as processed materials and consumer goods. Raven's title also circles back: home to Chinese mine laborers in the 1880s, "China Town" now describes the town of Ruth and its American inhabitants.[3]

Smithson's spiral offers a model for Raven's epistemic concerns as well. Describing the phenomenological experience of his monumental artwork *Spiral Jetty*, Smithson writes: "Purity is put in jeopardy. I took my chances on a perilous path, along which my steps zigzagged, resembling a spiral lightning bolt."[4] According to John Coplans, Smithson ensured just such an encounter with *Spiral Jetty* when he "ripped up the boulders so that the pathway couldn't be negotiated smoothly."[5] Raven's animation evinces a similar zigzag across the landscape. Her montage, in its frame-to-frame twitching and narrative digressions, disrupts any experience of sublimity. This effect is exacerbated by the images themselves, which are close-up views and mundane perspectives rather than grand, scenic panoramas. Accordingly, *China Town* disallows the passive reception of time and space. Locomotion across the land and through its images becomes labored; progress requires an active piecing together on the part of the viewer. *China Town*, considered on the global scale that it depicts, similarly portrays the supposed miracle of economic development as an uneven series of specialized efforts, zoned places and discrete histories; any appearance of uniform development or shared destiny is revealed to be a fabrication. KM

1  See Michelle Langford, "Alexander Kluge," in "Great Directors: A Critical Database," *Senses of Cinema*, http://archive.sensesof cinema.com/contents/directors/03/ kluge.html, and Stuart Lieberman, "Why Kluge?" *October* 46 (Autumn 1988): 5–22.
2  See Robert Smithson, "The Spiral Jetty" (1972), in *Smithson: Collected Writings*, 143–53, and Jennifer L. Roberts, "The Taste of Time: Salt and the *Spiral Jetty*," in Tsai, *Robert Smithson*, 96–103. Roberts relates *Spiral Jetty* to the artist's conception of time as a crystalline growth, cumulative and sedimentary. In his essay, Smithson describes the experience of *Spiral Jetty* as descending to a "surd state" and the film he made about the earthwork as "a spiral made up of frames" ("Spiral Jetty," 147, 148).
3  Roberts also considers the relationship of *Spiral Jetty* to the nearby Golden Spike National Historic Site, which marks the site of the completion of the First Transcontinental Railroad in 1869. The construction of the railroad's western leg by the Central Pacific Railroad relied heavily on immigrant Chinese labor, which in turn, also produced America's earliest Chinatowns. Roberts, "Taste of Time," 98–99.
4  Smithson, "Spiral Jetty," 147–48.
5  John Coplans, "Robert Smithson: The 'Amarillo Ramp,'" *Artforum* 12:8 (Apr. 1974): 42.

# Santiago Sierra

**Submission (formerly Word of Fire)**  October 2006/March 2007
Documentation of an action, Anapra, Ciudad Juárez, Chihuahua, Mexico
Two-channel digital slide projection, black and white, silent,
1:20 minutes (channel one), 78:20 minutes (channel two), looped

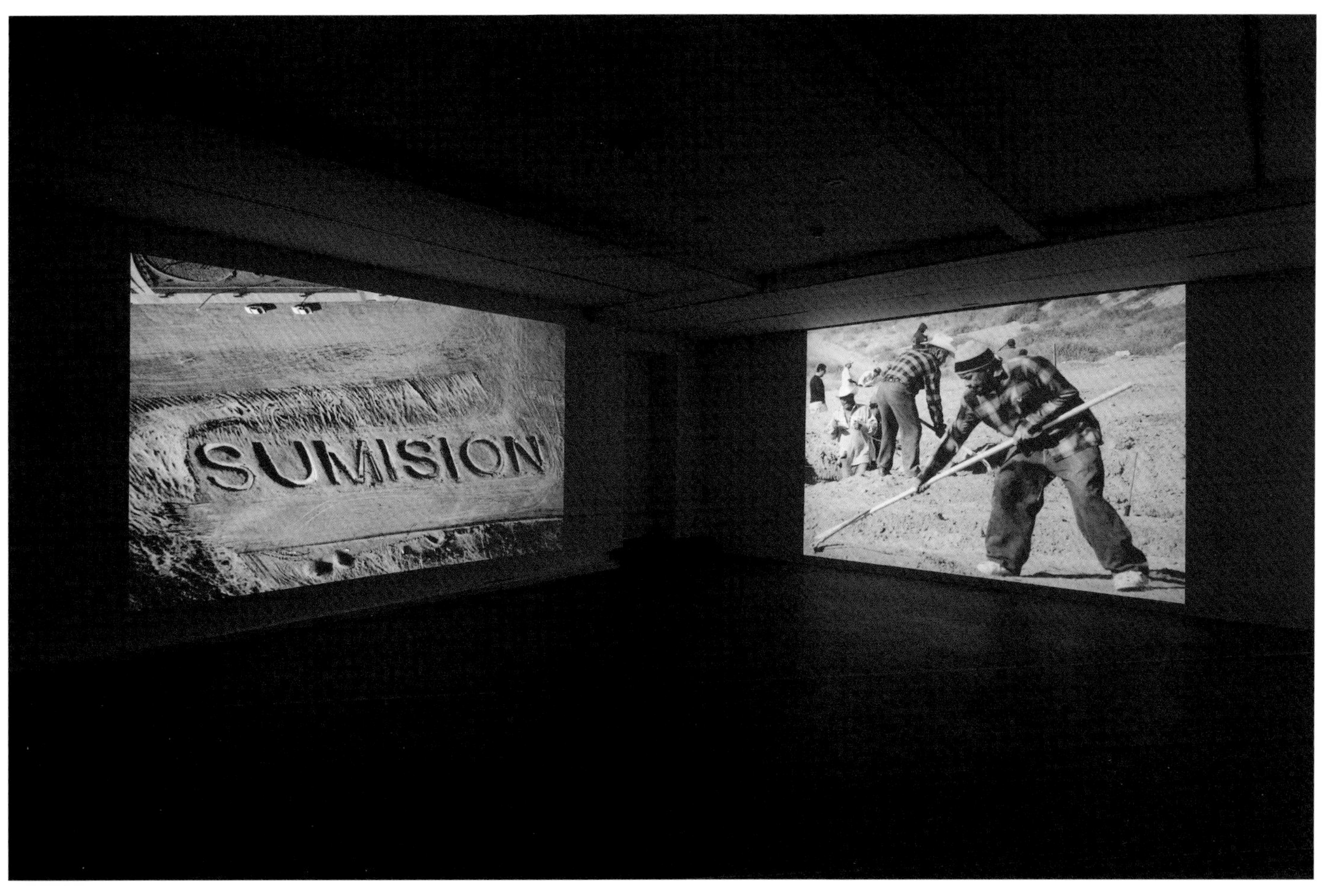

Installation view of *Submission*

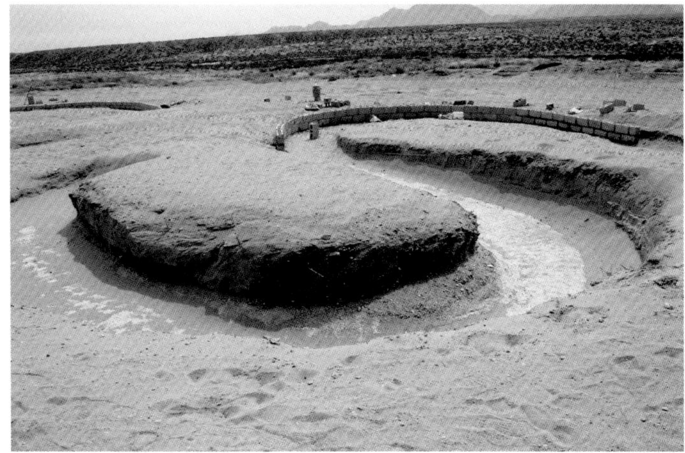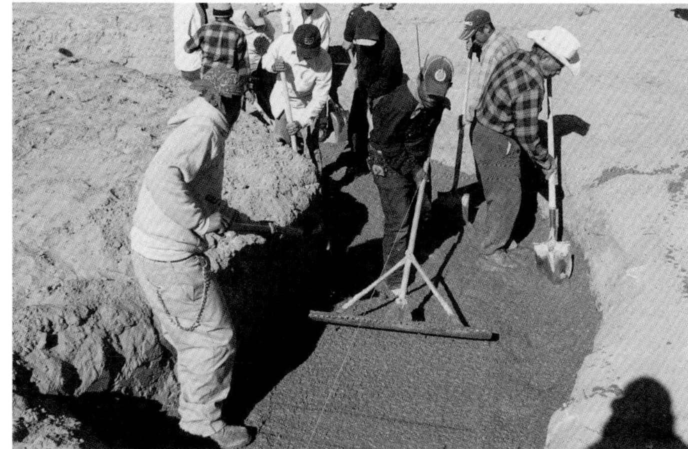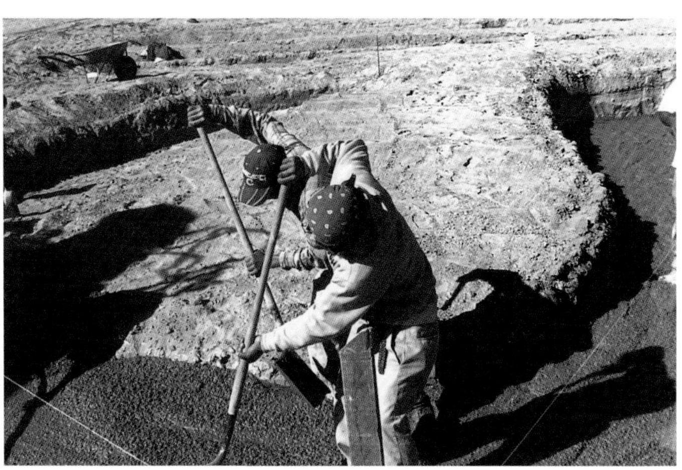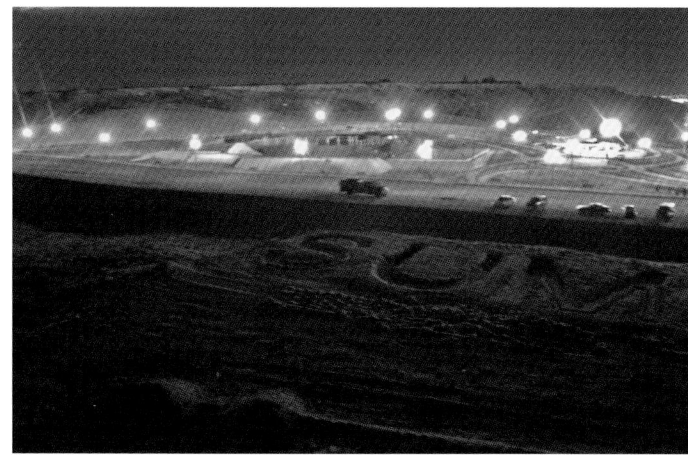

Slides from *Submission*

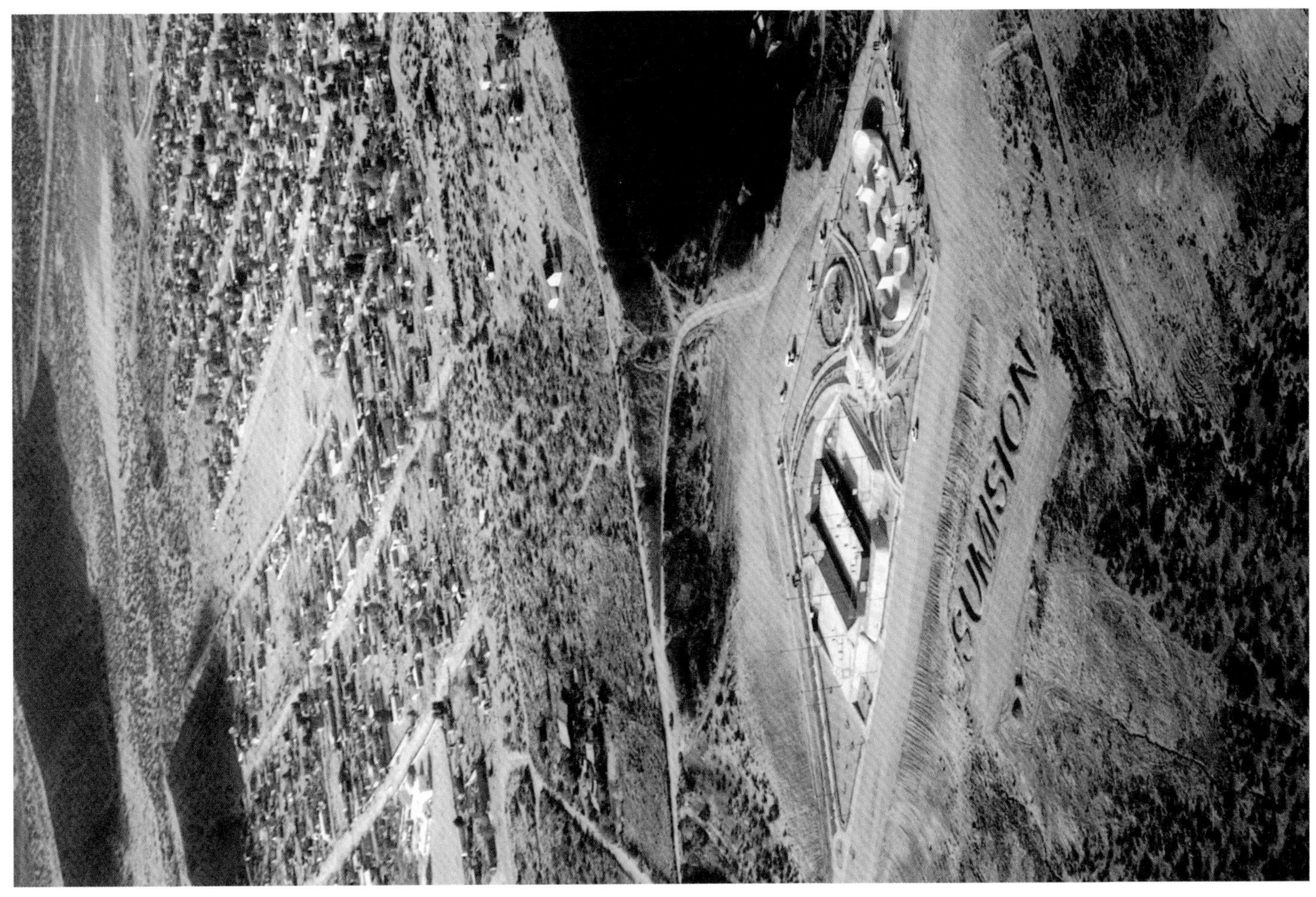



Slide from *Submission*

In 2006, Proyecto Juárez, an independent arts initiative based in Ciudad Juárez, Mexico, commissioned a number of site-specific projects near the United States-Mexico border. Santiago Sierra's *Word of Fire* was to be the first project developed for the series. The original proposal called for the word *sumisión* (Spanish for submission) to be engraved in letters nearly fifteen meters (fifty feet) high into a desert plot just outside the impoverished settlement of Anapra. Each of the letters was to be lined with concrete, filled with a gasoline mixture, and set on fire, at which point the flaming word would be recorded and broadcast over the Internet to viewers worldwide. The project was never realized as planned, however, because local authorities intervened before the word was ignited, citing a questionable concern for the work's environmental impact.[1] The documentation of this canceled project thus became the material for Sierra's later installation, titled *Submission (formerly Word of Fire)*.

The strong reactions garnered by Sierra's work are not surprising, given the intensity of his provocations. Sierra makes extremely difficult art. Many of his projects involve day laborers performing menial, stressful, and even humiliating tasks for deliberately meager pay. In the year 2000, for instance, Sierra paid men in Cuba to masturbate in front of a video camera, prostitutes in Spain to have a line tattooed across their backs, and two heroin addicts in Puerto Rico to have a ten-inch line shaved into their heads. In such works, Sierra brings into galleries and museums the otherwise invisible experience of (often) exploitative labor practices. In the process, the very act of looking at art becomes implicated in the exercise of economic power, and Sierra's audience is rendered guilty and uncomfortable.

Given the artist's direct engagement with issues of power and remuneration, one cannot easily discuss his work without mentioning the writing of Karl Marx, particularly his theory of labor value. According to Marx's formulation, labor under capitalism is assigned an abstract exchange value, and it is in part through this abstraction that the products of labor become alienated from the workers who make them.[2] Sierra's artwork mimes this abstraction, turning the concrete labor of his hired workers into art objects, while simultaneously placing those laborers (sometimes physically, other times in representation) in the spaces where his art is consumed. This engagement with

capitalism's quantification and instrumentalization of the time and bodies of workers tends to dominate readings of Sierra's work, and although it is central to his project, it is not the only process he investigates. Beyond remuneration and labor, for instance, *Submission* deals more directly with issues of history and life on the political and cultural border.

What started as a burning word in the Mexican desert now exists as two soundless, black-and-white digital slideshows projected onto intersecting walls. One of the slideshows depicts the finished word *sumisión* as seen from a plane flying above the Mexican desert. The other, significantly longer than the first, offers a somewhat linear chronicle of the excavation of the letters. This second slideshow also includes images taken of and around Juárez — urban landscapes, industrial parks, and even local land art. Together, these projections present the viewer with an endlessly shifting, shattered account of a land intervention that was never fully realized. As with much of Sierra's work, looking is a complex task in *Submission*. His disruption of the position of viewership, however, is unique to this particular installation. Each slideshow offers a different set of rotating perspectives that, seen together, resist the location of a single, primary site of spectatorship. Unlike many of his other installations, in which the roles of worker and audience are clear, it is not immediately obvious who is supposed to read *sumisión* or to whom the word refers. Museum and galley patrons are certainly the audience for Sierra's slideshows, but the workers who carved the word, as well as the residents of Anapra, are the land intervention's most immediate audience.

In this border landscape, the word *submission* has numerous, shifting points of reference, and it is inextricably bound up with questions of local and transnational power relations. Sierra offers a way into this complex social and political situation through a single image from the longer slideshow. It depicts another Juárez land intervention visible from El Paso: "CD Juárez, La Biblia es la verdad. Leela" (Ciudad Juárez, The Bible is the truth. Read it) painted in huge letters on the side of a mountain. By siting his own work nearby, Sierra transforms this statement of Christian authority into a marker of historical submission, calling attention to the oppressive history of colonialism, the modern reality of international capitalism, and the savagery of power imbalance on the border. It was the Spanish settlers, after all, who brought both Christianity and exploitative labor conditions to the region, forcing local populations to dig holes in the desert in search of precious metals. For his part, Sierra, a Spanish immigrant, put local residents to work digging holes as well, and there are certainly parallels to be drawn between gold mining and art fabrication. But it cannot be ignored that Sierra's laborers excavated the same land that conceals the bodies of hundreds of raped and murdered women — "las muertas de Juárez," the victims of a gruesome series of crimes that remain largely unsolved. Many of these women worked in maquiladoras — the foreign-owned, poorly-regulated factories where products are assembled at low cost and returned to their countries of origin nearly tax-free. In many respects, therefore, *sumisión* was inscribed on this landscape long before Sierra staged his work.

Like many of his contemporaries, Sierra is concerned with the organization of human relationships — primarily social and economic ones — but he does not overtly criticize the current (and largely asymmetrical) state of those relationships, nor does he offer a space for new strategies of engagement or new forms of collectivity to emerge. As the artist has said, "I don't believe that I begin from a critical position.... I don't see myself giving a lesson to anyone."[3] In the end, Sierra's position may be more agonistic than critical; however, it is in this agonism that he is perhaps most radical. Indeed, the response to his work to date suggests he is operating at the very limits of art-making — whether they be the limits of what audiences and institutions are able to bear, or the limits of the kinds of effective political critiques artists are able to make.[4] CR

1 "Sierra Censored in Mexico," Artnet News, Mar. 30, 2007, http://www.artnet.com/magazineus/news/artnetnews/artnetnews 3–30–07.asp.
2 See Karl Marx, *Capital: A Critique of Political Economy*, vol. 1 (New York: Penguin Books, 1990), 131–37.
3 Fabio Cavallucci and Carlos Jiménez, eds. *Santiago Sierra* (Milan: Silvana Editoriale, 2005), 74.
4 For a more hopeful reading of Sierra's use of antagonism as radically democratic, see Claire Bishop, "Antagonism and Relational Aesthetics," *October* 110 (Fall 2004): 51–80. For more on Sierra, see *Santiago Sierra: 7 Trabajos/ 7 Works*; Cavallucci and Jiménez, *Santiago Sierra*; and Eckhard Schneider and Santiago Sierra, *Santiago Sierra: 300 Tons and Previous Works* (Cologne: Walther König, 2004).

# Exhibition Checklist

**Jennifer Allora** (b. 1974, Philadelphia)
**Guillermo Calzadilla** (b. 1972, Havana)
Based in San Juan, Puerto Rico
*Land Mark (Foot Prints)*, 2001–2
12 digital C-prints, each 46 × 60.5 cm
(18 ⅛ × 23 ⅞ in.), AP 1/3
Princeton University Art Museum; Museum
purchase, Fowler McCormick, Class of 1921,
Fund (2009-147 a–l)

**Francis Alÿs** (b. 1959, Antwerp)
Based in Mexico City
*The Green Line: Sometimes Doing Some-
thing Poetic Can Become Political and
Sometimes Doing Something Political Can
Become Poetic*, 2007
Video installation with various components
Dimensions variable
Collection of the Los Angeles County Museum
of Art; Purchased with funds provided by
The Bernard and Edith Lewin Collection
of Mexican Art Deaccession Fund and the
Michael and Dorothy Blankfort Bequest by
exchange. Modified exhibition copy authorized
by the Los Angeles County Museum of Art
Courtesy of the artist and David Zwirner
Gallery, New York.

**Yael Bartana** (b. 1970, Afula, Israel)
Based in Tel Aviv and Amsterdam
*Kings of the Hill*, 2003
Video, color with sound, 7:30 minutes
Courtesy of the artist and Annet Gelink
Gallery, Amsterdam, and Sommer
Contemporary Art, Tel Aviv

**Andrea Geyer** (b. 1971, Freiburg)
Based in Freiburg and New York City
*Spiral Lands/Chapter 1*, 2007
Four panels from an installation comprised
of nineteen fiber-based photographs and
text; brochure with footnotes; three panels,
each 70 × 170 cm (27 ½ × 68 in.), fourth panel
70 × 230 cm (27 ½ × 90 in.)

Princeton University Art Museum; Museum
purchase, Fowler McCormick, Class of 1921,
Fund (2009-41, 42, 43, and 44)

**Joana Hadjithomas** (b. 1969, Beirut)
**Khalil Joreige** (b. 1969, Beirut)
Based in Paris and Beirut
*Wonder Beirut #6 (Rivoli Square)*, from
*History of a Pyromaniac Photographer*,
1998–2006
Lambda print mounted on aluminum,
70.5 × 105 cm (27 ¾ × 41 ½ in.)
Courtesy of the artists and CRG Gallery,
New York

*Wonder Beirut #10 (The Sea Shore)*, from
*History of a Pyromaniac Photographer*,
1998–2006
Lambda print mounted on aluminum,
70.5 × 105 cm (27 ¾ × 41 ½ in.)
Courtesy of the artists and CRG Gallery,
New York

*Wonder Beirut #13*, from *History of a
Pyromaniac Photographer*, 1998–2006
Lambda print mounted on aluminum,
70.5 × 105 cm (27 ¾ × 41 ½ in.)
Courtesy of the artists and CRG Gallery,
New York

*Wonder Beirut #15 (Rivoli Square)*, from
*History of a Pyromaniac Photographer*,
1998–2006
Lambda print mounted on aluminum,
70.5 × 105 cm (27 ¾ × 41 ½ in.)
Courtesy of the artists and CRG Gallery,
New York

*Wonder Beirut #21 (Beaches in Beirut)*,
from *History of a Pyromaniac Photographer*,
1998–2006
Lambda print mounted on aluminum,
70.5 × 105 cm (27 ¾ × 41 ½ in.)
Collection of Karim Tabet, New York

*Wonder Beirut #22*, from *History of a
Pyromaniac Photographer*, 1998–2006
Lambda print mounted on aluminum,
70.5 × 105 cm (27 ¾ × 41 ½ in.)
Collection of Mazen Makarem and
Dana Farouki, New York

**Emre Hüner** (b. 1977, Istanbul)
Based in Istanbul and Amsterdam
*Juggernaut*, 2009
Video, color with sound, 21:10 minutes
Courtesy of the artist and Rodeo Gallery,
Istanbul

**Matthew Day Jackson** (b. 1974,
Panorama City, Calif.)
Based in New York City
*August 6th, 1945*, 2010
Burnt wood and lead, 2.44 × 3.14 m (8 × 10 ft.)
Princeton University Art Museum; Museum
purchase, Fowler McCormick, Class of 1921,
Fund

**Lucy Raven** (b. 1977, Tucson, Arizona)
Based in New York City
*China Town*, 2009
Photographic animation, color with sound,
51:30 minutes
Courtesy of the artist
*Screened in conjunction with the exhibition*

**Santiago Sierra** (b. 1966, Madrid)
Based in Mexico City
*Submission (formerly Word of Fire)*, October
2006/March 2007
Documentation of an action, Anapra, Ciudad
Juarez, Chihuahua, Mexico. Two-channel
digital slide projection, black and white, silent,
1:20 minutes (channel one), 78:20 minutes
(channel two), looped
Courtesy of the artist and Lisson Gallery,
London

# Selected Bibliography


Andrews, Max, ed. *Land, Art: A Cultural Ecology Handbook*. London: Royal Society for the Encouragement of Arts, 2006.

Anderson, Benedict. *Imagined Communities: Reflections on the Origin and Spread of Nationalism*. London: Verso, 2006.

Appadurai, Arjun. *Modernity at Large: Cultural Dimensions of Globalization*. Minneapolis: University of Minnesota Press, 1996.

Arendt, Hannah. *The Origins of Totalitarianism*. 1951. Reprint, New York: Harcourt Brace Jovanovich, 1973.

Boettger, Suzaan. *Earthworks: Art and the Landscape of the Sixties*. Berkeley and Los Angeles: University of California Press, 2002.

Bradley, Fiona, ed. *Cities on the Move: Urban Chaos and Global Change, East Asian Art, Architecture, and Film Now*. London: Hayward Gallery, 1999.

Butler, Judith. *Giving an Account of Oneself*. New York: Fordham University Press, 2005.

———. *Precarious Life: The Powers of Mourning and Violence*. London: Verso, 2004.

———, and Gayatri Chakrovorty Spivak. *Who Sings the Nation-State? Language, Politics, Belonging*. London: Seagull Books, 2007.

DeLue, Rachael Ziady, and James Elkins, eds. *Landscape Theory*. New York: Routledge, 2008.

Demos, T. J. *Zones of Conflict*. New York: Pratt Manhattan Gallery, 2008.

Derrida, Jacques. *On Cosmopolitanism and Forgiveness*. Translated by Mark Dooley and Michael Hughes. Preface by Simon Critchley and Richard Kearney. London: Routledge, 2001.

Deutsche, Rosalyn. *Evictions: Art and Spatial Politics*. Chicago: Graham Foundation for Advanced Studies in the Fine Arts; Cambridge, Mass.; London: MIT Press, 1996.

Devji, Faisal. *Landscapes of the Jihad: Militancy, Morality, Modernity*. London: Hurst, 2005.

Feher, Michel, ed. *Nongovernmental Politics*. With Gaëlle Krikorian and Yates McKee. New York: Zone Books, 2007.

Franke, Anselm, Rafi Segal, and Eyal Weizman, eds. *Territories: Islands, Camps, and Other States of Utopia*. Berlin: KW Institute for Contemporary Art; Cologne: Buchhandlung Walther König, 2003.

Godfrey Mark, T. J. Demos, Eyal Weizman, and Ayesha Hameed. "Rites of Passage [Roundtable Discussion]." *Tate Etc.* no. 19 (Summer 2010).

Griffin, Tim. "Remote Possibilities: A Roundtable Discussion on Land Art's Changing Terrain." *Artforum* 43:10 (Summer 2005): 288–95, 366.

Hardt, Michael, and Antonio Negri. *Multitude: War and Democracy in the Age of Empire*. New York: Penguin, 2004.

Harvey, David. *The New Imperialism*. Oxford: Oxford University Press, 2003.

———. *Spaces of Hope*. Edinburgh: Edinburgh University Press, 2000.

Heller-Roazen, Daniel. *The Enemy of All: Piracy and the Law of Nations*. New York: Zone Books, 2009.

Kastner, Jeffrey, ed. *Land and Environmental Art*. London: Phaidon, 1998.

Kwon, Miwon. *One Place after Another: Site-Specific Art and Locational Identity*. Cambridge, Mass.: MIT Press, 2002.

Lefebvre, Henri. *The Production of Space*. Translated by Donald Nicholson-Smith. Oxford: Blackwell Publishing, 1991.

———. *State, Space, World: Selected Essays*. Edited by Neil Brenner and Stuart Elden. Translated by Gerald Moore, Neil Brenner, and Stuart Elden. Minneapolis: University of Minnesota Press, 2009.

Linebaugh, Peter. *The Magna Carta Manifesto: Liberties and Commons for All*. Berkeley and Los Angeles: University of California Press, 2008.

McKee, Yates. "Haunted Housing: Eco-Vanguardism, Eviction, and the Biopolitics of Sustainability in New Orleans." *Grey Room* 30 (Winter 2008): 84–113.

Manacorda, Francesco, and Ariella Yedgar, eds. *Radical Nature: Art and Architecture for a Changing Planet, 1969–2009*. London: Barbican Art Gallery; Koenig Books, 2009.

Markonish, Denise, ed. *Badlands: New Horizons in Landscape*. North Adams, Mass.: Mass MoCA; Cambridge, Mass.: MIT Press, 2008.

Mitchell, W. J. T., ed. *Landscape and Power*. 2d ed. Chicago: University of Chicago Press, 2002.

Mosquera, Gerard, and Jean Fisher, eds. *Over Here: International Perspectives on Art and Culture*. New York: New Museum of Contemporary Art; Cambridge, Mass.: MIT Press, 2004.

Retort. *Afflicted Powers: Capital and Spectacle in a New Age of War*. London; Verso, 2005.

Sassen, Saskia. *Territory, Authority, Rights: From Medieval to Global Assemblages*. Princeton, N.J.: Princeton University Press, 2006.

Smith, Stephanie. *Beyond Green: Toward a Sustainable Art*. Chicago: Smart Museum of Art, University of Chicago; New York: Independent Curators International, 2005.

Smithson, Robert. *Robert Smithson: The Collected Writings*. Edited by Jack Flam. Berkeley and Los Angeles: University of California Press, 1996.

Solnit, Rebecca. *Savage Dreams: A Journey into the Hidden Wars of the American West*. Berkeley and Los Angeles: University of California Press, 1994.

———. *Storming the Gates of Paradise: Landscapes for Politics*. Berkeley and Los Angeles: University of California Press, 2007.

Taylor, Chris, and Bill Gilbert. *Land Arts of the American West*. Austin: The University of Texas Press, 2009.

Thompson, Nato, ed. *Experimental Geography: Radical Approaches to Landscape, Cartography, and Urbanism*. Brooklyn, N.Y.: Melville House Publishing; New York: Independent Curators International, 2008.

Wagner, Anne M. "Being There: Art and the Politics of Place." *Artforum* 43:10 (Summer 2005): 265–69, 346.

Weizman, Eyal. *Hollow Land: Israel's Architecture of Occupation*. London: Verso, 2007.

# Contributors

**Uriel Abulof** is an assistant professor at Tel-Aviv University's Department of Political Science. He was a Postdoctoral Research Fellow and a teacher at Princeton University's Liechtenstein Institute on Self-Determination of the Woodrow Wilson School of Public and International Affairs 2007–9. He received his Ph.D. in International Relations from the Hebrew University of Jerusalem (2007), and was subsequently a Fulbright Scholar at New York University and Princeton University. Uriel has taught at the Hebrew University, led various web-based educational projects, and is currently an editorial staff member and writer for the *Eretz Acheret (A Different Land)* Hebrew Journal. He currently works on the role of political ethics in intercommunal conflicts, specializing in ethnicity and nationalism, with a focus on the Middle East, Canada, the Balkans, and South Africa. His recent article, to appear in the *International Studies Quarterly*, compares the existential uncertainty of two ethnonational communities: Israeli Jews and French-Canadians.

**Alex Bacon** is a Ph.D. candidate in the Department of Art & Archaeology at Princeton University. He holds a BA in the History of Art and Women's Studies from the University of Michigan, Ann Arbor. He is co-editor, with Hal Foster, of an anthology on Richard Hamilton and is currently serving as the research assistant for the Ellsworth Kelly catalogue raisonné project. Alex has delivered a number of papers on such artists as Brice Marden, Yayoi Kusama, Agnes Martin, and Gilbert & George.

**Kelly Baum** is the Haskell Curator of Modern and Contemporary Art at the Princeton University Art Museum. From 2002 to 2007, she was the assistant curator of contemporary art at the Blanton Museum of Art at the University of Texas at Austin. She is the author of numerous brochures and catalogues on contemporary art and has published in such periodicals as *October* and *The Princeton University Art Museum Record*. She has also curated several exhibitions, including *Carol Bove* (2006), *Jedediah Caesar* (2007), *The Sirens' Song* (2007), *Transactions* (2007), and *Body Memory* (2008, with Joel Smith).

**Rachael Z. DeLue** is an assistant professor in the Department of Art & Archaeology at Princeton University. Her area of specialization is American art, with particular focus on landscape representation, intersections of art and science, and the history of African American art. She is the author of *George Inness and the Science of Landscape* (2004) and co-editor, with James Elkins, of *Landscape Theory* (2008). Current projects include a book on the twentieth-century American painter Arthur Dove and an essay that considers the roles of beauty and agency in the work of Kara Walker and Michael Ray Charles.

**Margo Handwerker** is a Ph.D. student in the School of Architecture at Princeton University. Prior to her doctoral work, she was the Curatorial Assistant of Modern and Contemporary Art and the Curatorial Assistant of Prints and Drawings at The Museum of Fine Arts, Houston. She holds an MA in Art History, Theory, and Criticism from the School of the Art Institute of Chicago.

**Jonathan Levy** is assistant professor of history at Princeton University. He studies the history of American capitalism. His work has been supported by grants from the American Council of Learned Societies and the Mellon Foundation, and has appeared in *The American Historical Review* and *Wilson Quarterly*. His book, *The Ways of Providence: Capitalism, Risk, and Freedom in 19th-century America,* is forthcoming from the Harvard University Press.

**Michelle Lim** is a Ph.D. candidate in the Department of Art & Archaeology at Princeton University. Her dissertation project, *Navigating Floating Worlds*, explores how curatorial strategies have influenced the production, exhibition, and consumption of contemporary Chinese art between 1979 and 2009. Michelle is also an independent curator and critic. Her writings include articles and reviews for the *Asian Art News* and *World Sculpture News* as well as essays for the Princeton University Art Museum's exhibition catalogue, *Outside In: Chinese × American × Contemporary Art* (2009). On the curatorial front, Michelle is collaborating on the documentation of *Visions & Illusions: Reconstruction of a City*, an exhibition held at the St. James Power Station in Singapore in 2004. In 2009–10, she was a participant in the Whitney Independent Studies Program.

**Yates McKee** is a Ph.D. candidate in Art History at Columbia University. An alumnus of the Whitney Independent Study Program, he has taught courses on contemporary art at The Cooper Union, Parsons The New School for Design, and Ohio University, in Athens. His work has appeared in venues such as *October*, *Grey Room*, *Art Journal*, and *Third Text*. Yates is also co-editor of *Nongovernmental Politics* (Zone Books, 2007).

**Kurt Mueller** is a Critical Studies Resident at The Core Program, Glassell School of Art, at The Museum of Fine Arts, Houston. He has contributed criticism to *frieze*, *Art Asia Pacific*, *Art Papers*, and *Art Lies*, where he is Assistant Editor. Kurt has curated exhibitions at the Glassell School of Art and the Blanton Museum of Art, in Austin, TX. He received his MFA from the University of Texas, Austin, in 2008 and his BA in Visual and Environmental Studies from Harvard University in 2002. He attended the Skowhegan School of Painting and Sculpture in 2008.

**Chris Reitz** is a Modern Art History graduate student at Princeton University. His primary areas of interest are contemporary art and European movements of the 1920s and 1930s, with a particular focus on transnationality and the evolution of global capitalism. Before moving to Princeton, he worked as an independent curator and project manager for Public Art Fund in New York City. His work to date has included gallery exhibitions, publications, and research projects in the United States and Europe.

*Nobody's Property: Art, Land, Space, 2000–2010* is published by the
Princeton University Art Museum and distributed by Yale University Press,
New Haven and London.

Princeton University Art Museum
Princeton, New Jersey 08544
artmuseum.princeton.edu

Yale University Press
P.O. Box 209040
302 Temple Street
New Haven, Connecticut 06520-9040
www.yalebooks.com

This book was published in conjunction with the exhibition *Nobody's Property: Art,
Land, Space, 2000–2010*, organized by the Princeton University Art Museum, on
view October 23, 2010, through February 20, 2011.

*Nobody's Property: Art, Land, Space, 2000–2010* has been made possible by the
National Endowment for the Arts; the Virginia and Bagley Wright, Class of 1946,
Program Fund for Modern and Contemporary Art; the Frances E. and Elias Wolf,
Class of 1920, Fund; the Sarah Lee Elson, Class of 1984, Fund for the International
Artist-in-Residence Program; and an anonymous foundation. This publication has
been supported by the Andrew W. Mellon Foundation Fund for Publications and
the Elizabeth Firestone Graham Foundation. Additional support has been made
possible by the Partners and Friends of the Princeton University Art Museum.



Managing Editor: Jill Guthrie
Project Editor: Jane Boyd
Assistant Editor: Sophie Williams

Book design, composition, production: Binocular, New York
Separations and printing: E&B Engelhardt und Bauer, Karlsruhe, Germany
Binding: Josef Spinner, Ottersweier, Germany

This book was typeset in DIN and printed on 150 gsm GardaMatt.

Frontispiece illustrations: page 2: Andrea Geyer. *Spiral Lands/Chapter 1*, detail;
page 10: Matthew Day Jackson. *August 6th, 1945*, detail; page 44: Jennifer Allora
and Guillermo Calzadilla. *Land Mark (Foot Prints)*, detail; page 64: Emre Hüner.
*Juggernaut Mindmap*, detail.

ISBN: 978-0-300-14928-9
Library of Congress Control Number: 2010929423

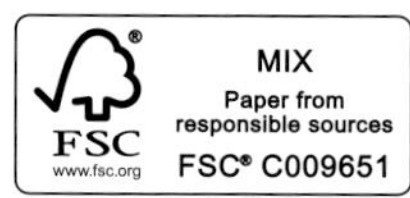


Printed and bound in Germany